795EN

I0375139

URBAN LOBBYING

Mayors in the Federal Arena

URBAN LOBBYING

Mayors in the Federal Arena

by

Suzanne Farkas

New York University Press
New York   1971

UNIVERSITY LIBRARY
Lethbridge, Alberta
8039

Copyright © 1971 by New York University
Library of Congress Catalog Card Number: 77-124523
ISBN 0-8147-2550-3
Manufactured in the United States of America

To
ANDREW, BRADFORD, ROBIN,
AND ROSE

Contents

LIST OF APPENDICES

Acknowledgments

I wish to thank Sidney Wallach, Bruno Schachner, Carol Kahn, Rose Scotch, and Nancy Castleman, without whose editorial assistance this manuscript might well have been comprehensible only to its author.

My deepest appreciation and acknowledgment of gratitude goes to those whose intellectual guidance enabled me to write this book: Professor Wallace Sayre, my primary sponsor, and Professors Robert Connery, Bruce L. R. Smith, and Warner Schilling. I also want to thank Professor Demetrios Caraley who encouraged me; Professor Robert Wood for giving me more of his time than he could really afford; Professor Don Haider for his thoughtful and thorough comments that helped me revise my initial text; and Professor Irving Kristol for his advice at a time when I needed the courage to submit the manuscript to a publisher without starting all over again.

However, it was only because of the graciousness of the mayors, federal and local officials, urban lobbyists, and staffs of the urban interest groups mentioned throughout that enabled me to carry out the project. I am especially indebted to Hugh Mields, John Gunther, John Feild, Patrick Healy, William Sorrentino, and John Barriere who suggested new sources of information, new people, new insights, and new ways to deal with the federal bureaucracy.

To Professors Sidney Burrell, H. Mark Roelofs, Alfred de Grazia, James T. Crown, and John G. Stoessinger I owe a more general debt for their intellectual influence in first sparking my interest in political science and for serving as models for me during those student days when one gropes for clarity of thought.

Bruno Schachner and Ben Bartel offered loving, skillful, and insightful assistance at many critical times. And to Carol Kahn, whose talents I could not have done without, I owe the comment that her "calmness and candor are commensurate with her competence and commitment."

Many other people, more than I can possibly thank, and some that I cannot possibly thank enough, contributed their interest and energy to this book. I am sure that many authors feel the disquieting combination of an urgency to communicate gratitude and a fear that they have left someone out. As a result of this anxiety, my final thanks must go to my friend and colleague, Professor Annette Baxter, who has promised to soothe my chagrin in case I did.

Suzanne Farkas

September 1970
New York University

URBAN LOBBYING
Mayors in the Federal Arena

CHAPTER I

The Urban Crisis, the Urban Lobby and the Conference of Mayors

THE second edition of Webster's Unabridged Dictionary and the even more comprehensive thirteen-volume Oxford English Dictionary record "urbanization" only as a sub-word. It is defined, irony of ironies, as relating to a process of making "urbane," presumably making more civilized what theretofore had been less so. Additionally, it refers to transforming a town or village into a larger aggregation, namely a city.

Only some forty years after the date of these publications, urbanization has become an everyday word and means the process of becoming citylike. This process has bred a host of difficulties which are among the most urgent and complex confronting social scientists. Problems which are the offspring of urbanization have formed an entangled family of relationships. Embracing each other in exasperating symbiosis, they have been given a collective name: "urban problems." To note just a few, there is urban congestion; urban pollution; urban transportation; urban waste disposal; urban slums; urban poverty, and urban unemployment; and perhaps most threatening, urban riots and urban bankruptcy.

This is an ominous progeny, a school, if not of outright scandal, certainly of scandalous elements.

Along with this curriculum, urbanization has gone hand in

hand with attempts to "urbanologize" about the full range of
phenomena it has spawned. "Urbanologize" means to include the
whole mesh—or is it mess?—of grave head-shaking about our
cities as well as imaginative ideas for their recovery; of jeremiads
and predictions of doom as well as of utopian visions of a City of
God; of pipe dreams and "non-negotiable" demands along with
hard-boiled, down-to-earth judgments that alone can lead, and
then only with difficulty, to practical proposals. This urbanization has generated a flock of experts who are the urban planners,
urban sociologists, urban geographers, urban economists, urban
anthropologists, and urban political scientists.

All have become familiar figures. Each one is busy according
to his own discipline assembling data on matters connected with
cities and offering interpretations of the unsavory bouillabaisse in
the urban locale. Since the term "urbanologist" is reserved for
those who seek theoretical insights into urban problems, one can
perhaps use the broader term "urbanist" for all those who deal
with urban problems on a decision-making level, in short, who
attempt to translate policy prescription into social reality.

Among these urbanists the urban lobbyists—groups, individuals, and institutions which constitute the "urban lobby"—have
come to occupy a position of mounting importance because of the
difficulty of the tasks they are called to perform. Their importance is readily apparent from a consideration of how much depends on the accuracy of their judgment, for they must cull that
which makes sense in political and operational terms from all the
suggestions pouring in from the various fields of urban disciplines.

They must extract those sets of facts, attitudes, and proposals
that can be collectively highlighted and then most dramatically
represented as an urban interest. This urban interest—amphorous
and lacking in historical tradition and self-evident content—must
then be converted into a practical program. Finally, it must be
put into terms which have legislative appeal and can command the
ultimate legitimacy: the financial resources necessary for implementation. While still giving nod to the biblical caveat "except the
Lord keep the city, the watchman waketh but in vain," the urban
lobbyist addresses his most fervent petitions to the federal
government.

No full examination of urban lobbying seems to have been

attempted before, and even the present study covers only urban lobbying by organized interest groups in relation to the federal government. In the congery which collectively makes up the urban lobby, the United States Conference of Mayors (USCM) has been one of the leading entities. It has had the longest experience in the process of extracting from among many analyses of urban problems those of greatest immediacy and of determining which can successfully be pushed towards remedial action. The unusual nature of this organization and its total immersion in the most important aspects of urban lobbying mark it as an appropriate example from which to generalize about representation of the urban interest in Washington.

Urban interest representation as referred to here is concerned with how federal-urban priorities are determined, and the substance of federal-city aid programs affected by skillful consensus-building between urban public interest organizations and sectors of the executive and legislative branches of the federal government. Inevitably the question arises how there can be, in the first instance, a successful structuring of agreement among the many interests of the many cities, the plethora of urban pressure groups, and the manifold urban-related bureaucracies of three levels of government. Assessment of urban interest representation also calls for comparing the effectiveness of the politics of confrontation with the politics of consensus, or mutual accommodation, as alternate strategies to obtain national solutions for urban problems in a contest with other claimants. A choice between these strategies has been one of the most persistent dilemmas facing the urban lobbies.

A study of urban lobbying is at the same time an attempt to investigate an area in political science which warrants further attention: the phenomenon of intergovernmental pressure groups as instruments of social change and as communication tools within a complex federal structure.

As an organization of mayors, the USCM is an intergovernmental lobby which attempts to make the federal government aware of the local variants of proposed national programs. By providing local perspectives on national activities aimed at cities, it serves as a counterweight to federal concepts of urban priorities. The influence of federal programs has become a crucial variable in the politics and power structures of local communities. These programs come replete with federal guidelines that leave less and less room for the interplay of local forces to control their own domain. If politics is defined as the competition over the allocation and uses of resources, the flow of federal funds into cities widens the arena of urban politics to the federal level. Thus the $1,321,197,760 of federal funds in the expense budget of New York for fiscal year 1970–1971 represents the extent of decisions that were made in the federal arena outside of New York City and therefore not subject to sole control by its own political processes.

In this context, one can assert that urban politics can no longer be understood without consideration of the federal variables. Urban lobbies are the links between the two decision-making processes as well as the points where they become tangential. They are intergovernmental pressure groups which try to influence the federal input and to determine the urban context into which national policies should fit.

There is more than one urban lobby; yet the nature of its membership makes the U. S. Conference of Mayors (USCM) the lobby that best illustrates the complexities of lobbying for the urban interest, and gives its operations special impact. Moreover, it is a special breed of interest group which affords the opportunity to examine an organization which is at the same time private in character, and in a sense, governmental. It is private because it is a voluntary association acting as a pressure group, and it has no formal relation to governmental institutions. It is governmental in character because it is constituted entirely of the highest elected public officials of the largest cities.

Its unique make-up suggests that the USCM has a kind of built-in political impact, whose potential political leverage should be considerable. The overlapping constituencies of the President, Senators, and Congressmen with those of the mayors imply great federal "vulnerability." The electoral support and public approval the mayors are capable of withholding or delivering have a potentially significant effect on a large number of voters who might determine the political future of federal policy-makers. A President would thus hesitate to provoke unified unfavorable reaction by the mayors. The mayors can also provide legislators with information on local political climates; they can publicize a Senator's attitude towards urban issues, or they can "groom" a city for a President in an election. Their influence also impinges on those federal administrators who need cooperation from the cities for their own programs. Moreover, since the membership is elective and therefore constantly changing, the policy views of the group can be expected to reflect changing views and demands of the electorate at any given time. This electoral sensivity to the collective political mood and major expectations of the voters gives the USCM as an intergovernmental lobby a special mandate for social change and a more likely capability to effect it—at least theoretically.

Thus it may be surmised that a membership of elected public officials should differentiate the USCM from other interest groups. Postulating further, its access to federal decision makers should be easier, its influence greater, and its internal cohesion more difficult to maintain. The stakes of its actions are higher and more complicated because they involve subtle interactions at all levels of government. Public officials lobbying other public officials should be able to benefit from the possibilities for interchange in the same political dialect. On the other hand, in urban affairs the range and divergence of possible positions are so great that speaking the same language may not be synonymous with seeing eye to eye. Hypotheses, however, are notoriously treacherous guides to insights.

The question must therefore be squarely posed and investigated: What are the consequences of this kind of membership for the internal dynamics, political strategies, and policy goals of an interest group, especially one dealing with expanding critical social problems? Perhaps by focusing on the phenomenon of "government organized into interests acting on government," and by untangling some of the intricacies of the relationships among groups of elected chief executives, traditional interest groups, Presidential task forces and those called "intervening elites" in the policy-making process, the scope of organization theory may be broadened.

This kind of inquiry seems especially amenable to approach through political systems theory as a method of identifying and evaluating the interaction patterns among participants in the

making of federal-urban policy. The regularity, the intensity, and
the content of their interactions will determine whether these
participants form a coherent, or even a discernable, political subsystem within whose boundaries federal-urban policy is produced.
Finally, in weighing the policy-producing capacities of the urban
lobbies and their institutional allies, it might be possible to assess
whether their ability for conflict management can withstand the
stresses resulting from the urban crisis of the 1960s and the
foreseeable 1970s.

Urban Lobbying and the Urban Crisis

In discussions of urban affairs it has become convenient to
rely on a shorthand of phrases: "comprehensive goals," "cohesive
urban interest," "objective priorities," "urban crisis," "national
urban policy," and others. These catchwords are often more
confusing than clarifying. When scrutinized for meaning they
diffuse into "shade without color, shape without form, force without motion." [1]

What, for example, is a "comprehensive goal"? Do urban
areas have, in reality, cohesive and united "interests" that are
both applicable to individual cities and at the same time generalized
enough in scope and content that they are also appropriate for
national, uniform treatment? How "objective" can policy ever be?

But more significant for urban lobbying is whether the urban
crisis has an operational definition, whether it means something
that can be acted on. Is it a problem likely to be solved? Is it a
condition to be endured? Is it a crisis? And if so, is it "urban?"
Is it an objective condition or is it a subjective reaction, a presumed cause of unfocused mass anxieties?

The concept of the urban crisis includes a qualified "yes" to
some aspects of all of these questions. On one level it is that crisis
which was brought about by the collective sense of outrage
following the emergence in the 1960s of the city as a political
issue. But the urban crisis is nonetheless real in that it denotes
something people experience. Beneath the surface of their anxieties
is the fear that the urban crisis is a condition which must be

grimly endured—either because it is so much more than a single crisis, because solutions to its constituent elements are not politically feasible, or because its components are more national than "urban."

There are prominent urbanologists whose analysis of the urban crisis into constituent and historical elements have the effect of defusing the sense of urgency for action. Problems of racial conflict, of social class inequities, of population density, of crumbling family structures, of persistent unemployment and the permanently unemployable, of turbulence among the poor, have come to be catalogued as the Monday morning laundry list—frequently accurate but without much directive inspiration. The notions that the large city has always been inimical to civilized and democratic values or that it has suffered from deterioration of life style with each new immigrant wave, are sometimes taken as indicating that the urban crisis is an overblown issue. By projection they imply that some problems will disappear as today's poor are absorbed into middle class status as were the poor of yesterday, and some problems must be lived with as permanent aspects of an intensively interacting society.

But the most provocative contention for a discussion of urban lobbying is that government action directed at the urban crisis is futile, since one cannot by legislation convert an "urban mob" into an "urban citizenry." [2]

Some urbanologists may take comfort from the thought that nature can be left to run its course. The urbanist—the urban lobbyist—however, is not content to be a mere spectator and insists on pressing for remedial action, as this is his responsibility.

Pointing out that the urban crisis has political, economic, social, racial, and moral aspects does not suggest that as a public issue, it is insoluble. It merely demonstrates that the urban crisis is complicated far beyond what its name implies. True, it may not be susceptible to treatment by traditional incrementalism, that is, by just pouring in more and more money or by merely enlarging some project to mammoth proportions. Such an approach may have little utility for cities, and it may run afoul of the problems which distributive politics pose for the federal government. A fixed quantity of resources has to be distributed among widely dispersed interests according to estimates of constituency support of the traditional pressure blocs—farmers, city dwellers, business, labor, and so on.

As perceived by the urban lobby, it is the simultaneous presence and co-mingling within our large cities of so many problems and situations of discomfort, coupled with the fact that cities are strategic centers of commerce, communications and political interaction, that make the urban crisis at once urban, national, and critical. It is true that the American political system is often confused by complex situations, and that it is slow to respond appropriately to challenge. However, the urban lobbyist insists that the urban crisis is at a "decisive time of peril that still presents the opportunity for change." [3] To him, response is imperative, and trying becomes almost as important as achieving. After all, "trying" is his profession.

The term urban crisis as used in the remainder of this discussion is a concept which governmental institutions employ to analyze reality and shape public policy. In any event, the urban lobbyist would like to employ the concept in this manner. In this sense, then, one can say that an urban crisis exists, and that it is a set of problems of which some may be susceptible to amelioration.

As a set of problems, the maladies of urban America require a diagnostic approach before they are brought to the formal political institutions for therapeutic action. Specifics must be distilled, priorities drawn up, and feasibility of particular federal programs for urban areas estimated.

But perhaps the most important task of the urban lobby is the need to keep the public conscious of the urban crisis. At the local level, a continuous reminder that we have an urban crisis can stimulate greater realization that community conflict should "converge at a point of commonweal." [4] At the federal level, it should induce an urban-conscious attitude toward legislation and a realization of the need to evaluate the implications for urban areas of federal actions and of failure to act.

It is true and unfortunate that, historically, the federal government has not had much urban orientation. Until recently, we have been a largely agragarian nation. One result was that there existed no cohesive decision-making machinery to define the specifically urban problems and to relate them to the total national economy and condition. Nor has their increased importance in the 1960's brought about a commensurate increase in the allocation of federal resources. Thus the early attempts to cope with the urban crisis were little more than a succession of improvisations, further bedeviled by a quagmire of red tape. Moreover, the absence of an "urban attitude" toward the early federal-city programs meant that they did not operate in a policy context addressed to the strains caused by the rapidity of transition from an agricultural nation to an urbanized society, and to the consequent transposition of major concerns to blight over barley, pollution over poultry, and slums over surplus farm products.

The urban lobby, of which the United States Conference of Mayors was the first example, has tried to provide the missing orientation. It has made itself responsible for much of the essential diagnosis and for developing a sense of urgency to provide federal remedies. All urban lobbying is, of course, in part concerned with defining what is urban as well as with judging which problems are appropriate for federal action and, among them, which require the most—and most immediate—attention. This calls for a fine acumen for balancing needs against the mood of Congress and the President, and for matching any proposal for dealing with an urban problem with a popular political issue, that is, one that can get the necessary appropriations.

Agreement among the urban groups on the direction of overall policy is a first essential if urban lobbying is to be effective. Urban lobbying requires awareness of minute administrative and legislative details, and sometimes battles with administrative agencies to change past practices despite the ego investment of the bureaucracy in charge. Clearly, too, representing the urban interest calls for formulating new proposals and for considerable frustration tolerance while the proposals are bounced from office to office, from one legislative committee to another, buried, resurrected, and then, hopefully, after much travail, enacted into law. Each step requires a new round of bargaining, supplication, coalition-building, pruning of issues, calibration of political possibility, and unrelenting watchful guidance. Thus, urban lobbying, a responsibility of enormous dimensions, makes imperative a process of firm and continuing power-management.

The difficulties of the urban lobbyist are increased by the necessity to project the justifying and unifying idea of urban lobbying—representation of the *total* urban interest. Since almost 70 percent of the population live in urban areas, the urban interest would appear to encompass most of the interests of American society. What then, distinguishes "urban" from "national?" If urban interests could be spelled out simply as "the interests of the vast majority of urbanites," this would not solve the problem. Most things will impinge on urban dwellers, if only negatively; even the ostensible exclusively rural interest in farm subsidy is deceptive. Since subsidies on farm products affect the prices that the urbanite has to pay for food, the urban slum dweller cannot leave farm-subsidy policy solely to a Congressional Committee on Agriculture.

Representation of the urban interest by the constellation of groups that make up the urban lobby is a far more difficult process than the representation of an interest by other pressure blocs. A lobby such as the National Rifle Association, confronted with the possibilities of firearms control legislation, has a single, clear-cut objective. In contrast, the urban interest groups must select issues and concentrate on those which seems most promising, no single one of which can be solved without sharp impact on many others. Onto each of these issues they must sculpt the the specifically urban profile to prove that it is an appropriate urban concern to the satisfaction of a multiple audience: their own members, local governments, urban electoral constituencies, other urban lobbies needed as allies, and the hoped-for majorities at all the necessary stages of the federal decision-making process. A kind of schizophrenia is a standard occupational hazard for the urban lobbyist; he must keep one eye on what he thinks is most needed and the other on what he can realistically hope to get. Neither becomes clear until after he has marshaled available pressures and enlisted effective allies. These processes in turn require their own priority and strategy judgments in an endless cycle of vigilance.

The conceptual nebula of urban interest representation are of small concern when compared to the operational difficulties. The commonly held view that there is, or should be, such a thing as a "comprehensive national policy" behind some specific issues highlights some of these with a clarity that is somehow depressing.

Daniel P. Moynihan, Chairman of President Nixon's Council on Urban Affairs, urges action towards a national urban policy. As he puts it:

> Social responses to changed social requirements take the form in industrial democracies of changed government policies. This has led, in the present situation, to a reasonably inventive spate of program proposals of the kind the New Deal more or less began and which flourishd notably in the period between the Presidential elections of 1960 and 1968 when the number of domestic programs of the federal government increased from 45 to 435. Understandably, however, there has been a diminution of the confidence with which such proposals were formerly regarded, at all events by their sponsors. . . .Hence the issue arises as to whether the demands of the time are not to be met in terms of policy, as well as program. . . .In a word, ought a national urban crisis to be met with something like a national urban policy? [5]

Yet Moynihan himself points to the difficulties when he mentions the number of interests and programs that would have to be encompassed by such a national urban policy.

How does one weave 435 separate programs scattered through numerous agencies of the federal bureaucracy into one coherent national policy? Even the most obvious questions are difficult to answer. Shall all urban programs be in the Department of Housing and Urban Development? Should national policy for urban air pollution programs be forced into a shot-gun marriage with projects for urban renewal? A random listing of elements of the urban crisis makes it clear that there are so many different issues, interests, and problems involved that to speak of a single national urban policy in operational terms becomes as obscure as the concept of "goals for America." Put too broadly, it becomes meaningless. In reality, ". . .there is never a single all-embracing policy in any area . . . Decision-making presupposes some known and agreed-upon objective . . . to be maximized . . .

Choices on alternatives . . . involve incommensurables, conflicting objectives to be balanced, and the clash of different conceptions of the public interest." [6]

Still, to point out the innumerable variants for a single, all-embracing, federal urban policy is not the same as denying the possibility of complementary federal policies. As Frederick Cleveland points out in *Congress and Urban Problems*, "Congress has adopted statutes formulating basic policy to govern federal involvement in urban affairs . . . urban problems can appropriately be considered a distinct—though not isolated—field of public policy . . ." [7]

There are policy clusters of sufficient cohesion to warrant consideration as one or another set of observable congeries such as "housing and urban renewal policy" or "urban mass transit policy." This enables analysts to combine several urban policies into related groupings, or to point out the discontinuities among them. Urban lobbies and interest groups have helped to produce these federal urban policies and programs and have labeled them as distinctively "urban." Whether these are ideal programs for ameliorating urban ills or whether they are, in fact, even in the interests of large cities remains open to question.

An examination of urban lobbying inevitably becomes a multiple investigation of how a great diversity of urban interests is represented, of how urban interest groups prevent the concerns they represent from becoming so broad as to be meaningless or so balkanized as to make consensus impossible, and of how they are able to choose from among an almost infinite number of urban interests those for which they can propose politically meaningful, actionable demands. Even when a general agenda is agreed upon, the program capability and lobbying impact of urban interest groups may be even further restricted when the specifics of a program must differ for each city.

The diversity of urban interests and all that this implies for purposes of representation pinpoints the single most important aspect of urban lobbying: the need to structure consensus for building a coalition capable of obtaining political results. This requires arranging alliances within a multiple constituency, obtaining acquiescence among several levels of government, and bargaining for trade-offs between political competitors.

Governments of large cities are headed by politicians who reflect the full spectrum of political diversity within the national political system. Yet without their reasonably united support urban programs would never get off the ground. By its very composition the United States Conference of Mayors is the fulcrum for collective urban lobbying since it brings together the heads of the 435 largest cities. Actually, the cities themselves are the members of the USCM, but they are represented by their mayors. Set up originally in order to structure consensus among them, its purpose, once they have reached agreement, is to magnify and bring to bear the full weight of their lobbying impact by deploying their combined political leverage with Congress and with the federal administrative agencies. There are obvious obstacles to quick agreement among elected public officials from cities in the North and in the South, from conservatives and liberals, and from Democrats and Republicans, especially when each has distinctive political skills, different electoral constituencies, a prima donna disposition, a varying yen for a national audience, and sometimes competing political ambitions. Yet this group nevertheless manages to achieve convergence of ideas on a surprisingly wide range of issues.

Despite what has been suggested as the USCM's inherent advantages from mayors' shared electoral constituencies with federal elected officials, there are still more Congressmen from small and medium-sized cities than from the urban giants, more Senators from states with few large cities than from those in which metropolitan electorates preponderate. In recent years there is also increasing attention directed to the suburbs since their voting behavior is gaining importance in elections. For these reasons urban programs need the support of the smaller cities and their Congressmen and Senators. The smaller cities, aware of the bargaining possibilities conferred by the more broadly-based political support they collectively represent, have organized as a lobby called the National League of Cities (NLC). Neither of these two "generalist" urban lobbies acting alone could have conclusive impact. Standing together, especially when joined by the Urban Coalition and the more specialized urban groups such the National Housing Conference (NHC) and the National Association of Housing and Redevelopment Officials (NAHRO), they can have substantial influence upon federal urban programs. Their reasoned presentations, it must be remembered, are the distillations of the demands that reverberate among the tumultuous urban masses.

Congressional Committees prefer that the primary bargaining between the USCM and the NLC on the content of urban proposals take place before their formal submission to Congress. This is recognition of the legitimacy and importance of these groups as representatives of the urban interest. Since their combined support can usually make or break a federal urban program, this practice of Congressional Committees betokens a realization of the desirability of this combined support and the extent to which the two organizations contribute to the substance of legislation. Finally, it suggests the role of these groups as conflict managers whose skill can be deployed to relieve the formal governmental institutions of part of that burden.

Much federal-city legislation, especially that concerned with housing and urban development, reflects both the trade-offs between the large and small city groups and the indispensible compromises made with them by the cast of characters which participates in every such program—from the White House, from executive agencies, and from Congress. The Model Cities Act is a good example of this kind of legislative mix. It was diverted from its original purpose, supported by the Mayors' Conference, of pouring massive funds into the total physical and social rehabilitation of a very few hard-core slums by the need for League support, in return for which funds were included for smaller cities. As a result of horse-trading in connection with the Model Cities Act, the League supported the rent supplement section favored by the Conference in return for Conference support of the new towns provision desired by the League. The President, in turn, included in his bill a request for more general urban renewal money as a quid pro quo for support by these two groups for *his* priorities. The establishment of the Department of Housing and Urban Development, as will be shown later, is another example of the structuring of consent first *within* the Conference, the League, the housing lobby, and federal institutions, administrative and legislative bodies, and subsequently *among* them. These examples are given in order to stress the intricacy of the consensus-building engaged in by urban lobbying groups, the necessity for this process, its reflection in federal programs, and on top of all this, the inherent fragility of the consensus.

The intricacies of urban lobbying cannot be overstated. It is a paradox, however, that the convolutions in the process of obtaining the necessary consensus are best emphasized by under-statement—that is, by describing only some of the steps taken by only one of the participants in federal urban policy-making. With the Conference of Mayors, attempts to arrive at mutually accept-able goals, or at least, confluence of direction, begin in an elaborate and simultaneous process of exploring the views of each individual mayor and his attentive public, his staff, his urban development agencies, his local bureaucracies, his city council, and some of the more influential local interest groups. Each mayor takes soundings from his Congressional delegation, his Senators, his state legislators, possibly his Governor, and from other mayors in his own and other states. Usually his strategy includes touching base with the leaders and most active members of his own political party at several different levels in its organiza-tional structure. He may also consult in some manner with other political parties and with prominent opinion leaders, especially if he is either a fusion mayor or hopes in the future to be a candi-date capable of attracting multiple endorsements.

Each mayor keeps his ears (and doors) open to all those whose financial or political support might be needed at election time. Both the individual mayors and the USCM as an organiza-tion attempt to gauge the most likely opposition to an issue at hand and try to compensate for it, to co-opt it, or to lessen its opportunities for mobilization. They make advance projections of probable reactions by the media and of significant groups within the constituencies of strategically-placed Congressmen and Senators. They forecast the response of the spokesmen for the major functional categories of political, social, and economic concern typically present within urban areas (labor unions, busi-ness associations, professional and civil rights organizations, etc.). There is an exploration of the position the President is likely to take; feelers are put out to the executive agencies with which individual mayors or the USCM has close ties, and to the appro-

priate Congressional Committee chairmen. At the same time, the
process of determining and of reconciling cleavages and differences is taking place both within the Conference of Mayors itself,
and among the Conference, other urban interest groups, Congressional and executive staff, committees, agencies, and key federal
officials. All of these latter participants are also engaged simultaneously as individual actors in the same exploration as that described
above for the USCM—but each from his own perspective.

The pattern of activities and interaction produces innumerable
permutations and combinations. To achieve any stability, they
must all converge on a proposal that is unknown, and perhaps
unknowable, in advance.

The many urban interest groups all have slightly different
approaches, with the USCM and the NLC having the most generalized outlook. In particular issue areas, more specialized groups
may take the lead, for example, the National Housing Conference
and the National Association of Housing and Redevelopment
Officials on housing. The other core urban groups will generally
coalesce behind them. The result of alliance building is, of course,
to offer a legitimacy to whatever is being proposed. The American
political tradition is based on the idea that the accumulated
decisions of large numbers of people deserve some representation.
When those most concerned with federal-urban policy are united
in their aims, the federal government is obliged to be an attentive audience.

The multi-group presentation of urban problems also means
that priorities have been allocated, and that agreement has been
reached on them. In the world of political expedience, it is vital
that a proposal be presented to government in such a way that
it can be acted on and implemented without undue difficulty.
Since a disparate range of ideas cannot be translated into urban
legislation, some "nuts and bolts" basic work must be done by
one or more of the organizations concerned so the presentation
can be clear, cogent, and concise. The nebulae of "urban interests"
are refined, directed, shaped, explained, packaged as a cohesive
plan, and only then delivered to the appropriate formal policy
institution. Getting proposals to this point, and working for
their passage, is the job of the USCM and its allies. Thus the

function of this labyrinth of consensus-weaving for urban lobbying is to produce politically meaningful results.

The efficacy of consensus politics as practiced in this way has been called into question by that body of opinion which maintains that this strategy is "dead." "Alive" (and certainly more lively), is the politics of confrontation. It sharpens conflict by raising the most intensely felt issues and can press claims of an ideologically unsullied constituency. It avoids the dilution of its concerns by avoiding the idea of bargaining within a coalition of mutual back-scratchers. In contrast to the gymnastics of confrontation, the politics of consensus manages conflict by avoiding the most hotly-contested issues. It aims for a broad constituency which, by finding the lowest common denominator for mutual goals, bargains to form coalitions with other groups to achieve results which, although they represent compromises, will endure. In confrontation politics, small "splinter" interests (usually only sporadically if noisily organized), present "non-negotiable" demands, and conflict among them must be resolved *within* the formal political process. This in many ways resembles a European multi-party system in which voters are organized on the basis of a few, intensely-held ideological views and the process of coalition and compromise takes place in the legislature rather than among the electorate. Political pluralism in America is instead reflected in consensus politics, whereby highly organized groups aggregate related, though not identical, interests, and arrive at a point of acceptable decision by settling on "something for everybody." Few are ever either completely satisfied or completely dissatisfied.

The advocates of confrontation politics are saying that obeisance to pluralism, aggregating consent, softening the issues to their lowest common denominator has not worked. They point to the urban crisis as evidence. The adherents of consensus politics reply that bringing people under the same umbrella, making them feel "part of the show," is the only peaceful way; despite present conditions, much, they claim, has been done.

The challenge has been squarely posed to the urban lobbies: should they continue to try to reconcile conflicting interests and present government with a "consensual" package of proposals?

Or should they experiment with the new politics by choosing a single most important urban issue and pushing it to its "most ideal" resolution—even at the risk of having to cash in on all their political chips?

A tentative hypothesis is that confrontation politics—although possibly yielding good results for some—may be inappropriate for the urban interest. For the urban interest the confrontation politics of the 1960's, by splintering the issues, ended up with something no longer "urban." In demands to "free the Black Panthers," or in marches on Washington to demand jobs, issues may be sharpened. But in the process there is also a fragmentation, an obscuring rather than an accentuation of essentially "urban" aspects of the demands. Urban interest groups have become craftsmen of consensus precisely to avoid this liability. The idea of an urban program supported by a multi-faceted urban constituency is too likely to be lost if the emphasis shifts to particulars and specifics. Perhaps by dramatizing only what is genuinely representative of mutual and overall urban interest can the urban crisis retain the high profile in public attention that it finally developed in the 1960's. The politics of the particular, while at times susceptible to confrontation and to the tentative acceptance of so-called non-negotiable demands, obscures the urban crisis elements as such even if limited objectives are for the moment attained. It may in fact be easier to act on a minute, specialized emotional goal. It is far less complicated for the authorities to turn over a hospital to a group of Young Lords than to tackle the knot of historical, political, social, and economic factors whose interaction gave rise to the urban ghetto and to the Young Lords and the Black Panthers in the first place.

In short, although confrontation politics and dramatic demonstrative actions may, in some cases, accelerate action on an urban program, they probably cannot expand the base of support necessary for its maintenance. Dramatic strategies, productive for a flickering moment, tend to become counterproductive in the long run by alienating the officials they push into action. The urban lobbies are sensitive to the fragility of democratic consent. They must prevent whatever obscures the urban crisis as a public issue and what might hinder coming to grips with its wider and more complex aspects.

Inter-governmentalism

It took almost thirty years of persistent effort before urban interest groups could bring the condition of the cities to the present level of federal consciousness. It is a cliché to call the modern metropolis environmentally untenable. From time immemorial, cities have been both the pride and the problem children of society. In the United States, however, it was not until the 1930's that remedies for their plights and blights began to be fashioned on the national, rather than exclusively on the local level. Urban problems came to be a subject of direct concern to the federal government. The occasion for this shift was a national catastrophe, namely, the Great Depression which impoverished the cities as well as large parts of the country's population. Price supports were given to farmers, and something had to be done to keep the cities from fiscal collapse as well.

In 1933, President Roosevelt decided that municipal bankruptcy and rampant unemployment should be dealt with as part of a national recovery program. Even the New Deal programs, however, were not primarily directed to problems of cities *per se* but at unemployment in general. Still, the programs for housing and public works that were instituted marked the beginning of direct federal-city relations. These programs were the ancestors whose progeny is an ever increasing number of federal aid programs operating in metropolitan areas.[8] Nevertheless, most of these forerunners continued as piecemeal measures directed at particular functional difficulties. They were not designed to cure urban problems as such, and urban ills were not even identified as separate phenomena.

There is no doubt that the urban component of federal programs has by now received increasing attention as a specialized field of public policy and that the new direct federal-city relationship which has emerged has altered the structure of American federalism by elevating the cities to *de facto* "third partners in federalism."[9] The primary support for this new relationship came from the Conference of Mayors. This group has influenced the institutional structure of American federalism through its

emphasis on direct federal-city relations that bypass state governments, the constitutionally-intended intermediaries. Bypassing the
state government receives ideological support from the USCM's
insistence on municipal home rule. It views direct federal-city
relations as a means of avoiding unsympathetic and uninformed
consideration of urban problems by rural-dominated state legislative bodies. To the extent that cities can discharge what were
once state functions, they render state government less important,
certainly in a lesser middleman role. Moreover, "states have been
bypassed, and doubtless some have used this as an excuse to avoid
their responsibilities of providing the legal and governmental
conditions under which urban problems can effectively be
confronted." [9]

The question of which spheres of action belong to the city
and which to the state is a constant source of friction among
cities, states, and various interest groups involved with either or
both levels of government. The National Association of County
Officials prefers to have the dealings of the federal government
with the cities channeled through the states. The USCM argues
for direct federal-city contacts and contracts. The real controversy
is about who will control the purse strings and patronage of
federal aid. There is some evidence that the USCM has been
successful in securing federal funds directly for the cities. This
pressure group is of particular interest to the analyst of federalism
because of its effects on inter-governmental relations—their substance, their direction and their process. Certainly as pervasive
and pertinent as its inter-governmental effects are its inter-governmental *features*—the nature of its membership (cities through
their mayors), the target of its activities (the federal government),
the beneficiaries of its results (local municipal government), and
the status of its main competitors (state governments). This kind
of inter-governmental pressure group and its role in the political
process is as yet a little-explored phenomenon and merits more
attention.

If the Conference of Mayors is typical, it would appear that
the inter-governmental urban pressure group, operating in a more
concentrated area than does its closest state counterpart, the
Governors' Conference, serves a highly specialized and unique
combination of functions. It is more than an interest aggregator,

representative and lobby. It facilitates and expedites communications and transactions as a liaison between the three different levels of government in a revised federal structure. Its machinery is adapted to its composite role. To interpret the needs of the cities to the federal government in the legislative and administrative areas, the Conference has an office in the nation's Capitol where a full-time staff drafts bills, evaluates new ideas, consults with Congressional committees, arranges hearings, screens testimony and structures impressive lobbying coalitions. It suggests new administrative regulations, or amendments to old ones, and it provides the Administration with data on how existing programs are functioning. Not least, it also provides forecasts of probable demands for additional funds from the federal coffers.

Like a traffic policeman on a two-way street, it also sets itself to interpreting the federal government to the cities with information and advice on existing federal-city aid programs and with assessment of the political ramifications these programs are likely to have on and in individual cities. It keeps its members informed of new legislation and administrative rulings and advises them of the significance of changes. And, when difficulties arise over the implementation of a federal program for cities, it becomes the mediator and the agent of both collective and selective bargaining between member cities and the federal government.

The USCM plays a further role as a channel of internal communication among its own member cities through the services of its permanent staff, through annual meetings and workshops, and through publications that report how one or another city copes with problems that are more or less endemic to large population centers. It also prepares studies and describes experiments of a wide range of interest for local officials.

A significant acknowledgement of the importance of the intergovernmental pressure group as liaison between levels of government is the requirement imposed by the Federal Bureau of the Budget pursuant to Presidential executive order that executive agencies consult with the Conference of Mayors, the Governor's Conference, the National League of Cities and the National Association of Counties about all major administrative regulations affecting federal urban programs or involving relations among the three levels of government. The effect of this requirement

was to give to the inter-governmental lobby a formal position
as part of the federal decision-making machinery and to make
official its role as a vehicle in the conduct of urban affairs among
sovereign and semi-sovereign units.[11]

It is particularly desirable for cities to have urban interest
groups implanted as consultants within the federal government in
light of the effect of federal programs on the power structure
and politics of local communities. Urban lobbies have a large
stake in infusing local preferences into the federal policies that
so directly relate to them. In the 1960's, little concerning urban
government and its politics was unaffected by some form of
federal input. Models of community power structure popular
with political scientists because they elucidate the process of
urban government by placing it within a theoretical framework
become less precise as the federal variables effecting local choices
and constraints become more prominent.[12] Who gets what, how,
and why out of the rival claims of local officials and bureaucrats
is now, if not largely settled, certainly to some extent pre-
ordained by federal programs that are available, by how much
federal money is allocated, and by what autonomy-reducing
guidelines are imposed. That this federal involvement changes
unpredictably yet constantly as to amounts of monies allocated
to cities, as to the number, kinds and qualities of programs authorized, or as to the federal personnel located in regional and local
field offices to exercise some form of supervision even further
accentuates the effects of federal presence in the cities. There is
an ongoing reshuffling of the relative influence of community
leaders, of the status of different groups, and of the scope of
activities of individual local administrative agencies.

The complications are such that one can see the irony of a
reversal of judgments. In the 1930's the cities were insisting that
only the federal government could solve their difficulties. In the
1970's blame for failure to mitigate the urban crisis is attributed
to federal "red tape," an accusation that was bound to follow
the requested federal intervention.

But it is important to realize at this juncture that although
the urban lobbies have been fairly successful at diverting financial
resources from the federal government to uses of the city, these
resources are diverted in the form of legislation authorizing specific

programs. These programs may have unintended and unanticipated effects, as happened with some programs fought for by large-city urban lobbies. An example will bear on the discussion of the inter-governmental lobby as an advocate of social change.

The USCM's interest in relief and in public housing for the core city, combined with relative inattention to the long-range consequences of the Federal Housing Administration's (F.H.A.) mortgage program, may have compounded rather than alleviated urban problems. Public housing, coupled with relief, made the cities attractive to the immigrating poor and created gigantic unforeseen demands for service. The most likely source of taxes to pay for the services, the middle class, was helped to escape the city tax collector by the F.H.A., which financed suburban homes. In addition, the USCM's focus on renewal of commercial districts as opposed to residential areas may have exacerbated what became an acute housing shortage, and its relative inattention to the availability of sites or financial aid for relocation of those displaced by either commercial or residential renewal increased the political problems and group discontents with which the mayors later had to deal.

On the other hand, in addition to unforeseen problems, there have been unforeseen advantages. The concentration of the blacks in the central cities gathered them into a geographically compact area, enabling the consolidation of electoral power. This permitted the black minority to become a politically effective voting bloc within cities, potentially better able to assert itself within the American political system. Although the social upheavals of the 1960's catalyzed by some of the leaders of this minority in urban centers across the nation appear threatening to those who are living through them, history may reveal "the black problem" in a different perspective. To paraphrase Irving Kristol, the social protest of the urban blacks may infuse the cities with a new vigor and purpose. "Who else would care enough to try?"

Local Government as an Interest Group

Since urban lobbying involves interests groups of officials from one level of government pressuring demands upon officials

from another level of government, it is a process which raises
interesting questions pertaining to the role of government institutions in a pluralist democracy and to traditional organization
theory.

The pluralist model of democracy offered by political scientists as a frame of reference by which to understand American
politics makes several assumptions of great importance for democratic theory. It suggests that a vast bureaucracy remains responsive to grass roots sentiments because of ready access to
government by the governed through interest groups representing
numerous demands, occupations, persons or economic interests.
These organizations bring together and articulate to the government the shared attitudes and desires of their members. Representation by interest groups is especially important for the concerns of geographically dispersed minorities because of the disadvantages for dispersed "interest" built into the electoral system.

To supplement group representation and in order to remain
in office, competing elites within the government seek to anticipate the needs of the public and respond to them. Government
itself, according to the pluralist model, acts as arbitrator, mediator
and agent of reconciliation among conflicting interests. It has no
substantive interests of its own except to maximize support and
legitimacy for its regime by presiding over an "equitable" allocation of resources among its constituents, Thus, the public interest
"is not some kind of pre-existing platonic idea; rather, it emerges
out of differences of opinion, reasonably propounded," and relies
on some notion of "the Democratic Principle as the supreme
arbiter of conflict." [13]

Looking at the phenomenon of urban lobbying, one finds
government lobbying government for independent interests of
its own, although sometimes coinciding with interests of its
constituency. Referring once again to the relationship between
the federal government and the Conference of Mayors to illustrate the point, one finds that two sets of public officials each
with its own constituency, legal standing, and independent source
of public authority, compete with each other over the allocation
of resources. If the lobbyist and the lobbied are both made up
of elected public officials, democratic theory can subsume the
process under the rubric of "representation," whereby those

chosen by one constituency attempt, in the name of that constituency, to influence those chosen by another.

This is perhaps a simplistic view; government acting on government does so with interest and reasons of its own that are sometimes far removed from (although not necessarily conflicting with) those of the governed to whom it is theoretically accountable. That there are policy implications of government acting on its own behalf is suggested, for example, by the lobbying activities of large-city mayors (through the USCM) directed at the poverty program. Through a series of amendments to the Economic Opportunity Act, "local government as a pressure group" succeeded in placing local Community Action Agencies—private community groups authorized to receive federal funds—under the control of local government. These agencies were originally intended to be private groups which could use public funds to organize their communities politically, and to involve "maximum feasible participation" by the poor. However, local public officials acting collectively as an interest group succeeded in eliminating possibilities for using poverty program funds for political action and in ensuring that the poor could participate only to the extent that local government could still control the program.[14]

Similarly, the possible divergence between the interests of government and the interests of constituents may be seen in the attitudes of the inter-governmental urban lobbies (especially the League and the Conference) towards representation of metropolitan areas. Speaking as officials of government, these groups focused their attention on municipalities as presently constituted, and on government over which the officials had, and hoped to keep, legal jurisdiction. However, as urban problems become more complex and as numbers of individual cities in one geographic area tend to act inter-dependently as a "megalopolis," the question arises whether the fragmented, individual city approach to urban affairs helps or hinders intelligent social planning. Is government acting on government limited in its capacity to consider the metropolitan area as an urban interest by virtue of the vested concerns of the urban inter-governmental lobbies? If so, the 1968 Presidential task force report on urban problems which recommends a form of federal-city tax sharing favoring those cities willing to institute some type of metropolitan area consolidation implies that the inter-governmental urban lobbies may be reinforcing an outdated approach by their insufficient emphasis on regionalism.

Government influencing government for interests of its own has been legitimized as an idea by its institutionalization in the Advisory Commission on Intergovermental Relations (ACIR). The ACIR is a part of the executive branch of the federal government, and its members are representatives from country, city, state and federal government. Within it, interests concerning public policy come into direct conflict. This ratification in ACIR of a governmental interest *per se* by a democratic system seems at variance with democratic theory.

What are these governmental interests, and to what extent do they receive priority over constituency interests? To what extent does local government shape these policies of the federal government which apply to itself? Is it healthy for government to be self-referent?

Viewed from a different perspective, government representing interests of its own appears merely as another aspect of interest articulation in a democracy. It becomes part of the idea of functional representation by interest groups and bureaucracies which supplement representation of sections of population (numbers) in Congress, of national majorities in the Presidency, of states in the Senate. Local government represented by interest groups might even be considered a necessary and natural analogue to the representation of states in the Senate, especially now that the cities have become all but constitutional partners in federalism. Yet it still seems reasonable to ask whether, when government comes to Washington as an interest group, it has priority over private interest groups in its access to federal decision-makers? If so, how much does its political leverage derive from overlap of electoral constituencies and shared responsibilities for operating federal programs among officials of the levels of government involved. How does government lobbying government capitalize on *ipso facto* legitimacy derived from the electoral process, a factor not shared by other groups? Does its special status make a governmental interest group a particularly desirable ally for other interest groups to an extent which enables it to extract special concessions for its support?

A membership of elected officials may be a liability as well as an asset to an interest group. Ostensibly, at least, it may place an inherent limitation on the group's range of activities, preclude it from participation in party politics and election or make it necessary to avoid certain controversies. How is group cohesion maintained when its policies come into conflict with the constituency needs, political ideology or ambitions of individual members?

Discussing urban lobbying in terms of group theory, and looking at the relationship between the urban interest groups and the establishment of the Department of Housing and Urban Development, one observes that Professor David Truman's insights as to how governmental institutions change in response to the activities of pressure groups have even further application. Truman's description of the growth of associations and their entrance into politics to adjust relations between private sectors and government also applies to one level of government acting on another.[15] In other words, within the federal-state-local hierarchy, an array of governmental interest groups rises to achieve equilibrium in inter-governmental relations.

This, along with the more general assertion of the relevance of urban interest groups to federal urban policy, becomes both timely and open to question when considered against the background of the argument emerging in the 1960's that group theory is outdated and no longer useful to an understanding of the allocation of values. According to this body of opinion, interest groups as discussed by scholars such as David Truman, V. O. Key, and E. E. Schattschneider are defunct because they no longer perform their functions adequately. Lewis Dexter, Roger Bauer, and Ithiel de Sola Pool point out, for example, that interest groups often fail to perceive their own interest.[16] Many lack adequate staffs and channels of communication to keep abreast of developments in Washington and to keep their members informed. Only highly organized groups with cohesive memberships and sharply defined goals are able to take advantage of access to the federal government. Moreover, as the later work of Schattschneider points out, the whole array of interest groups has an "upper-class bias" and therefore leaves out the interests of that part of society which most needs representation.[17] Theodore

Lowi adds to this dialogue by exposing a conservative attitude toward change by all established groups.[18] Given these indictments, how well do the urban lobbies express the interests of their members and of their ultimate constituencies? For example, does a membership made up exclusively of mayors give the USCM an upper-class bias? Do large constituencies of blue-collar workers and ghetto dwellers create a countervailing influence? Still another opinion on the role of pressure groups comes from the advocates of planning-programming-budgeting systems (PPBS). They think that ideally, policy should result from "overall planning" as opposed to "collision of interest." [19] Their argument is that a systems approach creates an opportunity to make choices on the basis of "objective merit," or, at least, on the basis of a greater ranger of alternatives; by contrast, they view the choices of special interest groups as lacking in scope, imagination, and information, and involved in the backdoor bargain politics of smoke-filled rooms. Furthermore, the argument goes, agencies that use systems analysis develop greater in-house capabilities to make sophisticated policy that meshes with all related programs, which in contrast to the limited policy-making capacities of groups, provides a possibility for gauging the organizational requirements of society as a whole.

A third hypothesis about the role of interest groups is that these traditional pressure groups are being displaced by "intervening elites," who usually enter the policy process attached to an *ad hoc* task force. These intervening elites are, as Professor Robert Wood describes them, a "fairly numerous, recurrent species, holding some skills or positions certified through some gateway procedure, possessing political influence, and though not formally or highly organized, exhibiting empathy." [20] Combined in the form of a task force, they are defined as a group of experts, marshalled to bring enlightened, impartial and politically unencumbered expertise to bear on an issue while at the same time representing broad sectors of society. Such intervening elites are called into government to offer high-level policy supposedly as a counterweight to bureaucracy and interest groups. Like the university research center, *ad hoc* task forces are playing increasingly large roles in the policy-making process. Is group politics, therefore, an anachronism? Have the urban lobbies had to adapt to changed conditions of policy-making by task forces and intervening elites, or are those so intervening merely another form of organization of the traditional interest groups operating under more progressive names?

An Urban Policy Subsystem

A political system, or subsystem, is defined by social science systems theorists as a persistent pattern of relations involving power and authority which results in the allocation of values.[21] But this definition does not adequately reveal all the elements which must be present. To be correct in an assertion that policy decisions about a particular issue area (such as federal urban policy) are made by a policy subsystem distinguishable as a policy-producing network, it is necessary to show several things. First, most major decisions affecting that area must be made by the interaction of certain "hard core" participants, those with the deepest and most continuous involvement. Second, identifiable linkages and communications patterns must exist among the actors. These interconnections must form the basis for shared attitudes, and the participants must address themselves to the same policy agenda. They must speak the same language, understand it in the same terms, and think of themselves and of each other as participants in a continuing dialogue. In short, a political subsystem must exist in the consciousness of its participants as well as from the perspective of an outside observer or according to a definition by systems theorists.

During the 1960's, Moynihan's plea for a national urban policy was also made in the mass media, by intellectuals, by ordinary citizens and by public officials. These demands for a national urban policy both assumed the existence of decision-making machinery having the qualities of an urban policy subsystem that could convert urban programs into urban policy and at the same time offered a host of suggestions for new institutions that would bring them into being: a Congressional committee on urban problems, an "urban think tank," or permanent Presidential "urban advisory councils" (in response to which President Nixon established the Council on Urban Affairs and the Office of Intergovernmental Relations). These proposals imply that a policy subsystem for federal urban affairs does *not* as yet exist, or if it does, that it is inadequate. In any event, from the demands for a "national urban policy" one senses a general suspicion that the urban aspect of federal policies has been fortuitous, an accidental fallout of general legislation. The existing formal research which bears on the machinery for federal urban policy-making divides equally on both sides of the discussion. The question persists: is there, or is there not, a federal urban policy-making subsystem which fits the definition here discussed?

The question has been examined by Professor Harold Wolman who finds that a federal urban policy-making subsystem does exist with respect to housing policy.[22] By contrast, Frederick Cleveland, in *Congress and Urban Problems*, finds that no such subsystem exists, at least not with respect to urban policies in Congress.[23] To discover what mixture of sources, initiatives and concerns are usually reflected in federal urban legislation, Cleveland asks:

> Does policy and tactical leadership normally come from the members of Congress and their staffs? From interest groups professionals? From executive officials or White House staff? Is there a concentration of urban specialists located on Capitol Hill, perhaps attached to a Congressional committee? Or in the Department of Housing and Urban Development? Or in the headquarters office of one or another interest group? [24]

Had Cleveland, in fact, looked in all of these places, he would have found an element of policy-making and leadership in each, and discovered in them a clear pattern of interaction and consultation among them all before a bill is formally submitted. In *Congress and Urban Problems* only early legislative "case" histories are examined by several authors, *viz*: on federal aid to airports, water and air pollution, juvenile delinquency, food stamps, and mass transit.

Given the limits of his investigation and choices of legislation, the conclusion Cleveland submits is not surprising. Most of the programs examined by Cleveland were relatively new insofar as they pertained specfically to urban areas. When they were first enacted, the patterns of interaction among urban interest groups, Congressional committees and others with jurisdiction over these programs were not yet fully established. Moreover, no study in the series examines the Banking and Currency Committees, or their relationships to the USCM, the NLC, and HUD. Nor is there a study of housing and urban development, the longest established area of federal activity in urban affairs.[25] It appears finally that the examined policy battles involved themes of only peripheral interest to large cities at the time the legislation was written.*

In light of this, it seems that further research might lead to different conclusions. It would appear reasonable, in checking whether an urban policy subsystem exists, to examine the relationships between those urban interest organizations, Congressional Committees, and Executive agencies most deeply and *continuously* involved with the best established federal urban programs. The substantive area of major, if not exclusive concern, should be housing and urban development, and the organizations which should receive most attention are the USCM and its ally, the National League of Cities. They have a history of continuous dealings with the Administration, Congress, the House and Senate Banking and Currency Committees, through which most urban-oriented legislation must pass, and the Department of Housing and Urban Development and its constituent agencies which administer more programs of interest to cities than any other Department. Primary attention must be devoted to the linkages between them that make for their continuity: overlapping membership, rotation and overlap of staff, formal and informal communications channels, and policy-making committees on which all of the participants are

---

* Examples of this include: the intended beneficiaries of food stamps were the farm interest and the Southern counties, not the urban poor who were to receive the food stamps. Aid to airports is primarily an airline interest and a national defense interest. Programs for control of water pollution (until the rise of "the environment" as a political issue in the late 1960's) were primarily for the benefit of conservationists and sportsmen. They were of concern only to those small cities that were in need of federal loans to build sewage plants because a poor credit rating prevented them from raising the necessary funds by the traditional method of bond issues.

represented. The process by which federal urban policy evolves, the structure of the decision-making arena, and the special capabilities and limitations of those who interact within it are all of major importance for the content of that policy. Examining the federal urban policy-making process in this context may reveal at which point in federal decision-making demands for urban programs can be most profitably expressed, and whether the present arrangement of authorities in the area of urban legislation can tolerate the anticipated stresses.

Urban lobbying, the emergence of inter-governmental pressure groups, and the organization of elected public officials into private associations are all aspects of a response to the comparatively recent release of the spending power of the federal government. The New Deal programs of the 1930's planted seeds of intensified rivalries among state, county, and local government officials over the allocation and administrative control of federal funds. The growth of direct federal involvement with urban problems stimulated a concommitant growth in the number, organizational quality, and spectrum of concern of interest groups impinging on federal urban policy. The history of the emergence of these groups will illustrate how they provide the nucleus for an ever-expanding urban policy network.

CHAPTER II

Emergence of
an Urban Interest Network

THROUGHOUT American history, "self-reliance" has been an article of faith. While occasionally rejected (as in protective tariffs) it has stood up through the years as a kind of treasured national possession. Up to 1933, the prevailing attitude, where it was significantly expressed, was that municipalities should be self-supporting. If there were problems beyond their own management competence, local governments were expected to deal with the federal government through their states. The urban interest groups that were in existence before 1933 were concerned with city government reform, and, in some cases, as in the formation of the National League of Cities, with the relations between a state government and its cities.

By 1932, however, it was clear that the financial structure of the country was close to disintegration and that municipal governments were near paralysis—as little able to support themselves as were individuals and even economic giants throughout the nation. The tradition of city "self-reliance" began to fade immediately following President Roosevelt's commitment to use the spending and regulatory power of the federal government for national recovery. Like the economic interest blocs of prior decades, the cities depended for their rescue on a general federal bail-out.

This process made them competitors with all other applicants and recipients of federal first-aid and in due course led to signifi-

cant changes in many formerly stable relationships. Those between
the cities and their rural-dominated state legislatures, though abra-
sive, had a certain primitive, accepted viability. The remedial efforts in the wake of the Great Depression disrupted these relations
and little by little induced radical changes in those between the
federal and state governments.

It should not be surprising that federal participation entered
what was formerly only the business of the state, if that. The rapid
proliferation of city problems and the clearly demonstrated incapa-
city of state legislatures to deal with the urban disasters within
their jurisdictions combined to bring forth associations of urban
interest groups determined to change relations between the federal
government and the cities. For it is well established that as a pattern in the process of political change, disturbances in society
which disrupt established relations lead to the formation of organizations which serve to stabilize the particular disruption.

The creation of the United States Conference of Mayors con-
formed to this historic pattern. It came into being to encourage
the beginnings of a federal-urban involvement and continued in
order to expand that involvement. It has endured because an instrument was imperatively needed to structure an urban policy
network for guiding federal participation. The rationale for the
permanent organization of the USCM was clearly its resolution of
February, 1933,

> that a permanent organization offers the only opportunity for
> a continuous inquiry into municipal questions in order that—
> the needs of municipal government will be properly presented
> before public and before Congress and the President.

In June, 1932, Mayor Frank Murphy of Detroit called a meeting of fifty mayors of the largest cities to draft a plan under which
the federal government would share the cities' burden of unemployment relief. This was the first time that the large cities had
come together to influence national legislation. They intended to
go beyond generalized pleas and petitions—to present a specific
program to the President and to press for its adoption.

In 1933, the large-city mayors met again to consider their financial plight in the wake of a general collapse of municipal credit. Out of this meeting came the formal organization of the Conference of Mayors. There was now an aim even broader than the new endeavor to safeguard the interests of cities as these might be affected by federal legislation. On top of its role as first city lobby of its kind, it became the first official liaison agency for fostering cooperation and direct communication between the cities and Washington, and among the cities themselves. Surprisingly, unlike many political institutions whose original functions tend to change over time, those of the Mayors Conference have remained what they were at the outset.

It was not the first group to concern itself with specifically urban problems, nor the first organization of municipal officials. At the time, however, it was the most important, and others in the family of sibling groups into which it was born quickly developed close working relations with the USCM. Several of them had grown out of the reform movements of the early 1900's and had a "professional" or "research" orientation towards improved city government. Some were "single purpose" groups developed in response to newly-apparent urban needs such as housing and welfare. Others were formed by functionally related public officials who wanted to share experiences and promote inter-city and inter-governmental communication. Still others had been prodded into existence by the federal government. The most important of the older groups, in terms of continuous involvement with urban matters and their relevance to the 1970's, were the National League of Cities (NLC), the National Housing Conference (NHC), and the National Association of Housing and Redevelopment Officials (NAHRO).

The NLC, until the 1960's called the American Municipal Association, had been established in 1924 as a national federation of state leagues of cities. At first it might appear that the NLC made the USCM unnecessary. It operated as a city-state lobby; the standard roadway, up to that time, conforming to tradition. However the insufficient weight of the large urban centers in the League along with its failure to achieve a united front eroded its potential for exerting the necessary influence. In fact, recognizing this liability, and foreseeing the need to become more involved with the federal government, the League's Director in 1931 warned that "either this organization will fulfill that need, or some new organization will arise to do so."

Another of NLC's limitations was structural. Mayors belonged to it only indirectly through membership in their respective state leagues. When Mayor Murphy called the first meeting of large-city mayors in 1932, he also invited the NLC, which replied that it could not take part as an organization because its constitution required it to be an association for service to *leagues* of municipalities. NLC's members were the directors of state leagues of cities, not the mayors. They lacked the prestige that presaged access to the highest level of government. Moreover, the NLC was dominated by small and medium-sized cities, while many cities were not members at all during its first ten years. In some states the basic membership units, leagues of cities, did not even exist. As appears from its proceedings of 1933, the NLC seemed to be aware of the difference. Its President, taking note of the first meeting of the Conference of Mayors, reported to his organization that

> Such an organization [USCM] would have considerable prestige and influence. As our organization is working along similar channels, it is essential that there be the closest relationship between the [NLC] and the National Conference of Mayors.

At its meeting the following year, the NLC decided that it, too, would become involved in national policy. Following the lead of the USCM, it passed resolutions calling upon federal agencies and Congress to help cities meet relief needs and to finance emergency public works measures. The two organizations now coexisted, sharing some of the same purposes and often working together so that for several years the facilities of the NLC were utilized as a common secretariat.

The National Housing Conference was formed in 1931 as a lobbying group to organize a drive for public housing. Unlike the USCM its purpose was fairly limited. Its membership, on the other hand, was more diverse, and consisted of community leaders, professionals, and public officials involved in housing. The NHC was also to serve an essential role as clearing house and policy base for national and local leadership in support of legislation. Because its membership included other organizations (while USCM was restricted to mayors and NLC to state league directors) the NHC therefore became the group through which labor, religious, social welfare and, later, civil rights organizations pursued their policy goals in the housing area. President of NHC, Nathaniel Keith, stresses that on specific issues it "frequently cooperates with the National Association of Home Builders, the United States Savings and Loan League, the National Association of Interest Savings Banks, and similar groups."

The National Association of Housing and Redevelopment Officials (formerly NAHO) was founded in 1933 and is, as its name indicates, a voluntary organization of public officials concerned with state and local housing. These public officials, in contrast with USCM members, are appointed rather than elected, and unlike USCM and NLC, NAHRO is not a lobbying group. It aims to be a clearing house for information on low-cost housing and to aid in the development of procedures for supervising, constructing and operating public housing projects. NAHRO provides consultants to help cities organize their local public housing agencies, and to draft enabling legislation for state public housing agencies. These legislation drafting activities brought NAHRO into a close relationship with the National Municipal League (NML), a "civic association" type of voluntary urban group whose expertise lies in drafting "model" state and local laws. From its inception, NAHRO has been an ally of the USCM.

NAHRO is limited in its ability to influence legislation because it is a tax exempt group and the Internal Revenue Code prohibits it from devoting "substantial" funds to political lobbying. However, although not a lobby group *per se*, it has been of considerable help to the federal government in formulating housing policy. As early as 1932 it had developed a comprehensive housing program for the United States which, as later amended by consultation with other interest group colleagues, is reflected in much of the early federal housing legislation.

Although the USCM, NLC, and NAHRO were the most visible participants in the early urban policy network, several other groups were also formed in the first third of the twentieth century. The National Municipal League, the International City Managers Association, the American Association of Public Welfare Officials,

and the American Society of Municipal Engineers were all concerned with some aspect of policy of interest to urban areas. Still
others had been organized under the sponsorship of the federal
government itself. The Municipal Finance Officers Association was
formed in 1906 under the auspices of the Census Bureau in order
to give the federal government better and more uniform statistical
data on municipal taxes, expenditures, and debt. Similarly, the Civil
Service Association of the United States was formed under government auspices to improve relations with and secure information
from localities.

Most of these organizations shared a number of difficulties:
lack of funds for permanent secretariats or for staffs capable of
providing year-round services. Several acquired a poor image, as
when their annual conventions were regarded as "joy rides" at
the taxpayers' expense. While there was in time improvement in
some of these conditions, one difficulty in particular was inherent,
and still persists. The rapid turnover among member officials who
were the leaders of municipal governments continues to cause
problems for several groups, especially the USCM.

These groups not only shared similar purposes and problems;
they were also linked together by a web of overlapping memberships and officers, by recurrent contacts on *ad hoc* committees and
advisory boards, by joint activities, by reliance on similar sources
of funds, and eventually, by proximity of location. John Stutz of
Kansas, who helped organize the NLC, was also Secretary of the
City Managers Association and Director of the Kansas League of
Municipalities. The central figure in the configuration, however,
was Louis Brownlow, who belonged to so many of these early
organizations that he became in his own person a major interorganizational contact point. To establish even closer cooperation,
he brought the groups together in Chicago and formed a central
secretariat to provide services for all of them, to establish still
other groups, and to encourage an inter-dependence by which to
insure that, as a collectivity of urban groups, they could fully
cover the field while allowing each to concentrate on its speciality.[1]

In 1930, Brownlow prevailed upon the Spellman Fund to give
its financial support to the American Association of Public Welfare
Officials so that this group could better meet relief and unemployment needs. Subsequently, with Brownlow's guidance and encour-

agement, the Spellman Fund provided grants to so many urban-oriented organizations (both the public official and the "service" types) that the urban interest groups became even more closely linked together.* A persistent pattern of relations was taking shape.

Louis Brownlow, John Stutz, and Charles Merriam of the University of Chicago, had for years been working to set up a central "institute for municipal government" that would, as far as possible, bring together organizations of local public officials. In 1930 a delegation was sent to the Governor's Conference Convention to request that this Conference incorporate within its own secretariat, the Council of States Governments, a meeting place for public officials. This was for the purpose of having state and city officials participate in an experiment in inter-governmental cooperation. The Governors objected to the proposal because it would have meant accepting foundation funds, so that Brownlow's "meeting place for public officials" had to be set up without them; the Public Administration Clearing House (PACH) was established in Chicago shortly thereafter.

A common center for both city officials and state chief executives might have bridged the communications gap and aborted the sense of mistrust which even now exists between them. The fact is that such distrust feeds the already intense rivalry between state and local chief executives as to which level of govrenment ought to get most federal money and have greater administrative jurisdiction over federal programs. "Tax-sharing" proposals to have the federal government redistribute tax revenues and permit states and cities to use these unearmarked funds as they see fit, have been held up for years. The mayors of cities and the governors of states cannot, it seems, resolve the struggle as to what proportion of the coveted funds each should receive, and whether the city share should first go through the state. Had Brownlow's original plan

---

* The Municipal Administration Service, set up at the National Municipal League, had a board on which both NLC and the City Managers Association were represented. Brownlow himself had been President of the Leagues of Municipalities of Virginia, Tennessee, and New Jersey. He also was a member of the Advisory Committee of the National Housing Conference and President of the International City Managers Association. In 1930, Brownlow and thirteen others organized the Regional Planning Association.

been implemented, would the public interest groups still have aligned themselves into "state" and "urban" camps with respect to almost every policy issue? Perhaps! The competition might, however, have been less intense and the deadlock broken well before now.

Once established, PACH began to gather around itself as many organizations of public officials as it possibly could, including those which already had inter-connections: the International City Managers Association, the American Public Welfare Association, National League of Cities, Municipal Finance Officers Association, American Legislation Association and the United States Conference of Mayors. PACH, again with the financial support of the Spellman Fund, then helped encourage or establish still other groups—NAHRO and the American Society of Planning Officials, for example. As Brownlow put it in his personal history of these progressive steps, *A Passion for Anonymity*, many of the groups in the original Chicago circle are "now self-supporting and are integral and important parts of the American government (albeit not official)." [2]

There are many examples of interlocking directorships and interrelations among these early urban groups and between them and the federal government.* Richard Childs, President of the National Municipal League, was also a trustee of PACH. Herbert Emmerlich, Associate Director of PACH, was an early Commissioner of Public Housing. Paul Betters was both Executive Director of the NLC and Secretary of the USCM in 1933. In 1934, he became Executive Director of both organizations. These groups were generally coordinated by Brownlow and PACH to work with the federal government in the planning and operation of the public works program of the National Industrial Recovery Act (NIRA) of 1933. The Act made provision for two prongs of the attack on the depression: an industrial effort to be administered

---

* The USCM has sponsored the establishment of other organizations which became connected with the urban groups: the United States Conference of City Health Officers, the National Institute of Government Purchasing, and the National Institute of Municipal Clerks. It is also affiliated with the International Union of Local Authorities and the Inter-American Municipal Organization. Thus, it has a network of associates which form targets for coalition-building activities.

by Harry Hopkins, and a public works program under Harold Ickes.

The urban groups, especially the USCM, extended their help in launching the operations of the NIRA. It was necessarily a multi-agency program—as most programs that affect urban areas continue to be—with all the attendant difficulties of coordinating various federal bureaucracies. Hopkins and Ickes themselves were unable to agree on who was to spend what, and where, for which relief and public works. Hopkins wanted more grants and fewer loans; Ickes wanted more loans and fewer grants. Frances Perkins, then Secretary of Labor, was flooded with letters and telegrams. Every state, county, city and village needed a bridge, a school, something. But, as Brownlow described the prevailing situation, they submitted no plans, no cost estimates, no time estimates. Ickes called in Brownlow to help and learned to his surprise that Brownlow had already set up his organization, PACH, to coordinate the "Chicago groups" in order to help the Administration in planning, establishing priorities, allocating resources, and communicating with localities on the public works program.

The development of all of these interrelated groups, their clustering around PACH as a joint secretariat, and their coordination through Brownlow to work with the federal government was, in looking back, the real beginning of a federal urban policy network laboring to become an urban policy-making subsystem. Little by little a persistent pattern of relations emerged among groups and individuals inside and outside the federal government that established the agenda items and level of debate; that allocated priorities and resources; and that provided the interlocking network without which no urban programs or urban policy can operate effectively.

Other steps which expanded the policy-making capacities of goverment, in keeping with the growing capacities of private groups, continued this process of a slow evolution of an urban policy subsystem. There was the Budget and Accounting Act of 1921, and the Reorganization Acts of 1939 and 1946. There was the development of a method for the central clearance through the Bureau of the Budget of agencies' legislative proposals and budgets so that they fit more coherently into the President's overall programs. There were the agencies set up by the National Housing Act of 1937 and their later amalgamation into a Cabinet-level Department of Housing and Urban Development (HUD). The creation of the Housing Sub-committees and the Government Operations Committees of Congress were still other building stones in the construction of a constellation of institutions which could hopefully form a subsystem for decision-making on federal-urban policy.

As these necessary elements were developing, the interest group structure of the urban network took on its present form. It is multi-centered, with each group having a particular and distinguishing task to perform as well as a share in some functions with others. It is directed towards improving municipal governments and setting up communications among public officials both vertically betwen city, state and federal levels, and laterally among cities in different states. It brings municipal problems before Congress and assists the federal government in carrying out specific programs in urban areas. The relations among the urban groups, usually functionally cooperative, have been at the same time intensely competitive. This rivalry among the generalist urban groups and the more specialized ones, along with the competition between mayors and governors, between urban-oriented interest groups and their state-oriented counterparts, and generally among elected and appointed public officials throughout the political system explain the many internal changes and strategies within groups and the qualified effectiveness of the urban policy coalition.

Of all groups in the "Brownlow-Chicago" circle that participated in the early public works and relief programs, the USCM played the most important role. During the Roosevelt years it acted as the President's liaison office with the cities, and served him, in effect, as a "city brain trust." It was also the agency through which other groups offered their services. After the NLC made municipal finance consultants available to the USCM, cities applied to the USCM for NLC consultants who would help plan the financing of their expected share of federally supported projects. By an arrangement with the American Public Welfare Association, the USCM also was able to provide a free consultation service on the welfare problems of individual cities.

Moreover, the USCM circulated to mayors and city administrative officers information and materials published by other urban-oriented groups that shared in the task of mobilizing cities for the government's recovery program. Copies of the first loan applications from the Emergency Public Works Act were reproduced by the NLC and distributed through the USCM. NAHRO published a stream of pamphlets on public and low-cost housing and researched comprehensive programs for demolition of unsafe and unsanitary dwellings; these publications were dispatched by the USCM for the mayors to circulate among city offices concerned with building inspection, with health, and with fire prevention. NAHRO and the USCM also offered a joint field consulting service to help mayors carry out the recommendations put forth in the pamphlets. In this way, the two organizations cooperated in services to their own and each other's members, each group concentrating, of course, on its own area of expertise. These links were illustrative of an emerging issue subsystem.

The early activties of the USCM during the 1930's and 1940's, in their nature and scope, made it an important factor in the launching of the National Recovery Program by preparing the cities for a relationship with the federal government of a kind to which they had not been accustomed. It was in this period that the organization had perhaps its greatest impact as a pioneer in urban programs. The USCM came to be a kind of "secretariat" for the federal government, almost an unofficial "Department of Urban Affairs." During 1933 it was the only group capable of functioning in this way and warranted the judgment that it was potentially the group most likely to "lead" in any support system for federal urban policy. In the early 1930's its work in creating a basic national housing act and an urban renewal program "set the basic thrust of the Conference," according to the USCM's present Director. After World War II it acquired more refined tools.

The USCM's earlier strategies are here chosen in preference to contemporary examples as a focus for more intensive study because the 1930's were the years of the earliest direct federal fund allotments and of landmark urban development legislation. A case study dating to this period may therefore prove more revealing. Since the USCM still "covers the same bases," contemporaneity is not sacrificed and the ways in which urban lobbying works can be illustrated with historical objectivity.

Urban Lobbying; the Early Years

The USCM's activities vis-a-vis post-depression programs illuminate some of the functions and the potential importance of federal-urban lobby groups—especially one made up of mayors and thus holding "keys to the cities." The Conference's overall policy objective in the major recovery programs with an impact on cities —unemployment relief (the Emergency Relief Act of 1933), Public Works, the Highway Program of the National Industrial Recovery Act, and the Civil Works Program—was to involve the federal government directly, and above all to have it accepted that the welfare of the cities was a national problem. This meant a major policy innovation. There had always been dominant a political philosophy of circumscribed direct government intervention in promoting the public welfare. To the extent that the government had been active, it was mainly in terms of functional categories— interstate commerce, or agriculture, or labor, and not in terms of geographical areas, certainly not of population clusters such as "cities."

The USCM wanted the city and its problems to be considered as a distinct and separate "point-of-view" in arriving at political decisions, rather than simply as a subdivision of a state. The USCM's participation in federal programs prodded the federal government to take a new look, to acquire an urban perspective giving special attention to cities as independent entities, in terms of policy, legislation, and administration.

The Conference's course of action on these programs outlines additionally the supplementary policy commitments it was led to maintain and the roles and functions it still attempts to carry out. It follows precedents established in those early years for its main institutional targets, or arenas of effort. The derivative policies to which the organization is still committed are: 1) to press for a larger percentage of the federal contribution to federal-city matching fund programs; 2) to strengthen direct federal-city relations and programs; 3) to obtain outright grants as opposed to loans; 4) to bring about an assumption of federal responsibility for national problems such as relief, previously supinely assumed by the municipalities; 5) to institute federal policies whereby help would be extended to municipalities in their financial problems, and 6) to press for programs that would leave the cities maximum autonomy.

These distilled concerns suggest the answer to the question of what are the most crucial, i.e. real, interests of the generalist urban organizations (particularly those with city officials among their memberships) which distinguish their primary focus from that of others? Throughout the network of the generalist urban lobby groups run several common denominators that define the essence of urban interest representation. Most point with persevering insistence to a realization that what is more vital to the cities and of greater long range value than any other program or set of programs are the following: MORE MONEY (from practically any source, but within present political and legal circumstances, especially from the federal government); control and authority for city administrators over programs commensurate with their responsibility; grants given to cities directly rather than through states, in short, a way of acquiring home rule with federal assistance. The primacy of these preferences for unearmarked funds, political autonomy, and municipal home rule distinguishes the core of the general and the "governmental" urban interest from the more limited program-oriented objectives of more specialized and regular membership urban interest groups.

Congruent with these goals, the prime operational purpose of the USCM continues to be its drive to change the constitutional aspects of a federal structure which work to the disadvantage of cities. The federal government, for example, has the income tax power and has used it to an extent great enough to preclude substantial taxing of income by cities. State legislatures exacerbate this problem by their own taxes and by either prohibiting their municipal corporations from certain ways of raising funds or by imposing limits on amounts. In essence, cities want the same "home rule" status granted to states under the Constitution. The pressure for unearmarked funds is an attempt to filter out external (i.e. federal and state) dictation of local policy and program agenda. Thus since the 1930's, cities have pushed to become in essence "third partners in federalism."

This effort has brought to the USCM a number of distinctive roles. It serves as a representative of a large population segment;

as an information service for the federal government to help establish the factual basis for proposed legislation affecting cities; as a
pressure group exerting the political leverage of large urban constituencies on legislators and on the President himself; as a federal-
aids coordinator to facilitate the efforts of whatever city and
federal agencies are involved; as a "bureau of urban information
compiling and disseminating relevant data; as a drafter of the
actual texts, of "city oriented" sections of legislation and administrative rules (although only to provide policy input, not as a technical drafting service); and as chief liaison between the many
agencies concerned with urban affairs and the cities themselves.

These roles, along with the specific examples which follow,
reveal the *process* of urban lobbying as well as its substance and
some identifiable successes. This process of organized federal
lobbying by urban interests formed into groups was launched in
large part to allay the problem that the federal government did not
(and probably still does not) have the ability to interpret the
effects of its programs on cities without information from the
cities themselves.

It was the USCM which assembled the large-city mayors to
dramatize and call to the attention of the President and Congress
the necessity for federal action on the direct relief problem.[3]
Relying on the strength of their claim to represent 45 per cent
of the population, the mayors passed a resolution and petitioned
for action to the President, the Speaker of the House, and the
Chairmen of the House Ways and Means Committee and the
Senate Finance Committee. As a result the Conference was responsible for the inclusion of $3,000,000 in the 1932 Reconstruc-
tion Finance Corporation Act (HR4606) for direct relief and for
work relief, so much so that the USCM's entire resolution was
actually incorporated into the text of the final act. Since the cities
themselves had borne their own relief costs up to that point, this
was a major coup. Even before the relief bill had passed, USCM
Director Paul Betters organized the cities for immediate follow-up
action, a tactic which was both a subtle form of pressure and an
impressive show of efficiency. He advised mayors to make preliminary plans to avail themselves of the Act's provisions to relieve
unemployment in their cities "so that when the Act passes, funds
can be secured immediately." When HR4606 did become law of

the land the USCM staff could claim, as it did, that the new federal relief bill ". . . in its entirety carries out the USCM's resolution on unemployment relief passed in Washington." As a result, it said, "practically every large city is receiving financial assistance in meeting relief needs."

It became clear before long, however, that the Reconstruction Finance Act had other aspects not so beneficial to cities, and the Conference turned its attention to amending them. In February, 1933, it passed a resolution to petition Congress to liberalize the Act, in particular "to provide for definite financial aid *directly* to cities," and formally presented its petition to the Senate and House Banking and Currency Committees via both the Conference staff and a delegation of mayors who were important to the constituencies of Banking and Currency Committee members.

Under the Act, a city had to issue bonds as collateral against relief loans when the state did not itself apply for the funds that became available. A city project had to be self-liquidating in order to qualify for such loans. These provisions created problems which had not been clearly foreseen, but once raised, the Conference staff undertook to explain them to mayors, to Congress, and to Federal Relief Administrator Hopkins. Thus Betters met with Hopkins and arranged for a delegation of mayors to inform Congress that since the projects had to be self-liquidating, the enacted legislation could not be used by near-bankrupt cities that most needed such relief. This requirement was in fact sabotaging the avowed purposes of the relief program. The Conference also insisted on the elimination of the requirement that cities issue bonds against relief advances, contending forcefully that to do so would ignore the actualities of municipal financing. The cities were already over their heads in debt; some, moreover, had reached their states' constitutional limits on the bonds they could issue. Moreover, the Conference stressed, municipal credit was so bad that there was no foreseeable market for new bonds. Vast numbers of people could not even pay their taxes and local banks were refusing to lend to cities. "How" they complained "do you now expect us to issue bonds?"

The USCM was thus lecturing the federal government that its legislation had been written without knowledge of the true situation in the cities even while Congress was looking to the cities to embark on a large works program. The cities were not in a condition to issue bonds; they needed grants, not loans. Betters asked the mayors to do two things: to wire their Senators and Congressmen on the need for amending the Reconstruction Finance Corporation Act and to submit to the Banking and Currency Committees information on "how much money they had been able to get in short-term borrowing in 1933, what were the prospects of getting loans from local banks, and at what interest rate." As a result of this forceful presentation the Conference "secured repeal of the discriminatory sections of the Reconstruction Finance Corporation Act in the new relief act of 1933, which also made a further fund of $500,000,000 available for assistance to states and cities on relief."

Once the legislative phase of the relief program had been straightened out, Betters spent a great deal of time with Hopkins working on the program's operating details and securing his cooperation in seeing that state relief administrators dealt fairly with the cities. In August, Betters wrote the mayors urging them to notify him if they felt that their state agencies were not allocating an equitable share of relief money to the cities. In this way the USCM was insisting that its own members lobby for "right" defined for them by staff.

The public works activities of the Conference had substantial results. The public construction program that it sponsored in 1932 was embodied in Title II of the National Industrial Recovery Act of 1933. Of the $3,300,000,000 appropriated for public works, $1,000,000,000 was alloted to local governments. Moreover, the USCM succeeded in having 30 per cent of this money authorized as an outright grant as opposed to a loan. Then, by calling on strategically located mayors to contact those federal officials with whom they had special relationships, and by direct staff lobbying with the President, Congress, and Secretary of the Interior Ickes, the USCM secured, for the first time in the history of federal highway legislation, a section authorizing the use of federal highway funds within municipal corporate limits. More than $100,000,-000 of the $400,000,000 highway appropriation in the National Industrial Recovery Act went to the cities.

Again working through the Bureau of Public Roads and with

Colonel Spaulding of the Public Works Board, Betters succeeded in having written into the official regulations a requirement that each state allot at least 25 per cent of the funds it received under the highway provisions of NIRA to municipal highway projects. Betters wired every mayor urging him to contact his state highway department and put in a claim immediately, "so that the states would not spend all the money on *rural* projects." He included in his telegram a suggestion as to whom each mayor was to contact. The USCM thereby publicized the program for the federal government, as well as facilitating its use by the mayors. Finally, since the program was to be administered by state advisory boards that might not adequately consider the urban interest, Betters pushed through a requirement that at least one "city representative" sit on each of these boards.

Having demonstrated its ability to understand the ramifications of public works projects and to organize its members to implement federal programs, the USCM was then officially asked to share in drafting the rules and regulations of the Federal Emergency Administration of Public Works. It was also designated by Secretary Ickes as liaison office between the Public Works Administration (PWA) and the cities and, at Ickes' own request, it undertook an evaluation of how to speed up the PWA program. A description of Betters' job as official liaison man highlights the two-way role of the USCM in its service both to the cities and to the federal government. He was "to bring to the attention of the Public Works Administration those actual municipal problems which arise and to keep Washington thoroughly informed of the municipal angle."

Once the USCM staff had completed its study of how to accelerate PWA's program, a nation-wide meeting of mayors was called in Chicago for September, 1933, to focus national attention on the imperative need for greater speed to put more people quickly back to work. This maneuver can be interpreted as, among other goals, a utilization of the USCM by Ickes to lobby other sectors of the government on behalf of his program. Federal response, in any event, was to allot $400,000,000 for an emergency civil works program. Approximately $250,000,00 of this amount was expended in municipalities, reflecting acceptance of the USCM's proposal as to the proportion of quotas alloted to states which should be distributed to cities. The USCM also loaned the services of Betters to the federal government to assist in carrying out this program.

One activity of the USCM is particularly noteworthy because of its reciprocal utility for mayors, for Congress, and for administrative agencies. Before proposed legislation goes through Congress, the USCM gathers information from cities throughout the country on exactly what projects they would undertake and how much each project would cost if the proposed legislation were to be enacted and funded. This is indispensable information to Congress when considering a bill. Such research became a practice which proved vastly useful also for the mayors themselves; the assembled data is used by the federal administering agency as well, as a basis from which to calculate distribution of funds after a program is launched.

The subtle political pressures that can be applied by the USCM by virtue of its carefully compiled data relating to project popularity, cost estimates, and applications procedures are themselves fascinating, though not always obvious.

Much to the credit and satisfaction of the Conference as well as the NHC and NAHRO, the Public Works Act adopted USCM suggestions on many types of construction projects for slum clearance and housing and for municipal utilities. But of particular importance to the Conference was the fact that the President was authorized to make direct grants of up to 30 per cent of the cost of labor and materials. The legislation, however, did not make the 30 per cent grant feature mandatory. To prevent use of this ambiguity as a possible loophole the Conference adopted what proved to be an adroit pressure tactic: cities were told to make it clear in their applications that *all* of their plans and estimates were based on the certainty of receiving a 30 per cent grant. To force the issue further, Betters had the mayors submit projects that could be started within thirty days after the Act was signed. This maneuver was calculated to convince the Public Works Administration to give out the requested grants, on the basis that not to do so would hold up the entire federal program.

The PWA was in a vulnerable position with respect to this kind of pressure. As mentioned, it had designated the USCM as its special consultant and as a conduit through which its programs would be publicized and expedited. In a sense, then, it had been co-opted by its "clientele group," and in many ways dependent on it. For example, a booklet of special importance to PWA on "The Purposes, Policies, Functioning, and Organization of the Emergency Administration of Public Works," was written and distributed jointly by the Conference and the Public Works Administration. Part of the PWA's program elaborations (which the agency had authority to make under the initial legislation) were actually made by the Conference. Specifically, these were the lease method, the optional payment plan, the deferred interest and principle plan, acceptance of special types of collateral, and fair consideration of light plant applications. In fact, all circulars put out by the Public Works Administration were distributed to cities through the Conference.

The role of the USCM in the federal government's programs for relief and public-civil works has here been traced out in detail both to illustrate the capacities and importance of the group and to present a verbal cartography of urban lobbying that is also fairly typical. Several other lobbying type activities in these early years merit mention as well. For instance, the USCM and its allies acted as liaisons for the cities in their dealings with the Agriculture Department in its campaign to keep down food prices, with the Treasury Department on problems of municipal finance, with the Department of Labor, and with the Home Loan Bank Board (urging that loans be made for repairs as well as for construction). In the field of municipal finance, the USCM tried to obtain legislation authorizing the Reconstruction Finance Corporation to extend credit to cities on tax anticipation collateral and on tax delinquencies, but was unsuccessful in this effort. In studying bills introduced in Congress it carefully followed all federal legislation affecting cities such as the Federal Tax Act of 1933, the Tennessee Valley Authority Act, the Glass Banking Act, the Civilian Conservation Camps Act, and the Home Loan Act. All told, the USCM served as an "urban information bank." In 1933 alone, it collected data from dozens of different groups of city officials: from city treasurers on features of systems to permit installment payments of taxes; from police departments on fees charged for permits; from fire departments on charges for fire protection; from city auditors, building inspectors, budget directors, and many others.

Yet the prominence of the Conference during the first decade of its existence was the result of more than its value to the cities and the federal government and its service as coordinating agency through which other groups worked on New Deal Programs. There were ancillary influences and circumstances that surrounded the Conference during its early years and provided an environment in which was shaped the prime orientation of the organization and which probably also accounts for the fact that the NLC, NHC, NAHRO, and the USCM have remained separate organizations. The original environment out of which the urban policy sub-system emerged appears to have set the pattern for the system as it exists today.

It had been clear to everyone that the large cities were badly hurt by the Great Depression. They constituted therefore the forces of support, as well as of demand, for Roosevelt's large-scale public works programs. Since Roosevelt's policies alienated the traditionally more conservative rural and Southern Democrats as well as Republicans, some counterweight had to be found; Roosevelt fashioned his policies to tap the burgeoning national majorities in the heretofore "forgotten" metropolitan areas. Most big-city mayors at the time were Democrats, and many large cities were controlled by Democratic party machines. The large-city mayors controlled (and were controlled by) tightly knit party organizations which could deliver votes for their favored Congressmen, Senators, or Presidential candidate. In short, in the 1930's the large cities had political power; when the chips were down they used this political power to cash in for financial liquidity.

From this situation a relationship developed between the mayors of large cities and Roosevelt, built on a combination of party support and program support. The cities turned to federal government to bypass the unsympathetic and often uninformed consideration of city problems in rural-dominated state legislatures. In turn, Roosevelt needed, and got, the administrative and political support of the large cities, first to operate the National Recovery Program and later to mobilize fully for World War II. Political and administrative reciprocity, based on a membership of the highest elected public officials of large cities, gave the newly formed interest group, the USCM, a massive early strength.

These factors might have themselves been enough to foster the growth of a national association of the largest cities having the nation's chief executive as its main institutional target. There were, in addition, others to reinforce the relationship. Roosevelt's first term began the year that the Conference was organized; he was in office during the USCM's first twelve years. This unusually long period of continuity in policy and personnel in the executive branch enabled the Conference to develop dependable relationships and smoothly operating organizational patterns.

In 1934, the Conference elected Fiorello LaGuardia, the anti-Tammany Republican-Fusion mayor of New York, as its President. LaGuardia held the office from 1935–1945, a period during which Roosevelt occupied the White House. LaGuardia owed his election as mayor in part to Roosevelt. As a former Governor of New York, Roosevelt had been instrumental in bringing about the resignation of LaGuardia's predecessor, Tammany Mayor James Walker, following the disclosure of graft and corruption in the city government. That the President of the United States and the President of the Conference of Mayors had this bond helps explain the close relationship between the Conference and the federal government up to 1945, and adds further light as to how the USCM became the fulcrum of the emerging urban interest network during this period.

During this period also, the Conference made several important doctrinal commitments which were generally shared by its allied groups: commitments to the principle of increased federal spending and thereby, indirectly, to the idea of national economic controls; to the concept of direct federal-city relations and, in the process, to the by-passing of state governments; and to the idea of municipal home rule, and therefore to the attenuation of the powers of state government. Roosevelt's agreement with the first of these principles made the others viable since without federal money, there would have been little substance to direct federal-city relationships. Furthermore, Roosevelt had a knowledge of and sympathy for the problems cities faced in rural-dominated state legislatures. The doctrinal commitments became entrenched as Conference policy partly because the envisioned goals came within reach. The institutionalization of the USCM into the federal executive branch that occurred in the 1960's and which acknowledged and stabilized its position as an inter-governmental liaison organization thus results, in some ways, from accidents of history and from early political relationships which entrenched its power base.

In 1937, the Supreme Court upheld the Wagner Act and the Social Security Act, thereby opening the way for new avenues of governmental regulation of the economy. The early history of the Conference coincided therefore with a changing national policy that was complementary to its own goals; the second Roosevelt Administration saw the passage of the large scale public works projects, including public housing and slum clearance, that were high-priority objectives of the USCM.

The Housing Act of 1937 marked a transitional period for the Conference. Until then, it had been unchallenged as the most important and central lobby group in federal urban policy. In the late 1930's and 1940's, however, other groups broadened their area of collaboration with the government. Housing had been the special province of the NHC and NAHRO, so that these groups naturally became intensively involved with all aspects of the precedent-setting housing legislation that became part of federal urban programs between 1937 and 1949.

Moreover, both organizations broadened their scope of activities. NHC expanded its interests from public housing to low-cost housing in general. NAHRO broadened its concerns to include urban development. In addition, the post-war role of NLC expanded considerably. Its good relations with Congress helped make it especially effective in building support for urban programs, and its growth in membership and expanded research facilities strengthened its position among its group colleagues. It was not so much that the role of the Conference declined as that it moved away from occupying center stage as a larger urban policy network, with greater equality among participants, took shape.

The characteristics of this network were those of a coalition: the Conference, the NHC, the NLC and NAHRO (joined by labor and by the Public Works Administration) generally lined up on one side of an issue, while the more "conservative" groups such as the National Association of Real Estate Boards, the National Association of Home Builders, the United States Building and

Loan League, the Savings and Loan Associations, and the Mortgage and Banking Association lined up on the other. Thus Congressional hearings show that the USCM, the NLC, the NHC,
and NAHRO presented a united front in their testimony on all
proposed housing and urban development legislation between 1934
and 1949.

The USCM, NHC, and NAHRO, together with local housing
officials who came upon the scene under the Public Works Administration, undertook an extensive program of stimulating local
public concern over low-income housing. The landmark Housing
Act of 1937 incorporated the goals and program that had been
agreed upon and published jointly by NAHRO and the NHC in
1934 in a document entitled *Housing For America*. The initial
draft of the Act was accepted by Senator Robert Wagner as
drawn up by Ira Robbins, President of the NHC, and numerous
conferences on the bill were held among Wagner, the NHC,
NAHRO, and the USCM. The urban policy support groups outside of the government were especially important during these
years because public housing had little attraction for Roosevelt,
who preferred private ventures to direct government action on
housing. These provisons, of vital interest to cities, had to make
their way without Administration support.

During the Truman Administration, the Conference's attention
began to shift from the Presidency to Congress. According to most
literature on housing legislation, the Act of 1934 was basically an
Administration measure, the Act of 1937 more of a public interest
group project, and the Act of 1949 a joint effort of Congress, the
Administration, and the urban housing groups. Although Truman
was interested in urban legislation, the most important urban program during his terms of office was one in which Congress took as
great an initial interest as did the President. This was the Taft-
Ellender-Wagner Bill, which became the Housing Act of 1949,
the first step in federal aid for urban renewal. It authorized ex-
penditure of one billion dollars in the form of loans to cities for
planning redevelopment projects and for acquiring the property
that had to be cleared. The Conference still regards the passage of
this Act as one of its outstanding achievements. It not only supported the bill, but "put the strategy and substance of this act
together," with Betters, as Executive Director, working directly

with the President and his Cabinet officers. Although the 1945 bill was drafted by the National Housing Agency it was not an agency bill; in fact, the NHA Administrator Blandford showed little enthusiasm for it. More accurately it was drafted by the National Housing Agency in consultation with Senators Taft, Ellender, Wagner, the USCM, NAHRO and the NHC. All of the participating groups consider the urban renewal concept among their best achievements.

During the period 1940–1960 Congress became as important an institutional target for group lobbying as the Presidency had been earlier, and the USCM was no longer the secretariat for other groups. As the urban policy network expanded, there came about a division of labor for several valid reasons.

In the early 1940's the work of the USCM and its allies was concerned with mobilizing the cities for the war effort and with civil defense and defense housing. During the war, the federal government acquired more extensive (and coordinated) control of housing. It set up building priorities, saw to it that previously autonomous housing agencies worked together, and determined the occupancy and prices of defense area housing. The war, in effect, freed the Conference from the necessity of concentrating on the Administration and executive agencies because there was less need for organizational attention to coordination of federal programs. Moreover, the Housing Act of 1949 which eventually passed in substantially the form proposed by the Conference, required five years of effort concentrated on Congress by all of the major urban groups because, while Truman supported the bill in 1945, the Republican leaders in Congress were unsympathetic to public housing.

The controversy over the Taft-Ellender-Wagner bill centered mainly around its public housing aspects, and the chief concern of public housing specialist groups was the survival of the program itself. The USCM, however, developed a slightly different orientation from the other urban groups. Although it supported the public housing provisions, it was primarily interested in Title I—the original charter for urban renewal. This proposal authorized a city to assemble and clear slum land, and resell it on the open market for redevelopment. The federal government would pay the difference between the cost of assembling and clearing and the price paid for the land by a private developer. This combination was a rather radical concept at the time it was churning through all the essential political processes. In the opinion of several observers, the program itself scraped through without heated debate only because it became lost in the larger controversy over public housing. It has even been suggested that the public housing provisions acted as "a stalking horse for urban redevelopment," meaning that some groups, especially the Conference, deliberately escalated the public housing controversy to divert Congressional attention from the inherently radical aspects of the urban renewal measure.[4] This measure had been framed to have special appeal to the Republicans and to appear in sharp contrast to public housing. Private enterprise was projected as the major participant, and the idea of "slum elimination" did not provoke the same hostile outcries of "socialism" as did public housing.

It was during the debate over the 1949 Act that the difference in the ranking of priorities between supporters of public housing and supporters of urban renewal developed that still persists. The "renewers" (represented mainly by the USCM) won in 1949, not the "public housers" (represented by the NHC and NAHRO), who were continually forced to fight amendments designed to cut down the number of authorized public housing units.

Although giving highest priority to urban renewal, the Conference did support public housing, and the NHC, NAHRO, labor, and the other "housers" did support urban renewal despite their own preference and public housing. The point is that from 1949, there was a difference in priorities among urban lobby groups, and this difference came to produce increasing differentiation in the roles and identities of these groups. It is noteworthy that the urban lobby groups recognized that in building consensus among themselves and presenting a united front before Congress, they restrained skeptical Congressmen from using the divisions as excuses to delay both programs. They struck realistic bargains among themselves as to the "program mix" they would all support *before* appearing at Congressional hearings. Formal Congressional testimony reveals only slight differences in emphasis among the "core" urban groups, and offers no clue to the real distinctions.

The Housing Act of 1949 has now become a sacred cow for all those oriented towards "national goals" and "overall" policy directives. It sets forth as a national objective a comprehensive housing program and the realization of "a decent home in a good living environment for every American family as soon as is feasible." It further notes that "this objective cannot be achieved without a comprehensive, soundly planned slum clearance and redevelopment program." Some of the difficulties with the concept of a "national urban policy" continue to be highlighted by the ongoing debates over definitions and priorities implied in these objectives. How does one define "blight" so that it becomes an operational goal rather than a subjective reaction? Is a slum an area of social pathology or a group of buildings with overt structural defects? Does "decent homes," as a concept, allow for an open-end definition, as does a "suitable environment"? All of these phrases imply evaluation as well as measurable data. Judging by their difficulty of application and by the controversy they have provoked, they lack the clarity needed for purposes of public policy.[5]

The major significance of the Housing Act of 1949 however, was that it did establish the goals as outlines for twenty years of debate on "overall policy," and served as a catalyst for specialization of emphasis among different urban interest groups. The basic questions around which small, incremental shifts in public policy were to take place in the 1950's and 1960's became clear: what kinds of problems of relocation were being created by urban renewal projects for the displaced poor? Who should pay for relocation? How much of an urban renewal project must be residential renewal, aimed at housing-connected goals? How much was to be commercial, aimed at the goals or revitalizing central business districts and expanding the city tax base? What should be the percentage of federal contribution?

In two other respects the Act of 1949 set the boundaries of later debate on federal urban policy. First, the Housing and Home Finance Agency (HHFA) was established as a step towards consolidating the principal housing activities of the federal government and to bring agencies with distinct, even clashing orientations and different clienteles under a more central policy control. Here the pressure of the urban interest groups for general recognition of the importance of the urban aspects of policy culminated in the elevation of the HHFA to Cabinet-level status in the 1960's. Second, 1949 began the period of intensive "urban-oriented" activities of several strategically placed individuals in Congress with whom the USCM and its allies were able to establish close relationships over the years. Some have since changed their official positions, yet in 1969 they were still important links in the urban network by virtue of their long experience and continuing activities. Two examples are typical of the patterns that were developed to form the basis of an urban policy subsystem.

Senator Paul Douglas (Democrat; Illinois) began his many years of leadership in the field of housing and urban development legislation during the debate over the 1949 Act. He was then a freshman on the Housing Subcommittee of the Senate Banking and Currency Committee, itself a strategic locus for urban programs. He shared responsibility for managing the bill with Senator Sparkman (Democrat; Alabama), whose involvement with urban legislation spans a period from 1946 to 1970, at which time he is chairman of the full Committee. Douglas remained, until his retirement in 1966, on the Banking and Currency Committee, and was a key supporter of urban development legislation and an important friend of the NLC, NHC, NAHRO, USCM complex. His retirement, however, did not remove him from the field of federal urban policy. He served subsequently as a consultant on "Senate strategy" for the Urban Alliance, a constellation of support groups assembled by the Department of Housing and Urban Development and the USCM to obtain passage and funding of the Model Cities Program in 1966. In 1968, Douglas headed a Presidential task force on urban problems, the Douglas Commission.

Albert Cole is another example of one long linked with the urban network as legislator, executive agency chief, task force director, and as a member of one of the most important permanent Committees set up by the urban groups of representatives from all sectors of the urban network. Cole was active in the original urban redevelopment legislation of 1949 as a Republican Congressman from Kansas. Later he became Administrator of the HHFA and chairman of the Eisenhower task force on housing policies in 1953. During the 1950's, Cole was in close contact with

Hugh Mields (who has been on the professional staffs of the HHFA, the NLC, NAHRO, the USCM, and the Urban Coalition) and Mields credits Cole with saving the urban renewal program from budget cuts by the Eisenhower Administration. Cole subsequently participated in the USCM's working subcommittee on Community Development, one of the consensus building mechanisms of what became a loose urban policy subsystem.[6]

This mechanism was innovated immediately after passage of the 1949 Act, when the USCM formed a special committee on slum clearance to study the program and to help implement it. Many of its members maintained their relations with the Conference when they moved into positions of leadership within government or other interest groups. Richard Steiner, then Director of the Baltimore Redevelopment Commission, became a Federal Urban Renewal Commissioner; David L. Lawrence, chairman of the committee, then Mayor of Pittsburg, later became President of the USCM, Governor of Pennsylvania, a director of the Urban Coalition, and chairman of the President's Committee on Equal Opportunity in Housing.

The relationships the USCM developed with all of these men were of considerable importance to its activities during the Eisenhower Administration. During the Truman Administration, the urban interest groups devoted attention more or less equally to the President and to Congress. During the Eisenhower years, the cities had to turn to Congress. A present Conference staff member gives as the reason that "under Ike, there was no sense in fighting; Ike was not inclined to pay attention to cities, and insisted he knew nothing about them." According to a former chief staff member of the House Banking and Currency Committee, the urban lobbies spearheaded a Congressional coalition in an attempt to override Eisenhower's veto of the urban redevelopment bill of 1959, but failed. Of more significance for the urban lobbies during the Eisenhower years, however, was the elaboration of the role of the National League of Cities.

In spite of a Democratic Congress, the Conference, itself largely a liberal, Democratic group, found that it could not get very far with a Republican in the White House. The complex balance of power between a liberal Senate and a more conservative House, and the fairly even balance between liberals and conservatives within the two branches, made for a "politics of deadcenter," placing "an extra premium upon skillful legislative leadership from within Congress . . . . if the policy making machinery was to function effectively." [7] Here was an instance when the Conference had difficulty finding a strong Congressional ally to get its programs through the federal legislature. Having access through members who are political V.I.P.'s is not enough if the atmosphere is particularly unfavorable for programs labeled as "large city" ones. Some specialized groups have, in fact, a better overall track record, a testimony perhaps to the easier task of representing a single-purpose interest.

The Eisenhower years were therefore a time for consolidation for USCM. In the new political environment the NLC, representing the smaller, more conservative cities, could gain attention more easily, and it is significant that until that time the NLC did not become intensely committed to lobbying. Before the 1950's it was LaGuardia, as President of the USCM, who focused on federal-city aid programs while the NLC concentrated primarily on state aid programs for cities. However, once the NLC turned its attention in a "federal direction" in the 1950's, it became more articulate on urban needs than was the Conference. One reason was that the NLC had a more stable membership (state league directors, not elected mayors) and greater staff facilities. Another was that by having previously stayed out of the day-to-day exigencies of new programs, the NLC had been able to devote time to develop well thought-out, longer-range proposals. According to a USCM staff member, the NLC more clearly articulated local needs, and the Conference had not kept pace with the growth of federal administrative capacity which followed from the Reorganization Acts of 1939 to 1946.

The Conference had other problems in the 1950's. Its Directtor, Paul Betters, died and was succeeded by his brother, Harry. Staff members who worked under both have indicated that Harry was not as effective. He could not, they claimed, operate under a Republican regime. Moreover, he had come to USCM from the NLC, which had created friction between the two groups. During those years, therefore, each went its own way.

One outcome of this concatenation of events and situations

was that the Conference had very little to do with the *ad hoc* policy groups that worked on some of the more important legislation. In 1953, for instance, Eisenhower arranged for the administrator of the HHFA to hold a series of "hearings" around the country to gather suggestions and evaluations of new ideas for redevelopment, housing, and related urban matters. These "Administrator's Shirtsleeves Conferences," formally the *President's Advisory Committee on Government Housing Policies and Programs*, reported to the President in 1953. Significantly, the USCM was one of the few relevant groups that did not participate, and a proposal to which it was strongly opposed was allowed to become part of the *Report*. This, the so-called workable program requirement, was embodied in legislation in 1954 and still causes some difficulties for large city mayors.

Nevertheless, despite the slackening of the activities of the USCM in the 1950's, an impressive array of developments preserved and expanded the basic urban renewal consensus reached in 1949. Republicans were attracted to the idea of renewing the central business districts, and mayors from both parties (among whom Mayor Richard Lee of New Haven stands out) began to see possibilities for political support from business toward increasing city revenues by expanding the property tax base through "downtown" urban renewel. Having chosen a popular bipartisan, consent-producing issue on which to hang its hat in the late 1940's, the Conference was able, despite its weakened condition, to make some gains in the 1950's. One was that the Housing Act of 1954 permitted 10 per cent of grants-in-aid to be used for commercial renewal, thereby modifying the overwhelming emphasis on housing. (By 1968, the Conference was successful in raising the percentage to 35 per cent.) Moreover, a separate Urban Renewal Administrator was added to the HHFA in 1954. In sum, although the organization was not at peak productivity during this period, its goals were not abandoned. But by the 1960's, so many of the other urban groups were operating at a high capacity that it was no longer possible to tell, as it had been in the 1930's, whether the mayors were leading or following.

The NLC's activities during the 1950's did expand the interests of the urban groups into areas other than housing and urban renewal. Although the League's orientation was not that of the "large city group," its interest in water pollution control and highways opened these areas for future activity by the larger city lobby. Clearly, even in the "absence" of the Conference, the urban network could survive. Both the Water Pollution Control Act of 1956 and the Highway Act of 1956 were, according to participants, "put together as far as their city aspects were concerned, by NLC." The Water Pollution Control Bill was managed in the House by Congressman John Blatnik (Democrat; Minnesota), and drafted at his request by the NLC working with Jerome Sonosky, Blatnik's staff aide. The bill was a Democratic substitute for an Eisenhower measure. In addition to its appeal for sportsmen and conservationists, it was designed, according to James Sundquist to "appeal to a broad coalition of mayors who wanted financial aid for municipal functions." Thus, "their measure added to the enforcement features of the Senate bill a provision for $100,000,000 a year in federal grants for municipal sewage treatment works." [8]

As "spokesmen for mayors," the NLC then led the campaign for the grant program against the opposition of the Department of Health, Education and Welfare and a combination of Republicans who contended that cities would not need grant money for sewage treatment if they would assign it a high priority in their existing budgets. Industry groups were also opposed to the whole bill. To meet this coalition of opposition, ". . . the NLC polled its members and received what a staff member called an avalanche of letters favoring grants, which were sorted by congressional districts and sent on to individual Congressmen." [9] In this way, the League was able to sustain the urban interest in the Water Pollution Act.

The Highway Act of 1956 was also one in which the NLC, rather than the Conference, was to be the most active to protect the interest of cities. It organized a "Highway Information Group," composed of the National Association of Counties, the American Association of State Highway Officials, truckers associations, roadbuilders, and farm groups. In this way, the smaller cities and the suburbs together with the states, farms and counties —usually rivals of the USCM—affected the highway system legislation. The results did, as it turned out, add some complications for the cities, and the Conference of Mayors, for one, still feels the consequences of its failure to recognize some of the unfavorable implications at the initial stages of the Act.

Conclusion

When the federal government unleashed the forces of its spending power to counteract the Great Depression, it brought out newly intensified political contests for federal attention— especially competition between states and cities (governors and mayors). But rivalry was also increased between these chief executives on one hand, and their respective bureaucracies on the other. The growth of vertical relations between the city, state, and federal agencies involved in administering the same programs sometimes put the bureaucracies into alliances against state and local chief executives and legislative bodies.

Urban interest groups which arose to press their claims were themselves at once cooperative and colliding, reconciling their differences for political purposes but rivals for money for program goals, and sometimes for legitimacy from the same constituents.

The New Deal programs served as catalysts for a new kind of federalism in which cities formed *sustained* direct relations with federal government and intensive lateral relations with each other. The political circumstances of the 1930's nurtured an era of organized federal lobbying by cities (formed into groups) and by city interests. These lobbies emerged into an urban interest network, described as such because of similarity of purpose, division of labor, inter-group communication, and overlapping personnel.

USCM's activities vis-a-vis post-depression programs illustrate some of the functions and the potential importance of federal-urban lobby groups. The several roles played by this group— despite its unusual character as a private pressure group of elected public officials—are descriptive of the general process of federal-urban lobbying. Most of the groups engaged in this process act as traffic regulators on two way streets, serving both the cities and the federal government.

The success of the USCM in the 1930's, and following from that, the institutionalization of federal-urban lobbying, resulted not only from Depression needs and good tactics, but most important, from political circumstances which made the cities F.D.R.'s source of support and national majority. Democratic control of cities and a Democratic President, party machines which could deliver votes, the President's need to administer NRA in cities, and a 12-year relationship between F.D.R. and the USCM all combined as factors creating a climate favorable for federal programs in metropolitan areas. The 1930's and 1940's saw substantial achievements in housing and urban renewel legislation, much of the substance and success of which can be attributed to the urban lobbying groups. The coalition formed around this legislation and the legislation itself formed the basis on which most subsequent urban development legislation has been built. The difficulties in its administration and interpretation foreshadowed the difficulties encountered in the 1960's in grappling with the concept of a national urban policy.

The primacy of the USCM in federal-urban lobbying became balanced by the increasing activity, specialization, and diversification of other urban groups. The NLC began its period of ascendancy in the 1950's, and became an equal partner with USCM. The post-war role of NLC in building support for urban programs, its growing membership, access to media, and contacts with Congress have made it a necessary ally for USCM. In fact, it is hard to say which is the stronger group, especially in view of NLC's better relations with the Republicans, who have controlled the Executive for 10 of the past 20 years. But more important, the network of urban-oriented groups that emerged between 1930 and 1960 was beginning to take on the task of defining urban interests, urban problems, and urban possibilities.[10]

The purpose of this chapter has been to illustrate the nature and process of urban lobbying, using the USCM as the primary example. The expansion of urban interest groups and urban lobbying activity, linkages among the groups, and the possibilities inherent in this arrangement for future urban policy-making will be especially important for the 1970's. Based on new census data showing a more suburban concentration of population, and on

Nixon's state-oriented federalism, the large cities may find themselves needing all the leverage and unity they can achieve in order to maintain their share of federal attention. The extent to which these various urban groups can hold together under stress, however, will be in no small part a consequence of the strength of the interaction patterns which seemed to crystalize in the 1960's.

CHAPTER III

A Policy System
in the Sixties

THE difference in attitude between Eisenhower and Kennedy was so great that several urban lobbyists expressed the feeling, "When Kennedy came to power, the cities came back in too." The 1960's brought about a new rapport between the United States Conference of Mayors and the President as well as an expanded relationship between the Conference and the federal government's administrative agencies. The number of urban programs rose from 28 to 435. The President had his own staff of technicians and advisers on urban programs; the expansion of the Executive Office of the President created additional intermediaries between the Conference and the President. These new actors in the urban decision-making drama stimulated, in turn, a new method of operation by the Conference. "Betters didn't talk to Senate assistants and urban renewal commissioners," John Gunther pointed out. "He talked to Cabinet officers and to the President himself. But with all the new programs in the sixties, we had to get closer to the technicians. Administration of the programs became as important as their substance."

The proliferation of federal urban programs and their administrative machineries gave the Conference a new institutional target —the administrative agencies, and provided more room and more routes in which urban lobbying groups could maneuver. A natural

69

protective interest in the adoption and expansion of its own particular program led an agency to seek allies from urban groups whenever it had to turn to Congress for authorization of new proposals or urge the Bureau of the Budget to place its requests for appropriations high on the Executive Budget priority list,

If an urban group failed to form an alliance with an agency, it could also pursue its goal by playing on the standard rivalries between Congress and the President. Most important, when Congress wouldn't act on a policy request, it still stood a chance of implementation. Lobby groups could maneuver it through the Executive back door under the guise of "interpretation of regulations." Optimistic lobbiests noted that "when we can't change a policy, we change the way it's administered." But on the other hand, concommitant with the establishment of new urban-oriented executive agencies was the growth of new urban-oriented interest groups, each with its own special emphasis. It followed that the agencies also had more freedom for choice of political strategies. They could, for example, try to play off one urban clientele group against the other. Or, instead of allying with an interest group, with a Congressional committee, or with another federal agency, each administrative unit could ally with its analogous bureaucracy at the state or city level—not necessarily with the blessings of chief executives in either.

Thus, although the strengthening of governmental machinery for dealing with urban programs had the potential for solidifying the urban interest and its representation, the fluidity of coalitions could just as easily elicit rivalries between lobby groups, between mayors and their bureaucracies, housing and redevelopment officials, and entrenched commissioners, between different levels of government, or between a legislative and executive branch at the same level. Again, these multi-faceted and multi-layered rivalries are the greatest problem for cohesive, united-front urban interest representation. Thus, despite Kennedy's attention to cities, which did present great opportunities (and certainly a better climate than the Eisenhower regime), the opportunities had to be properly used—and proper use depended on building consensus.

The USCM was infused with renewed vigor in the 1960's under John Gunther, who became its Executive Director in 1961. He added highly qualified people to the staff and led in expanding the scope and depth of the group's activities. Relations with the National League of Cities also became closer: so close, in fact, that the two groups took practically identical policy positions and instituted a partial staff merger. This staff merger has particular historical interest. Louis Brownlow told Hugh Mields (according to Mields) that the USCM was initiated *within* the NLC (then AMA) by a dissident group wanting to do Washington lobbying. They broke away from NLC because at first, it wouldn't go along.* Once USCM began, however, Paul Betters, then Director of NLC, became excited by the idea of working with the mayors, and by the increase of access, power, and prestige he felt a group of mayors could have. He began working with USCM while it was still, according to Brownlow, loosely a part of NLC, then switched to become director of USCM instead of NLC. Although access and success are not necessarily synonymous, many, as Betters, have preferred primary affiliation with the Mayors Conference, perhaps with the expectation of greater access and political leverage.

Brownlow's story is that Betters pulled the USCM *out* of the NLC and made it completely separate because NLC was getting money from the Spellman Fund, and Betters was very annoyed at the elaborate accounting procedures it imposed on recipients of its support. The two groups thus started as one, got further and further apart, moved closer together in the early 1960's, and in 1969, finally again merged their staff organizations.

USCM and NAHRO had not worked very closely together between 1952-1962. In 1962, Mields came into the USCM as Associate Director, and made NAHRO members part of a new working subcommittee of USCM (the important Community Development Committee, mentioned at length later). This brought the two groups into greater contact. In the 1960's therefore, the USCM established closer ties with NLC, with NAHRO, and with the new groups—Urban America and the Urban Coalition—which were formed to carry out tasks in the federal urban decision-making network which existing groups had not been able to pursue.

*The story of USCM's genesis is told somewhat differently in Chapter II, but this is mentioned as an example of differences in interpretation by insiders, especially Brownlow.

In this newly-aerated political environment, the urban lobbies began to concentrate efforts toward expanding the range of issues in which they could advance a "city" point of view. By 1963, the USCM was also active in the urban-related fields of human resources, civil rights, poverty, and mass transit in addition to its established roles in housing and urban development. While these last continue to be its major areas of concern, the city lobby has by now also become involved in welfare legislation, air and water pollution control, manpower training, crime control, construction of health-care facilities, and highway planning. More and more issues are being defined as "urban," at least to the extent that urban groups identify them as such and stress this identification on policy-makers.

Other urban interest groups have developed agenda that are similarly expanded in scope of concern and also perhaps to an astonishing degree, similar in policy content. Together the urban lobbies have been insistently calling for a reordering of national priorities and demanding that the federal government preside as midwife in a rebirth of the cities.

Since the 1960's therefore, the conditions exist under which an array of policy-advocates and decision-makers in a particular issue area could legitimately come to be regarded as a subsystem for federal-urban policy.

To analyze the place of USCM in this array of participants, one must examine the environment in which they all operate, and stand off to inspect at least the broad outlines and qualities of the subsystem they form. This calls for a look at the main participants, an inspection of the intensity of their interactions and types of linkages, an awareness of the different roles played and a selection of major trends and development within the system.

The urban policy subsystem, although somewhat loose and porous, does have identifiable parameters and continues to branch out. It is a complex network of relationships among Congressional committees, individual Senators and Congressmen, executive agencies, units of the Executive Office of the President, a permanent Presidential "urban" staff, *ad hoc* governmental task forces, interest groups, mayors, independent lobbyists, and housing and development coordinators. Also, individual experts and consultants whose advice is sought so frequently that they, too, become a dependable source of idea input must be considered members.

The following are the major participants from the Executive branch of the federal government:

1) There is *the President*. Since the days of Franklin D. Roosevelt, with the sole exception of Dwight D. Eisenhower, the President has generally assumed a leadership role in urban affairs. His importance arises out of political realities. Presidents are elected by a national constituency that has increasingly crowded into and around the large urban centers. Even a President whose electoral success is based on a different political estimate as, for example, Nixon's reputed "Southern strategy," cannot afford to ignore the votes in the major cities. The cities have become clusters of social and political discontent as well as locations for innovative confrontation politics. The news media focus maximum attention on city developments so that for a Presidential candidate to snub the cities is, in lesser or greater measure, to risk acquiring a political liability. It has therefore become standard operating procedure for a President to have special assistants for urban affairs. President Richard Nixon has gone a step further, perhaps to offset inferences of an anti-urban stance, by creating a Council on Urban Affairs, with Daniel P. Moynihan as Chairman and an Office of Intergovernmental Relations that emphasizes the relating of urban concerns to other levels of government.

2) There is *the Vice President*. His office has become a "coordination center" for urban affairs. Lyndon B. Johnson, when Vice President, acted in this capacity for President Kennedy. In the present administration, Spiro Agnew is coordinating the urban staff and is responsible for directing the new Office of Intergovernmental Relations. The Vice President usually has his own special assistants for urban affairs who interact with the President's urban assistants, thereby establishing a situation of competing elites within the Executive Office staff structure for urban affairs. Moreover, the Vice President and the Chairman of the Council on Urban Affairs seem to have overlapping functions.

3) There is *the Department of Housing and Urban Development*.

Since its creation in 1965, replacing its constituent unit, the Housing and Home Finance Agency (HHFA), HUD has been the most important department of the Executive branch in the field of urban affairs. With its elevation to Cabinet status, most programs that deal with housing and urban development fall within HUD's sphere.

4) There are also *other Departments of the Government*, participants with "secondary" connections in the subsystem. Although not as clearly members of the system because they are not as concerned with urban matters as are the hard core groups and institutions, they are nevertheless not without importance. Their patterns of interaction with the more central actors are as yet in the development stage, but some of the programs that secondary participants administer are becoming increasingly important to urban areas. Such departmental participants include: a) the *Department of Labor*, that collects and analyzes construction statistics, helps recruit construction labor, and must enforce federal labor standards; b) the *Department of Transportation*, which administers mass transit since that function was removed from HUD, and, c) the *Department of Health, Education and Welfare (HEW)*.

5) A leading role is played by *the Executive Office of the President*. Several units of the Executive Office can be considered within the purview of the subsystem: a) the *Office of Economic Opportunity (OEO)*, because of the impact of its anti-poverty program on urban areas; b) the *Office of Emergency Planning (OEP)*, because of its mayor membership and its responsiblities as an official link for many levels of government, and, c) the newly formed *Office of Intergovernmental Relations (OIR)* which, according to Vice President Agnew, is to have increasingly expanded responsibilities. The Bureau of the Budget is not, strictly speaking, a member of the urban subsystem; yet it must pass on budget requests for all urban programs, and has a special staff to consult with urban groups and agencies.

6) Then, too, there is *the Advisory Commision on Intergovernmental Relations (ACIR)*, which deals with urban-oriented pro-

grams, suggestions, or research with respect to effects of and on federalism, or relations among multiple levels of government.

7) Finally there are *Task Forces*, such formally instituted although temporary units as the *National Commission on Urban Problems of 1968* (the Douglas Commission); or *the President's Commission on Urban Housing of 1968* (the Kaiser Commission).

In the Congressional cast the most important actors are:

1) *The House and Senate Banking and Currency Committees.* These committees, along with the Housing Subcommittee of the House (the Senate no longer has a Subcommittee on Housing), are core committees. Most urban legislation must come before them. Their members usually include Senators and Congressmen who either represent highly urbanized areas or who want to develop reputations as being urban oriented.[1] Most of them have long records of leadership in urban legislation, and often seniority within Congress.[2]

The stability of membership on these committees is of considerable relevance for the urban policy subsystem, making for continuity of policy and relationships and for the development of genuine expertise. The 1959 and 1969 membership lists reveal that of the thirteen members of the House Housing Subcommittee, six have been on the parent Banking and Currency Committee for at least ten years. The Chairman, Wright Patman, has been on the Banking and Currency Committee since 1937. The staff of the House Banking and Currency Committee, interviewed on this aspect, observed that "almost all the members on our committee are seniors members of the House."[3]

A continuity of committee staff adds to the cohesion and established interaction of the system. As of 1969, the Housing Subcommittee has had only two staff directors since the passage of the Housing Act of 1949: John Barriere and Kenneth Burrows. Carl Coan, Burrows' counterpart, has been on that Senate staff since 1960. All have had continuing, well-established relationships with the executive directors of the major interest groups in the subsystem. Since so much of the substance of urban legislation and administrative regulation is hammered out at the staff level, the staffs, including the general counsels of the Congressional committees, of HUD, and of the interest groups might be considered as a supplementing choral cast in the drama enacted with every attempt, successful or not, to pass new urban-related legislation.

2) *The House and Senate Appropriations Committees*, crucial for the actual funding of any legislation, naturally play major parts in the urban policy subsystem. Although traditionally the urban interest groups have focused most of the attention on the authorizing committees and had better relations there, now that a great deal of important legislation is already on the books, they are finally turning their attention (with limited success) to the funding committees. Since 1966, a markedly enlarged lobbying thrust has been directed at them.

3) *The House and Senate Committees on Government Operations*. These, especially the Subcommittees on Intergovernmental Relations, are important as the Committees exercising legislative oversight of HUD. The Committee hearings bring out an enormous compilation of information on the federal government's role in urban affairs. These committees, too, can be considered as having secondary rather than primary roles in the urban system.

The overlap and rotation of membership in the major Congressional committees can have a positive effect upon the system's coherence. Senator Muskie, as an example, has since 1959 been on both the Banking and Currency Committee and the Government Operations Committee. He became one of the Congressional members of the Advisory Commission on Intergovernmental Relations in 1967, and in 1969 was Chairman of the Independent Offices Subcommittee.[4]

It is not to be assumed from the above that all committees dealing with legislation important to urban areas can be regarded as members of the subsystem. Criteria for inclusion are the content, the intensity and regularity of relations among the participants, and the conscious awareness of themselves and of each other as urban interest specialists. The House and Senate Judiciary Committees handled the Omnibus Crime Control and Safe Streets Act in 1969, legislation of major interest to the cities. The files of the NLC and the USCM reveal that the Judiciary Committees worked very hard on this act. Nevertheless, there was no persistent pattern of relations, no set of shared attitudes, no firm grounding in a common experience between the Judiciary Committees and the long-time forces in the urban policy system. Frederick Cleveland found this to be true also of the Congressional committees dealing with the Food Stamp Act and with air and water pollution.

That these are not really *in* the subsystem may turn out to be an obstacle to sustained efficiency. Still, the interaction is constantly growing. Key members particularly are being inched into the orbit of a subsystem centered on a more urban orientation. What may appear as only a housing and urban development system of the dimensions described by Professor Harold Wolman, is developing into something more far-reaching. The web of affiliations steadily becomes stronger.

Outside of the executive and legislative branches of the federal structure, the core members of the subsystem remain the USCM, the NLC, the National Housing Conference (NHC), Urban America, the Urban Coalition, The National Association of Home Builders, the National Association of Housing and Redevelopment Officials (NAHRO). As in the case of the institutional participants from Congress and the Executive, there is also a secondary constellation of interest groups made up of organizations having more of a functional concern. These are not yet in the urban subsystem but may well become so as their interactions multiply and their key members develop more of an urban orientation. Already a number of them are allies of the core groups and share their often "liberal" attitude towards federal activities.* Included are such associations as the AFL-CIO, the

---

* The constellation of groups which usually form an opposition coalition includes the Council of State Governments, the Governors Conference, some bankers associations (such as the Mortgage Bankers of America, the United States Savings and Loan League, and the National Association of Mutual Savings Banks), the National Association of Manufacturers, the United States Chamber of Commerce, and the National Association of Real Estate Boards. Some object to the bypassing of state governments when the federal government deals directly with cities. Others object to large-scale federal spending or to spending priorities. Still others oppose the "banking" activities of the federal government.

American Society of Planning Officials, the American Institute
of Architects, some of the smaller veterans' associations, the
Americans for Democratic Action, the National Association for
the Advancement of Colored People, the Urban League, and the
American Institute of Planners. They may not fully agree on
the extent or method of federal participation, or on the desirability of one or another element of a program, yet the mutuality
of *general* goals when faced with the coalition which usually
opposes them is one of the forces which shape federal-urban
policy.

An outline of participants in the urban policy system such
as is here projected can at best be no more than impressionistic.
The core actors in the ongoing subsystem are involved in almost
every urban issue. The secondary actors, of course, vary from
issue to issue, and are never totally integrated in a subsystem.

Mayors and their staffs are also institutional actors in the
federal-urban policy scenario. They are to be considered separate
participants representing individual units of city government,
since their activities within the subsystem are frequently unconnected with those of the USCM. However, the chief executives of the cities, individual city lobbyists, and local redevelopment directors (or community development coordinators) are
linked together through the USCM, the NLC, and NAHRO, and
especially through the USCM's Community Development Committee.

Under different titles, many of the key aides to the mayors
bear the brunt of the responsibilities since it is they who represent
their mayors on this committee or attend interest group meetings.
There is a great deal of lateral communication from city to city
through these staff contacts.

It is also legitimate to define actors in the urban policy subsystem in terms of individuals who exercise authority affecting
policy output and who have persistent and intensive relations
with the group and institutional actors.[5]

A good example of a star role is Hugh Mields, Jr. He has
been a special consultant on federal urban programs to the
President's Commission on Urban Housing, to the city of San
Diego, to the National Urban Coalition, to the Redevelopment and
Housing Authority of Norfolk, Virginia, and to Mayor Lindsay's

Task Force on Housing and Neighborhood Improvement. He has served as Associate Director of the United States Conference of Mayors; assistant administrator for Congressional liaison, United States Housing and Home Finance Agency; assistant director for federal activities, National League of Cities; assistant director for urban renewal, National Association of Housing and Redevelopment Officials; economic analyst for the Housing Authority of the City of Milwaukee. He was formerly a member of the Air Pollution Program Grants Advisory Committee of the United States Public Health Service and the United States Bureau of Census Advisory Committee on the 1960 Census of Housing. In 1970, Mr. Mields is a partner in the consulting firm of Linton, Mields and Coston. Mields is retained by Chicago as the Mayor's special consultant on urban programs and represents the City of Norfolk, Virginia as its lobbyist.*

In his Chicago affiliation, Mields works closely with the head of the city's Congressional delegation, Dan Rostenkowsky. The Chicago delegation is more cohesive than most city-wide congressional delegations—probably attributable to Mayor Daley's control of his Democratic organization—and its dean is a ranking member of the influential Ways and Means Committee. These circumstances combine well with the responsiveness of the delegation to the wishes of the Mayor and Mield's special expertise on federal-urban programs to make an impressive arrangement for applying lobbying pressure.

Linkages Among Actors

Systems linkage is obvious when participants are in contact with one another directly, formally or informally, on matters of mutual interest about which they bargain or exchange information in a continuous process of interaction. A more subtle linkage occurs in a series of existential phenomena which, taken together, establish the reality of a functioning, constantly operative, inter-reactive policy subsystem. This complex of phenomena

---

* See Appendix III for list of other individuals influential in federal-urban policy.

includes: 1) overlapping policies, or confluence of goals; 2) overlapping membership and overlapping participation among groups
(including governmental institutions); 3) overlapping leadership
and rotation of leadership; 4) formal consultation; 5) loaning,
overlap, or rotation of staff; 6) informal exchanges of services
and formal joint projects; and 7) informal communications,
general "touching base," and constituency linkages.

These linkages and subtle meshings are important because they
demonstrate by the amount and intensity of interaction, and by
the shared attitudes and mutual experiences, that a subsystem
exists. All of the types of linkage discussed below occur very
frequently. The examples used for each type have been selected
from among hundreds of situations and are therefore illustrative
rather than comprehensive.

Overlapping Policy or Confluence of Goals

To speak of overlapping policy or confluence of goals is not
to imply that all policy-makers in the subsystem agree with each
other on all matters. It does mean, however, they they address
themselves to the same general agenda, with each expert still
maintaining his special area of interest. They enter into a dialogue
until some kind of consensus is reached. Evidence of this kind
of linkage is clearly apparent in the community of intent of
resolutions and public statements by the several participants.[6]
Two examples will be given—a general one to indicate congruence of attention and definition of the problem, and a specific
one to indicate that once members of a subsystem agree on the
nature of the general political dialogue, consensus on specifics
can occur.

First, all the core actors have agreed that there is an urban
crisis that requires a "national response" in terms of "allocation
of funds," "priority of attention," and "national urban policy."
All have called for a "reordering of priorities," and all have identified shortage of housing for low-income families as a primary
problem. All have developed a common language. Finally, almost

all have criticized the size of the defense budget. These common threads appear and reappear in policy declarations, from which excerpts follow:

ACIR (1968)

"urgent need for immediate establishment of a national policy for . . . future urban growth . . . federal involvement and assistance . . . assurances of an adequate range of housing;" "need for national unity . . . for identifying and targeting priority attention . . . to the urban crisis." [7]

Urban America (1969)

". . . new emphasis on the concept of priorities;" "proposals for large new urban programs" ". . . examine the enormous expenditures for guns . . ." "nation's tardy recognition of urban needs . . . ." [8] "The inadequacy of the nation's lower income housing is one of the most pressing needs today." [9]

USCM-NLC (in a joint statement 1968, 1969)

"Required national response" to "America's urban challenge," "the greatest domestic, *national* crisis," "the nation must face it by . . . reordering national priorities to assume the commitment of the kind . . . of resources required;" ". . . policy must keep faith with the commitment" to provide housing "units for low-income citizens . . ." [10] "Space, . . . military programs which prudently can be deferred." [11]

Urban Coalition (1967, 1969)

". . . must move without delay on urban programs. The country can wait no longer. . . . Particular emphasis is being paid the problem of new lower income housing . . ." [12] "Five to ten billion can be cut from our defense budget without diminishing . . . the nation's security." [13]

NAHRO (1968)

". . . great pressures demanding housing and urban renewal
are product of default . . ." ". . . the aggregate consequence is
a *national* problem" "greatest area of unmet need. . . in . . .
low-income families . . ." ". . . recognize . . . task . . . of
National Housing Policy." [14]

NHC (1968)

"The crisis of our cities and the severity of the housing problems of our ghettos [calls for] the establishment of a national
goal . . . recognize that the Vietnam conflict is a major
economic cost . . . NHC urges dequate measures to redress the
imbalance . . ." [15]

The Chairman, Senate Banking and Currency Committee, Senator John Sparkman (1968)

". . . Why the crisis of the cities? . . . Federal assistance came
too late . . . the problem today is the wide disparity in housing
conditions." [16]

The President (Nixon in 1969)

". . . having a policy in urban affairs . . . is a pre-condition of
success." [17] . . . goal of a decent home . . . and need for
specified number of units . . . has been endorsed by the
National Advisory Commission on Civil Disorders, the National Commission on Urban Problems and the President's
Commission on Urban Housing . . . problems in obtaining
an appropriate allocation of resources . . . from the viewpoint
of total national housing policy and goals . . .[18]

HUD, Secretary George Romney (1969)

". . . the most urgent domestic problem today is the explosive
tension in the core city . . . important . . . to establish urban

policy . . . as foreign policy . . . ask cities to establish priorities . . . greatest physical shortage is housing . . ." [19]

HUD, Assistant Secretary Lawrence Cox (1969)

". . . crisis in the low rent housing program clearly overshadows all else." [20]

Chairman of the Subcommittee on Urban Growth, House Banking and Currency Committee, Congressman Thomas Ashley (1969)

". . . the imperatives confronting our cities today require a . . . shift from defense . . . to urban needs . . . more housing for poor people . . . both the Administration and Congress for the first time are indicating a commitment to a comprehensive, rational approach to urban growth. . ." [21]

Congruence of more specific policy expresses the conviction that federally assisted low-income housing must be dispersed throughout a metropolitan area as opposed to remaining concentrated within the central city. This policy has been formally announced by officials of HUD, which has a task force to work out specific proposals, and by the ACIR, the USCM, the NLC, the Urban Coalition, the Kaiser Commission, the Douglas Commission, the Chairman of the Senate Banking and Currency Committee, Urban America, and the NHC.[22]

Policy overlap also occurs in Congressional testimony and as sponsorship by most groups of the same bills. The hearings on housing and urban development legislation since 1937 reveal the same core interest groups as *dramatis personnae* again and again in performances in which they read lines which differ only slightly. Significantly, the similarity of testimony is no accident. The groups reach a consensus among themselves before a bill reaches Congress. Their testimony is rehearsed until the contrapuntal chants of their variations on the same theme become a harmonizing chorus. That the resulting concert of voices is more than a superficial public front only temporarily drowning out inter-group rivalry is recorded by the institutional machinery which helps in bringing it about.

Listening to a re-run of one typical agreement-producing session, one finds that in 1963 the working subcommittee of the USCM's Community Development Committee spent much time working on a low-rent housing program drafted by NAHRO. The legislative recommendations resulting from the debate in this Committee are reflected in a compromise package that had used the NAHRO program as an initial stimulus for reaction and new ideas, and as a basis for eventual reconciliation of purposes (which although essentially convergent, differed in emphases). Attending these 1963 series of policy meetings were staff and members of the USCM, the NLC, NAHRO, the NHC, the staff directors of both the House and Senate Banking and Currency Committees, members of the staffs of Senators Joseph Clark and Harrison Williams, Congressman William Widnall, a counsel to the HHFA, and a former commissioner of the FHA. This informal *modus operandi* for finding the points of both commonality and possible compromise among members of an issue subsystem before urban programs are formally presented to the legislature is standard operating procedure; overlapping Congressional testimony becomes expressive of intra-subsystem consensus.

Another form of joint policy is the practice of publishing one another's resolutions, and activity reports. This form of taking notice of what cooperating groups do and say alerts members of one group to the work of its colleagues and erects more scaffolding from which to construct a shared point of view. The ACIR, for instance, reviews and discusses the reports of Presidential task forces;[23] the USCM applauds the positions and activities of ACIR and the Urban Coalition in its Newsletter;[24] the chairman of the Senate Banking and Currency Committee inserts the resolutions of the NHC in the *Congressional Record*;[25] the Urban Renewal Surveys of the NLC-USCM are attached to hearings on urban renewal legislation; USCM resolutions refer to the positions of the President, Congress, task forces, and other interest groups;[26] the NLC comments on reports of the ACIR, the Urban Coalition, and the USCM;[27] Urban America "take(s) notice of the official resolutions of both NLC and USCM."[28]

This is all part of a "support building" or "consensus building" blueprint, of which another form, although it is the same general phenomenon, appears when a group, including the governmental institutions, reviews, recommends and takes note of the articles, resolutions and books published by other groups in the same circuit.

These practices reveal at the same time a division of labor in that they permit each group to cover the field in the area to which its own past practices and customs as well as its research facilities and budget have directed it. Division of functions prevents a wasteful duplication of effort.[29] Different groups take on different assignments and as a result, play different roles with respect to the same policy. On low-cost housing, NAHRO wrote the original proposal; the USCM's Community Development Committee served as consensus builder; Urban America worked on technical aid and implementation; and the NLC and the USCM lobbied the members of Congress. And last, policy overlap can also be detected when urban groups present joint "urban affairs planks" to political party conventions. Since 1960 the USCM and the NLC have submitted such joint proposals for the party platform to the national conventions of both major parties; these form part of the recorded commitments to which most members of the federal-urban policy subsystem are pledged.

Overlapping Membership and Overlapping Participation

All the members of the USCM are also members of the NLC (although not all NLC members belong to USCM), and many members of both organizations are also active in Urban America. The precise list varies slightly from year to year as mayors enter and leave office. Overall, however, the memberships of both groups remain stable enough to warrant attention to the phenomenon as evidence of subsystem continuity. Taking 1967 as a sample, Mayors Allen (Atlanta), Barr (Pittsburgh), Cavanagh (Detroit), Collins (Boston), Currigan (Denver), Lee (New Haven), Lindsay (New York), Maier (Milwaukee), McKeldin (Baltimore), Schrunk (Portland, Oregan), Shelley (San Francisco), Tate (Philadelphia), and Tollefson (Tacoma) were involved in all three groups. In the same year Mayors Allen, Barr, Cavanagh, Collins, Daley (Chicago), Graham, Lindsay, Naftalin (Minneapolis), and Tate were all active in the Urban Coalition as well.[30] Mayoral membership of the Advisory Commission on Intergovernmental Relations in 1967 were Blaisdell (Honolulu), Maltester (San Leandro), Naftalin, and Walsh (Syracuse).[31]

All of the mayors active in these last three organizations (Urban America, the Urban Coalition, and ACIR) were also either on the Executive Committee or the Advisory Board of the Conference or the NLC.[32] ACIR (nominally in the Executive branch), has representatives from the federal, state, and local governments. The four representatives from local governments are suggested to the President by the Conference from among its members. They are therefore also members of NLC. Members of the ACIR, as well as members of the executive bodies of these groups, are all eligible for reappointment and usually keep their positions until they leave the mayoralty office. However, mayors do not become members of the Conference leadership committees (from which appointments are made to the other positions), before their second term in office by which time they are held to have demonstrated electoral "staying power." Consequently, there is considerable stability in the overlaps. In 1969 for example, one finds that three of the four ACIR members mentioned have been members since 1960. Similarly, of the nineteen separate "overlapping activists" listed for 1967 (some of whom overlap in more than one place), five were on the Executive Committee or the Advisory Board of the Conference as early as 1960 and remained there at least until 1968: Blaisdell, Daley, Lee, Maier, and Schrunk. By 1962, three more were added: Barr, Cavanagh, and Collins, and in the following year, Tate and Maltester. In 1964, Naftalin and McKeldin became members. And so the process of overlapping and interlocking continues.

Mayors who serve on other government commissions or advisory bodies are usually among the leaders of USCM or NLC. In 1967, the three mayor members of the Office of Emergency Planning were Barr, Currigan and Collins, who, as has been seen, were active in other groups as well. Mayor Barr, when President of the USCM in 1968, was also on the President's Commission for

Urban Housing. Continuing with further points of interaction, members of USCM and of NLC have been members of the President's Commission on Youth Employment, Civil Defense Advisory Council, Natural Gas Advisory Council, and the Federal Power Commission. In 1968, thirteen mayors served as an advisory committee to the federal government's Housing and Home Finance Agency, with Mayor Daley, as President of the Conference, spokesman for the group.[33] In 1969 alone there were seven to ten advisory commissions to HUD, all made up of members of the USCM, the NLC, the NHC, the Urban Coalition, and NAHRO.[34] The ramifications and possibilities for affecting decisions implicit in this "advisory commission" type of overlap are suggested by the postions of Mayor Maier of Milwaukee. He is on a HUD task force initiated in 1969 for making recommendations on how federally assisted housing can be dispersed more evenly throughout a metropolitan area. Maier, since he is also active in the USCM, the NLC, the Urban Coalition and Urban America, is a kind of personal conduit for channelling the ideas of the non-federal groups into the federal task force and as the task force's feedback into the various groups. Accordingly, it is not surprising that Maier was the author of the USCM's 1969 resolution on this topic.

The membership of the NHC also shows interesting overlap. It includes members of the Urban Coalition, Urban America, NAHB, NAHRO, the American Society of Planning Officials (ASPO), former Senators, Congressmen, HUD officials, city redevelopment officials, and mayors' assistants who are also active in the USCM and the NLC.

Still, while members of groups in the subsystem overlap substantially, that is only part of the total story. Rotation of leadership among governmental and non-governmental groups has perhaps even more significance since it provides the basis for a spillover and exchange of orientation. Such rotation is sometimes a key in analyzing a group's capabilities and limitations. It also assures channels of communications among various groups based on past relationships.

Overlap and Rotation of Leadership

Rotation of leadership is so widespread that one might assume that the officials of almost every governmental and non-governmental group in the urban policy field have had prior leadership experience elsewhere in the subsystem. Several cities often use a staff member or consultant of one of the urban groups as their lobbyist. Overlap and rotation also occur when new urban groups are formed by the older ones (as Urban America and the Urban Coalition, which will be treated in more detail later). Finally, a former public official from an institution that is part of the system may become a leader in more than one group at the same time.

William Slayton, for example, in 1970 Director of the American Institute of Planners, in 1969 was Executive Vice President of Urban America. He is a former consultant to the USCM and a former Commissioner of the United States Urban Renewal Administration. As of 1970 he is also a member of NAHRO and ASPO, and a Director of the NHC. David Lawrence, a member of the Executive Committee of Urban America, was formerly a President of the USCM, a member of the NLC, and Chairman of the President's Committee on Equal Opportunity in Housing. Trustees of Urban America include Andrew Heiskell, Chairman of the Urban Coalition, and John Gardner, its President. Urban America, before it merged with the Urban Coalition in 1970, had a staff which included people who had been with HUD, as well as several former members of local planning or redevelopment agencies. The President of the NHC, Nataniel Keith, is also a former Administrator of the United States Urban Renewal Administration and consultant to the USCM.*

The composition of the 1969 Board of Directors of the NHC is especially illustrative of the degree of overlap in the subsystem as it includes men who are mayoral staff, leaders in other urban groups, Presidential task force members, officials from HUD, members of Congress, and Congressional staff. William Rafsky,

* See Appendix II for more thorough analysis of rotation and overlap of leadership.

President of NAHRO, in addition to being a director of the NHC, is also a consultant to the USCM's working policy subcommittee. He is a former Development Coordinator of Philadelphia. In fact, NAHRO also has a membership which overlaps widely with that of other groups.

The overlap of leadership between the USCM and the NLC is more substantial than that of any other two groups. Since 1965, the combined Executive Committees and Advisory Boards of the two groups show an overlap of about two-thirds. Moreover, members of the Executive Committee or Advisory Board of the Conference who are not officials of the NLC are at least members. As noted, the same nucleus of mayors forms the leadership of the USCM and the NLC and provides members for special Presidential committees and consultants to executive agencies. When a former Congressman holds a leadership position in one of the urban groups, as Mayor John Lindsay of New York and Mayor Samuel Yorty of Los Angeles (both members of the USCM's Executive Committee), expanded opportunities are created for institutional access and closer relations among participants in the subsystem.

Leaders move from governmental bodies to urban groups as frequently as from urban groups to government. All the following mayors were active in the USCM and the NLC before becoming federal officials: Anthony Celebrezze (Cleveland) became Secretary of HEW; Hubert Humphrey (Minneapolis) became a Congressman, Senator, and Vice President of the United States; Don Hummel (Tucson) became HUD Assistant Secretary for Housing and Renewal Assistance for the Johnson Administration and Floyd Hyde (Fresno) became HUD Assistant Secretary for Model Cities under the Nixon Administration; Dorm Braman (Seattle), Assistant Secretary for Urban Systems and the Environment, HUD, under Johnson, still serves in 1970. Ralph Taylor, a Director of the NHC, also became an Assistant Secretary of HUD. Farris Bryant, past Director of the Office of Emergency Planning, became Chairman of the ACIR. Lawrence Cox, formerly a Director of the Norfolk Redevelopment Agency, a President of NAHRO, a President of ASPO, and a consistent member of the working policy subcommittee of the USCM, became Assistant Secretary for Housing and Renewal Assistance, HUD, in 1968.

Cox's assistant at HUD, ArDee Ames, has been legislative aide to
Senator Harrison Williams (Democratic; New Jersey), a member
of the "urban" concerned Banking and Currency Committee.

Ames is considered by both group and governmental participants in federal urban policy-making to be the primary initiator
of the program which authorizes cities to apply for federal funds
for purchasing "open space" land as urban parks. Ames says that
the idea was conceived while he was an active member of the
Regional Planning Association of New York. When he became
staff aide to Senator Williams, he participated in the USCM's
Community Development Committee. The open space program
was drafted in this committee and worked into the Community
Development Act of 1964. (Of course much of the credit for
this section of the Act went to Senator Williams, who sponsored
it hoping to enhance his reputation as an "urban" Senator). Thus
the open space program is a typical example of how ideas are
generated within the subsystem, filter through it, and link together
many participants in the process of bearing fruit, It resulted from
the combined contributions of the Regional Planning Association,
Ames, a Senator from a highly urbanized area, the Banking and
Currency Committees, HUD, and the Community Development
Committee of the USCM, and therefore also serves as a specific
example of this working subcommittee as a major linkage source
within the subsystem. When the 1963 USCM subcommittee
"processed" the open space program, it consisted of people from
the NHC, NAHRO, the USCM, the NLC, (Urban America and
the Urban Coalition had not yet been formed), past members of
the 1959 Democratic Advisory Policy task force on urban and
suburban problems, the 1960 Kennedy Task Force, city development administrators, consultants who were also general counsels
to the HHFA, urban renewal commissioners, staff members from
both Banking and Currency Committees, and members of the
staffs of individual "urban" Congressmen.

Informally constituted working subcommittees within urban
interest groups are common, and the USCM's Community Development Committee "subgroup" is a good illustration of these
loose but ingeniously operative mechanisms whereby under the
auspices of one group, consensus on ideas and specific legislation is
obtained from other governmental and non-governmental actors.

That other groups have similar internal task forces or *ad hoc* committees attended by people from other groups, from Congress, and from HUD further reinforces the capacity of the subsystem to produce policies that are viable and that have the required political support. The NHC has a "legislative policy committee, involving representatives from the other organizations . . . which develops legislative recommendations for our Board of Directors, our resolutions committee and our members." [35] NAHRO and the Urban Coalition have similar mixed-membership (or mixed attendance) working groups. [36] They are the major and continuous linkage phenomena and vehicles for consensus-building for federal urban policy-making without which this issue area would probably not qualify as a political subsystem.

Formal Consultation

Formal consultation takes place when officially constituted bodies considering federal-urban matters, whether temporary government advisory boards, task forces or permanent bodies such as the ACIR, include many subsystem members through either institutional or individual representation. Congressional members of ACIR are usually legislators whose committee appointments are on those Committees which are the major Congressional actors in the federal-urban subsystem—Banking and Currency, Government Operations, and Appropriations, Mayor members of ACIR have overlapping memberships in USCM, NLC, or the Urban Coalition. [37] Formal consultation also occurs when the meetings or conventions of any of the urban interest groups are addressed (or even merely attended) by other prominent subsystem actors who explain, elicit support for, or float "trial balloons" on urban policy. [38]

Publicized meetings between President Nixon and the urban lobbies, such as those which occurred while he was still President-elect, are indicative of the practice by urban interest groups of subjecting newly elected (or appointed) officials to a process of socialization, especially when the official is part of an institution which *per se* is considered part of the federal urban policy-making subsystem.

> Advance groundwork for developing urban policies . . .
> was started . . . in a series of conferences with President-elect
> Nixon . . . An Urban Coalition delegation including USCM
> Vice President . . . met with him . . . December 13 [1969].
> Picked by Mayor Beverly Briley of Nashville, National League
> of Cities President; a small group of Mayors who are active
> in both the USCM and NLC conferred with him there a
> week later.[39]

In 1969, Urban America undertook a project partially funded
by the Ford Foundation to draft an overall national policy on
urbanization. The committee formed to prepare this report included members of Congress, governors, and representatives of the
United States Conference of Mayors, National League of Cities,
and National Association of Counties. Any proposals on national
urbanization policy produced in this way would, inevitably, reflect the "inside" views of those who were already most intensely
engaged in the formal urban policy-making process and represent
still another aspect of their extensive interaction.

Similarly, the task force which prepared the revenue-sharing
proposals for President Nixon in 1969 formally consulted NLC,
USCM, and the President's Council on Urban Affairs.* This type
of consultation is sometimes spotlighted by considerable, often
advance, publicity as an effort to dramatize governmental concern
about the issue at hand with its "attentive publics." Consultation
with clientele groups by a task force is also a device for conferring
at least an ostensible legitimacy to its future conclusions. An-
nouncing the tax-sharing task force, Vice President Agnew made
the point that it would include

> . . . myself, White House Counselor Arthur Burns, Secretary
> of the Treasury David Kennedy, Budget Bureau Director
> Robert Mayo, Chairman Paul McCracken of the Council of
> Economic Advisers and Dr. Daniel Patrick Moynihan, We
> will work with the United States Conference of Mayors and
> the National League of Cities in arranging the participation
> of the Mayors.[40]

* See Appendix I for more elaborate examples of Formal Consultations.

Loaning, Overlap, and Rotation of Staff

Temporary loans, mutual uses, and rotations of staff among governmental and non-governmental participants in urban policy occur frequently and create further avenues of inter-relationship among actors. While this linkage has been treated in part by the earlier discussion of overlapping membership and leadership, it is here considered separately because of the importance of staff, or "middle level bureaucrats," in formation and execution of public policy. It is at this level of service that communications and everyday implementation are either facilitated or ignored.[41]

David Wallerstein, Assistant Director of the USCM's Community Relations Service, was "on loan" to the Office of Economic Opportunity (OEO) in 1966. Similarly, in 1965, the USCM's Committee on Community Development "borrowed" personnel to serve as special consultants to the working subcommittee. The subcommittee thus benefited from the inputs of the legislative assistant to Senator Joseph S. Clark, (an important figure in urban legislation), the Urban Renewal Commissioner and one of his staff, the former President of the NHC, the Presidential adviser on national capital affairs, the President of the NHC, and a staff member of the Senate Banking and Currency Committee.[42]

One particularly outstanding "loan" personality is Howard Moskoff, who has the urban perspective from a Presidential task force on urban housing and from the directorship of a semi-governmental corporation; he was Assistant Director of the Kaiser Commission and Director of the National Corporation of Housing Partnerships in 1968. Moskoff was loaned in 1969 to both the USCM's Community Development Committee and to the Urban Coalition's Housing Task Force. Norman Beckman "rotated" from Assistant Director of the ACIR in 1964 to Assistant Secretary of HUD.*

---

* See Appendix II for further illustrations.

Formal Joint Projects and Informal Exchange of Services

Some of the formal projects and informal exchange of services by members of the subsystem have already been noted. Other aspects of this form of linkages still merit mention. Some of the urban interest groups undertake studies officially requested by or contracted for by Executive agencies and Congressional committees. The joint USCM-NLC Surveys on Urban Renewal done for Congress or HUD is one conspicuous example of such connective role. In 1966, NAHRO also came to take part in this joint effort. Many of the NLC research reports are done under contract from a government agency. Similarly, a Congressional committee may ask the USCM to make a special survey. Or, the committee itself sometimes drafts its own questionnaires and uses the name and the distribution facilities of the USCM. Inherent in this situation are some of the same political considerations which occur when research bearing the name of the USCM has actually been done by the staff of a city that had a special objective.

In 1966, USCM carried out a major piece of research on local anti-poverty programs under an OEO contract. In 1969, USCM and NLC received a joint contract from the Department of Labor to hold seminars for mayors' assistants in 150 metropolitan areas aimed at improving local liaison with the Manpower Administration. The seminars were planned and overseen by the USCM, the NLC, and an interdepartmental committee.[43] Under still another joint contract in 1969 from the Department of Transportation, USCM and NLC began developing eight new case studies on mass transit.

Since 1968, the major publications of the Urban Coalition are produced by Urban America. Cooperating with HUD, in 1967 and 1968 the Nonprofit Housing Center of Urban America held a series of regional and "individual large city" seminars on new ideas for joint efforts between nonprofit and business groups for meeting the President's goal of 26,000,000 new and rehabilitated housing units in ten years,

In 1969, Urban America and the Urban Coalition jointly published *One Year Later,* an examination of the effects of the President's National Advisory Commission on Civil Disorders; Urban America and the USCM jointly published *The New City.*

Informal Communications, General "Touching Base" and Constituency Linkages

By far the greatest volume of communication among actors in the subsystem is informal in character and therefore hard to document. Nevertheless, such informal communication is one of the most stable, intensive, and important bonds. This has given rise to the increasing use of quantification in political science to gage interaction or to count transactional linkages. Because of its myriad forms and subtleties, no exact yardstick for measuring information transactions among urban interest groups is available. However, their unpublished files reveal that continuous and voluminous informal contact is maintained: letters to one group, individual, or governmental coparticipant in federal-urban affairs with copies for others; items of interest received by one and sent around for wider attention; memos of telephone conversations; minutes at meetings; records of appointments, notices of social gatherings.* The materials revealed something of the extent, the nature, the relevance, and the tone of informal communications, and shed considerable light on the frame of reference in which one participant views another. As pertinent elements in the criteria for determining the existence of a policy subsystem, these communications indicated keen awareness of a mutual investment and participation in a continuing dialogue which would affect federal urban policy. It is by no means unusual for speeches to be drafted by the staff of one of the core urban groups, delivered by a member of a second urban actor, at the meeting of still a third group in the total constellation.

A letter to Mields from a special counsel to the House Committee on Public Works illustrates some aspects of how the system communicates informally and how the previous affiliations of individuals acquire added significance.

---

* See Appendix III for samples.

Yesterday's meeting on air pollution produced a whole series of proposed revisions in the language of the House bill, and as a result, Fitzpatrick [prior counsel to the HHFA, consultant to the USCM, 1959 task force, and a director of the NHC] asked that you give some attention to such problems as soon as possible.

The hearings are scheduled to begin on September 10, with Celebreeze [Secretary, Department of Health, Education and Welfare; 1962 President of USCM] and Daley [Chicago Mayor] is tentatively set for the 11th . . .

Apparently Daley would be willing to recommend that technical assistance, federal air pollution standards, and an advisory board be put in the bill, but may not be willing to suggest . . . enforcement procedures, additional money and a different grant formula . . .

The major question of concern to Fitzpatrick was who was going to make these recommendations . . . and . . . who was to . . . writ[e] the testimony. Fitzpatrick felt that John Gunther [USCM Director] had best call Daley immediately upon hearing from you if you expected Daley to make these recommendations . . .[44]

The staffs of the various urban groups have, to an extraordinary degree, close personal and professional relationships. Referring to the other core groups the President of one urban group writes that "On the staff level, we maintain continuing liaison in most cases have had personal and professional relationships over a period of years."[45]

It is a statistically unmeasurable but highly significant factor that these relationships are not purely professional, developing solely from the necessity for repeatedly "touching base" with other groups and communication with government. They are relationships of a social nature as well. Some initially developed while the parties involved held federal office at the same time. The staffs of Urban America and the USCM "see each other socially quite a bit and . . . become involved in joint projects such as the creation of the Urban Coalition . . ."[46] William Slayton, President of Urban America, is a close personal friend of Patrick Healey, Executive Director of the NLC; of John Gunther, Executive

Director of the USCM; and of John Feild, national coordinator of the Urban Coalition. Mayor Tate of Philadelphia, a member of the Executive Committee of the Conference, is a close associate of Congressman Barrett, also of Philadelphia, Chairman of the Housing Subcommittee, and is said to work for Barrett in his election campaigns. Other organizations with which many members of the subsystem are simultaneously associated, serve as important informal meeting grounds. Many interviewees indicated that a considerable number of individuals belong to Americans for Democratic Action and that informal contacts at ADA meetings contributed to their images and expectations of each other in their respective formal roles.*

Conclusion

Once one identifies the people and the institutions concerned with urban policy at the federal level and has examined the interactions and linkages among them, a loose but reasonably identifiable urban policy-making subsystem appears in rough contour, despite persistence of the myth that there are no regularized decision-making patterns for urban affairs at the federal level.

The 1960's saw: 1) proliferation and elaboration of urban-interested groups, lobbies, government agencies, and general federal concern; 2) expansion and innovation in lobbying strategy to deal with new federal agencies, with Congress, and with increasingly important middle-level bureaucrats and staff; 3) changes in relations among groups, whereby USCM became closer with NLC and NAHRO, and two new urban interest organizations were formed (Urban America and the Urban Coalition); 4) growth in the functional capacities, division of labor, and spectrum of concerns (branching out from housing and urban development) within the urban network.

The urban interest network meets the criteria for qualification as a political subsystem set forth by systems theorists David Easton and Robert Dahl: a persistent pattern of relations involving power and authority which results in allocation of values. Major decisions

* See Appendix III for further examples of informal consultation.

affecting federal-urban policy are made by the interaction of distinguishable hard-core participants which are deeply and continuously involved, and identifiable linkages and communications patterns exist among them. These inter-connections form further bases for shared attitudes, and the actors address themselves to the same policy agenda; they are conscious of one another as colleagues in a continuing dialogue.

There are many and complicated rivalries among members; since the subsystem spans so many levels of government, it mirrors the intense competition of public officials at all stages. It is not a tightly organized, cohesive, "power elite" type, but a loose, flexible, and porous one. Individuals and groups can easily move in and out, and even core groups constantly change in their relative strengths. Moreover, it is a subsystem which has taken a long time to evolve—and might even be described as, so to speak, "on the brink of being and still becoming." Nevertheless, a concert of voices does direct what appears on the stage of federal-urban action.[47]

This subsystem provides the environment in which the urban lobbies function. The activities, strategies, and goals characteristic of each are shaped by the constraints and opportunities it affords. Conversely, since the attributes of individual actors effect the substance of policy and the capacities of the subsystem as a whole to produce decisions, the content of federal urban policy and the conflict management abilities of the subsystem itself are to be better understood by first thoroughly analyzing an individual participant.

The USCM is the only group in the urban network made up exclusively of mayors. Its membership underscores one of the most complicating and fascinating aspects of the federal urban policy subsystem, its intricate entanglement with federalism. This means there are three separate levels of government reacting to, demanding from, and exercising some kind of control over each other. The Conference is historically the most important as well as the most timely of the urban lobbies from which to attempt generalizations. It is the interest group that speaks for the largest cities, where the urban crisis is most visible, and it is a microcosm of the whole subsystem's difficulties in defining and representing urban interests and converting demands into policy. Its internal dynamics illustrate the problems of obtaining consensus for action from individuals and groups which have such a wide array of concerns, such a narrow range of agreement, and such a great potential for conflict. Selecting the agenda from the multitude of possible urban interests and structuring some kind of preliminary agreement on demands to be made on the political process is the way in which "urban problems" can be made meaningful to government so that it can act.

The continuing question is whether the urban policy subsystem can be expanded to provide representation for new and accumulating issues that have major importance to cities, and whether its present participants can respond to the increasingly pressing demands for a more active and generous urban policy. The answer depends on whether or not goals can be clarified and consensus can be broadened and reached at a rate commensurate with these demands. The possibilities for this vary with the degree of internal cohesion within each individual group. Group cohesion becomes especially important in the USCM in view of the widespread demand for "national urban policy," because a pre-requisite to any urban policy, national or not, is support from those responsible for implementing it—in this case, the mayors. The Conference, however, has the intrinsic poly-schizoid tendencies on national policy one might expect from a political grouping which reflects the same cross-cutting cleavages that exist in the American political system as a whole at any given time. The answer depends on whether or not goals can be clarified and consensus can be broadened and reached at a rate commensurate with these demands.

CHAPTER IV

Cleavage
and Cohesion

As a voluntary association of government officials, the USCM combines the norms of a civic interest group with those of a body of powerful public office-holders. The nature of its membership, one that has in a way been ratified by an electoral process, differentiates it in several important respects from other interest groups that lobby the federal government. It implies a kind of special legitimacy as well as a very broad concern for the social good, and the USCM capitalizes on this implicit validation. It is presumed to be motivated by a code of deference to the public interest powerful enough to draw its conduct above the level of the routine "special interest" lobbyists. By popular democratic mythology, public interest groups are the "good guys" who are *expected* to participate responsibly in the governmental process, whereas private interest groups are often regarded as the "bad guys," capable of converting, maybe even perverting, a claim of the public good into a private gain.

This characteristic, however, infers several questions about the USCM as an inter-governmental lobby. Does the apparent need for this body of elected urban chief executives, joined organizationally to lobby the federal government, suggest an even greater dispersion and fragmentation of power in the federal system than that of which one is already aware? The political complexities of these lateral relations within a theoretically hierarchical constitutional structure might be still another contrivance of Madisonian checks and balances that sometimes keep the gains of public policy at check-mate and its progress at the balance of a pendulum.

When the chief executives of one level of government become a discrete constituency of a higher or different level of government, can they also remain as completely accountable to their electorates as they would be if each were acting for individual needs? Or, the phenomenon might suggest that otherwise independent, unconnected elected officials should band together as a new class of professionals with those having analogous jurisdictions in order to govern more effectively in their own.

How, it may appropriately be asked, does "government acting on government" differ in its behavior from other interests acting on government? In classical organization theory, government is arbitrator and mediator among competing private concerns. In the case of the federal authority and the USCM, there are two sets of "government" each with its own constituency, official standing and source of authority, struggling over decisions determining the allocation of public resources. If government itself lobbies, does it exert pressure on behalf of a general public interest and in pursuit of a mandate from its immediate constituency as in its image in the popular myths of democracy? Or does an aberrant, independent "governmental" interest appear like a non-conforming child whose deviant behavior is hushed up by the family. Does "official status" held by individual members of a private group automatically confer more priority and ease of access to the decision-making process and thereby elevate an independent "governmental" interest above the specific function or issue-oriented interests of the more familiar types of lobbies?

It is with these broader themes in mind that one must approach a discussion of how the internal dynamics, strategies, and policies of the USCM are affected by the nature of its membership.

Clearly, the composition of the USCM affects its internal dynamics because it creates an inevitable condition—a low degree of dependable cohesiveness. This consequence, however, in its turn affects the entire urban policy-making subsystem. The organization cannot easily total up the influence that members as individual mayors may have on the behavior of other politicians and office holders. With respect to the group, this influence is noncumulative and non-additive, and is difficult to amass as solid impact for political leverage on the President, Senators, Congressmen, and administrative agencies. It is ironic that the lobby within the urban policy subsystem which has the greatest knowledge of the daily operational problems of the large cities cannot summon organizational influence commensurate with either its experience or its political potential.

It is normal for the USCM to encounter difficulties in presenting a united front—almost an occupational hazard. Every internal dissent diminishes its representational claims. In the absence of substantial majority backing or when its members persistently use their other avenues of approach to government, the organization is undermined.

The USCM's obstacles to developing consensus or even instilling strong organizational allegiance result from each members' personal political characteristics, leadership proclivities, and opportunities for individual access to the federal government and to the press. Especially potent are ideological cleavages. Democrats and Republicans, liberals and conservatives, large-city mayors and small-city mayors, Northerners and Southerners, nominally united under a banner of mutual group membership, remain Democrats and Republicans, liberals and conservatives, and so on—perhaps even the more so in direct reference to each other.

Decisions must be restricted to issues on which substantial agreement, or at least aquiescence, can be achieved. However, even an overview of the general centrifugal impulses which must be first neutralized and then redirected towards serious accommodation suggests that the legendary inertia in the "journey of a thousand miles" here applies as well to the trip of a single step.*

Lobbying is a process in which the expectations, capabilities, needs, liabilities, and political stakes of both the lobbyist and the lobbied are variables in the outcome both as facts and as mutual *perceptions*. The role of a participant in a policy subsystem is substantially defined and circumscribed by the way he is viewed by fellow participants, since their opinions can become fulfilled predictions. Interviews thus have an especially marked relevance

---

* The analysis that follows is based on intensive interviews and correspondence, direct observations by the author, and an extensive reading of published and unpublished documents and files.

for analyzing the USCM, and serve to provide multiple perspectives from which an organizational characteristic is perceived by some as an asset, by others as a liability.[1]

All those interviewed were asked to give their judgments as to a number of aspects of the USCM: its internal cohesion, and its utility and importance to the person or institution involved; the nature of its internal process and its policy output, and its specific, substantive contributions to federal urban policy; its policy-making potential, its visibility in the political process, and the characteristics of its staff; the frequency with which the mayors bypass the Conference to make direct contacts on their own, and USCM's relations with HUD, Congress and other groups; finally, its freedom of access to the federal government, and, above all, as to its strong and weak points.

To the question, "What is the greatest problem, or weakness of the USCM?," all replied: "low internal cohesion," or lack of unity, because its members are highly visible elected public officials. This is both fact and expectation. The tallest tower of strength built around mayors may prove to be only a tower of babble in a strong political windstorm.

In contrast with most interest groups, every single member of the USCM has personal as well as institutional access based on perquisite of title, on mutuality of electoral constituency, or on operating control of federal-city programs, to most pressure points of the federal government. In actuality, the Conference has to stand on the shoulders of its members for institutional access to the Legislative and Executive branches; one mayor expressed this by complaining that "the Conference uses him more than he uses the Conference." * The more usual relationship among interest group members, their active minority and staff, and government is that members of the group become politically significant *through* their organization. It speaks for them, gains them access to decision-makers, and delimits its membership as those like-minded people who wish to offset the disadvantages of a dispersed minority by banding together to assert some political leverage. By contrast, the USCM uses its more important members for its base of prestige.

Since they are not dependent on the Conference, many mayors

* This was not true in the 1930's.

deliberately cultivate their own independent links. It is good for one's political careers to have many federal contacts.

Of all the mayors interviewed, most indicated that they "did their own legislative and agency work," or "had their own lobbyist" for what was of greatest importance to them. Mayor Daley of Chicago, for example, turns to Hugh Mields as his Washington located consultant on urban problems and Daley is one of the most active members of the USCM. New York City employs its own Washington representative, as do most other cities that can afford to do so. Such supplementary lobbying arrangements diminish the importance of the Conference in the eyes of its own members and accentuate its centrifugal tendencies. Divergent viewpoints from established Conference policy are communicated by mayors directly to the very officials before whom the USCM wants to appear as single spokesman, and city lobbyists indicated that they pursued their individual cities' goals with little thought of their consistency with broad Conference policy.

Many cities enter into individual contracts with the USCM itself instead of with an independent lobbyist to look after their special interests. For this purpose, the Conference and the National League of Cities jointly provide a "Man in Washington" service. A staff member will usually represent more than one city in addition to serving in another capacity for the USCM itself. David Wallerstein represents Los Angeles and serves on the staffs of the USCM's Community Relations Service and its Community Development Committee. This practice is a countervailing influence to possible confusion provoked when member cities hire independent lobbyists; it also informs the USCM when members adopt a position in conflict with that of the organization.

Mayors who do not have their own lobbyists nevertheless make important contacts on Capitol Hill or with the Administration directly. Detroit is an example. Supplementing usage of the USCM for lobbying on matters of general urban interest, the Mayor "goes directly to the federal agency on administrative problems and works with his state delegation for Congressional relations." This practice is not to be construed as an affront to the organization, because a mayor must be aware of the fullest range of alternative actions and choose among them by weighing their political costs and benefits, however subtle. Cultivating direct vertical relationships between local administrative agencies and their federal counterparts is an expression of managerial savvy, and building personal cooperation from state Congressional delegations is the better part of political wisdom. Some of these contacts may become a mayor's allies in heading off interference on a federal-city proposal by his governor; some may even become the critical rung in his ladder to higher office.

The multiple considerations of mayors' political needs and choices and of individual cities' unique and varying interests in the specifics of a program earmark the USCM's chief utility as that of building lobbying coalitions for *general* urban legislation —urban renewal, mass transit, low-cost housing, or model cities. For more individualized projects—and there are many of them— a city lobbies in its own name. Chicago, for instance, is known for its special interest in federal funds for rat control and New York for its interest in raising cost ceilings in the rent supplement program. Direct communication between cities and the federal government is so widespread a form of lobbying that HUD officials comment on having "heard as much from individual mayors as from the Conference." One Texas mayor had an especially interesting analysis of the extent to which a mayor uses the USCM:

> Mayors who have great authority, that is—strong-mayor city governments—usually work with Washington directly. Those with city managers, 'weaker mayor' forms of govern-ment, and those with 'part time' mayors use the representa-tional short cut afforded by the USCM.

However, "strong mayors" also gain advantages from "united front" contacts by the USCM. In fact, since there is not necessarily a natural reciprocity of empathy between a mayor and a federal bureaucrat, lobbying through the organization is at times a better strategy. In the presence of cross-purposes, an individual mayor is easier to avoid than a group of them together. And although individual access to the federal government by its members does bring liabilities, in reality it has some positive as well as negative aspects. The greater the number of close and dependable rela-tionships between individual mayors and federal officials, the larger the pool of contacts available to be drawn upon for use by the group. This results in increased organizational access since the USCM, on its part, frequently turns to its mayor members to contact the Administration on its behalf so as to add political punch to its own efforts. On the other hand, federal officials "usually do not know whether the views expressed are consistent with, contradictory to, or merely supplementary to those of the mayors' organization." This lack of clarity makes appraisal of the ultimate base of support for the requests a matter of guess-work—or of extra homework. Urban lobbying as practiced upon and perceived by federal administrative agencies is a constant process of constant petitioning, often from undifferentiated sources.

While the urban lobby groups are useful to federal officials, especially in providing feedback on programs and in helping agencies calculate their base of support, federal executives do not want urban interest groups to completely supplant direct federal-city relations. HUD officials appreciate that some mayors direct their program suggestions and work out administrative problems with the HUD regional offices. Mayors themselves dis-play a sensitivity to federal resentment of over-use of lobby groups as "middlemen," explaining that "they like people to play by the rules," through the official hierarchy established by HUD to communicate directly with individual cities. Here is an ironic reversal. Direct federal-city relations, once demanded by the urban lobbies to circumvent states, has on occasion become a preference by federal officials to circumscribe pressure from the urban lobbies!

Since "keeping the lines open and busy" from the cities to regional offices, and directly to HUD officials in Washington, is looked upon with favor by both local and federal officials, the regional offices of HUD have now come to play a growing liaison role. In fact, in 1970 they are in the process of a reorganization to bring them even closer to the cities.[2] This does not necessarily diminish the liaison function of the Conference as such. There has been so sharp an increase in federal-city programs as to make it impossible for one institution to carry the burden of all the communications and transactions that a liaison role requires. The elevation of HUD's control capacities and the debut of its regional offices as significant factors in federal-urban interaction procedures may, however, by intitutionalizing still another access route, become a further disunifying influence within the USCM. HUD regional offices may also diminish the direct involvement of the Conference in problems of program operation. This could deprive the organization of some of the useful data which it uses to present an informed and coherent agenda to its members.

A nearly impossible, yet necessary task in the quest for internal cohesion in the USCM is that of trying to exercise leadership over the mayors. Organizational intelligence dictates that it attempt to influence what the mayors do and say, to get them to speak for the group in lieu of focusing attention on themselves, or to persuade them to forego an immediate but transitory value as against a broader look to the future. The staff has a natural status gap to contend with when it tries to direct members who are themselves accustomed to, and skillful at, asserting leadership on their own. The politics of actually leading, or so much as seeming to lead, is a signal for competition at all levels, whether for office or even if only to stand out in open debate. An interest group with a membership of high elected public officials does battle as an army of generals; there is absent the usual spontaneous division between followers and leaders that is common to other kinds of groups and almost an axiom in organization theory. Here, everyone wears all four stars! This creates the kind of universe in which the press enjoys encouraging a display of credentials and a competition in tactics of command which further irritates organizational collegiality.

As usual, the USCM June 1969 convention was widely covered by the news media. Item one: the Conference passed several resolutions on urban issues then being debated in the White House and Congress. Item two: the very next day five mayors—all prominent in their own right and in official positions in the Conference—appeared on "Meet the Press." [3] None emphasized what the USCM had agreed upon. Despite their positions within the group, some actually spoke out in opposition to the positions that the Conference had adopted.

When questioned on this odd behavior, the Conference staff pointed out that mayors need to play to their constituencies and have an aversion to suggestions of political self-restraint. In deference to this, the staff admittedly made no attempt to do so. Although the media billed them as "meeting in Pittsburgh to bring the needs of the cities to the attention of the federal government," the mayors did not discuss the USCM as an organization, the circumstances of the agreements reached or even refer to a unifying assembly of "urban interests" which could exert collective political force. The mayors, according to one staff member, "have a vested interest in disagreeing if it suits them." Their identity with what is in a sense their trade organization, comes a distant second, well below their Pavlovian response to the compulsions of their own importance.

The main difficulty, of course, stems from the mayors' tendency to use the organization as a platform from which to make themselves more conspicuous—to a home audience and to a national audience, if they have high political ambitions.

They want also to have high visibility before other federal officials. A possible administrative appointment may be in the cards after a term as mayor. The frequent opportunities for using the organization as a personal springboard seems, in fact, to be an aspect of Conference membership that mayors value most, and helps explain why membership on the Executive Committee is so much desired. There is always competition among the mayors, especially at the USCM annual conventions, for media attention and, for that matter, for the attention of political colleagues at and outside the Conference.

Proceedings at the Convention of June 1969 highlighted the effect of this competition on the formulation of group policy— a process which ideally should be thoughtful, deliberative, and collegial, and the reason for which the mayors were meeting. The USCM requires that mayors send their proposed policy resolutions to the Conference staff in advance of the sessions. Instead, some mayors saved their most controversial and attention-getting proposals until the convention was already assembled. Mayor Cavanagh of Detroit wanted the Conference to oppose by resolution President Nixon's plans for an anti-ballistic missle system. Mayor Daley of Chicago, hearing about Cavanagh's plan shortly before the meeting, prepared a substitute which would modify the impact of Cavanagh's resolution by expressing only disapproval of the high level of military spending. Neither of these was sent to the staff in advance. As a result, full opportunity for debate and informal discussion by other mayors was minimal.

The intrigue of the lobbying inside the USCM that attended the above incident diverted attention from planning for longer-range and more far-reaching lobbying outside the USCM. But the internal mechanics are not without interest. Cavanagh had known in advance he would not be able to win the Conference's endorsement, but intended to raise the issue nonetheless. News of Cavanagh's intention had "leaked" to the White House and to the press. At the opening session of the Resolutions Committee, Cavanagh requested permission to waive normal procedures in order to consider a matter of great national urgency. The press was clustered around him and the television cameras were poised. Daley and Cavanagh had both been circulating copies of their resolutions, and the other mayors were caucusing and calculating their own politcal stakes in supporting one or the other resolution. Such dramatic circumstances compelled a suspension of the rules. Cavanagh read his proposal. Although the other mayors were relieved when he suggested that it could be consolidated with Daley's as a compromise resolution, the interplay between Cavanagh and Daley took up one and one-half hours of the two hours scheduled to consider 26 policy resolutions, all of which had been circulated in advance.

To top it off, as soon as the Mayors of Detroit and Chicago had finished, they left the meeting taking with them the television crews, most of the press, most of the other mayors, and a good part of the staff of the USCM and the NLC. Only some 30 to 40 people stayed on to consider and debate the other resolutions in the remaining half hour.

This anecdote is significant because in many respects it typifies how centrifugal forces within the organization are exacerbrated by those from without. Conflict, of course, makes headlines; the press concentrated its attention on Cavanagh and Daley rather than on resolutions that represented a considered, consensual, group policy. The press ignored mayors who had done less visible but more organizationally practical work. In a sense, then, it was the press and not the USCM that really selected the issues that were projected before public attention.

There were other examples of the role of the press in setting the agenda and spotlighting some personalities while completely ignoring the others. This is a kind of "newsmaking" by the media. It provoked only the most phlegmatic of protests until 1969, when it became a militant theme for Vice President Agnew to spiral into a verbal guerilla warfare with the press. All in all, the real business of the meeting was ignored in favor of the more colorful, so-called newsworthy activities of two mayors out of over 400.

This is of course just the meat that jealousies feed upon and with each such instance, the possiblities for unity are reduced. Widespread resentment is generated and the organization's staff gets the blame for permitting "a clique" to run the Conference, for showing favoritism toward the cities paying more dues, for "not caring whether anyone else participates." In actuality the staff deeply resents such tactics.

The full story of the Cavanagh-Daley incident has still one more aspect worthy of notice in an analysis of the role of the USCM. It serves in some respects as evidence of the interest taken by the President of the United States in the policy positions arrived at by an organization of large-city mayors, even on issues not necessarily "urban." The White House had its liaison men at the Convention determined to defeat Cavanagh's proposal on the "anti-ABM" resolution. The Mayor's Convention was held during the very period when the President was trying to line up Congressional support for the ABM, and he did not want to risk a united repudiation by an organization with proven political effectiveness and an image of broadly representative power.

According to Cavanagh's staff he had several telephone calls from the White House. Allegedly, there was pressure also on Mayor Lindsay of New York. The resolution came up for a vote on the day just before the New York mayoral primary in which Lindsay was being opposed by a Nixon supporter on the Republican ticket. The Republican party line was to oppose the anti-ABM resolution. However, for Lindsay to do so would have jeopardized his standing with Liberals, and he was slated to run on the Liberal Party ticket. The guess was that Lindsay "would be in such a bind" that he would not appear, even though his staff said he expected to be at the meeting. He did not show up.

Administration representatives were sent to the Convention

in Pittsburgh to lobby individual mayors to support the ABM. The "President's men," as they were called, seemed to this author to be omnipresent, and to take on the aspects of an invading army. Vice President Spiro Agnew, scheduled to speak only at the Conference's luncheon, came into town a day early, "unannounced," to hold private meetings with some of the mayors.[4]

Clearly, then, the positions taken by the USCM are important to the President, and the mere possibility of a united stance by the nations' prominent mayors was enough to gain them considerable attention. Thus the centrifugal tendencies of this group of officials does not dissolve its political importance as much as would those same tendencies in some other pressure group. But the episode also shows that "outsiders" both try to take advantage of the ease with which the mayors can be split, and, to the extent that they call upon superseding political allegiance, are the cause of some aspects of its internal dissension. Moreover, the Administration did not work through the staff or the official leadership bodies of the Conference, but through individual mayors, so that in a sense the group was not given a chance to be cohesive.

One final general cohesion-reducing factor in the USCM is the instability of membership caused by the turnover of mayors at election time. Changes in membership also affect the relative strength of ideological viewpoints. The USCM staff estimates that there is a 10 to 15 per cent membership turnover each year.[5] This inherent instability of course causes greater discontinuities when it affects the organizations' executive committee than when it alters general membership. Therefore, the group's leadership committees are usually selected from mayors with proven electoral staying power. However, there can be unanticipated upsets. Thus, in 1969, many mayors who constituted the organization's leadership announced that they would not run for re-election, and the USCM lost five of the 12 mayors who, as officers and members of the Executive Committee, had been the principal activists for many years.[6]

Political Cleavages

Conference members tend to factionalize along the lines of North-South on civil rights issues, liberal-conservative on issues bearing on "federal participation," and small city-large city on issues such as mass transit, rent supplements, and civilian review boards.[7]

Consider the continuing current of the North-South, very civil, persistent, civil war. This is a cold war, not only between states, but between states-of-mind and once in a while, flares up into a war of words. The North-South division on most civil rights issues was sharply demonstrated at the 1964 annual meeting. Early in 1963, President John F. Kennedy asked Conference support for civil rights legislation that he planned to introduce in 1964. He was especially interested to have each city set up a bi-racial community relations commission. On the advice of John Feild, then a member of the President's Commission on Equal Opportunity, he decided to address the USCM's annual meeting. He did so at the Conference in Hawaii on June 9, 1963, in an exhortation to the mayors not to consider the problems of race relations from a sectional point of view.

"I am here, in short," he said at that time, "to discuss with you a problem which is not local, but national, not Northern or Southern, Eastern or Western, but a national problem, a national challenge." [8]

He was followed by David Lawrence, then Chairman of the President's Commission on Equal Opportunity in Housing, and a former Mayor of Pittsburgh who had been President of the Conference from 1950 to 1953. "All of us," he appealed, "and I certainly mean those of us who live in the North as well as those whose homes are in the Southland—have an urgent obligation to provide the leadership and the hard work needed to bring about equal opportunity, which I believe is our moral obligation." [9] Member mayors accustomed to lobbying the federal government had been, in turn, lobbied *by* it in a strategy using the prestige of a popular President of the United States and an appeal for union by a former President of their own organization.

The staff of the Conference was eager to support the President. It wanted not only to have the USCM pass a resolution in favor of the President's plan, but also wanted to establish a Community Relations Service to help cities set up their own commissions and to engage in the study of methods by which to reduce racial tensions. Several obstacles were predictable—the opposition of Southern mayors to any civil rights resolution, and the opposition other mayors would face on their home grounds to the funds required to establish such commissions. Another obstacle was that cities without racial problems were reluctant to finance a service for those that did, and, according to Gunther, only 200 of the 435 Conference members had Negro populations of 7,500 or more. Conference policy had been to avoid accepting outside contributions in order to preserve its semi-public nature. More basically, mayors were generally not receptive to injunctions as to what they should do, and the USCM staff by both tradition and treaty, was constrained from ardent advocacy of anything.

There were procedural problems as well. The USCM was normally disinclined to set up permanent committees. It had only one, the Community Development Committee, to evaluate the effects of current legislation on cities. A standing special function committee would set a precedent. That in the end the Community Relations Commission was established and funded, despite all these obstacles, is eloquent testimony to the political skill of Conference leaders in managing the highly flammable conflicts which result from the Northern-Southern cleavages within the group.

Here an important organizational practice proved useful. The Resolutions Committee was in session and was by custom flexible enough to consider not only resolutions submitted in advance, but by a two-thirds vote, additional resolutions as well. Copies of such resolutions are customarily distributed to the members on the first day of the Convention meetings to allow some opportunity for study.

This time the resolutions presented by the Committee contained one entitled "Equal Opportunities" that urged passage of "a civil rights bill." It had been drafted by the USCM staff and came up before the Resolutions Committee without prior distribution to the full membership. It made no reference to any specific civil rights bill, although the Civil Rights Bill of 1964 was then before Congress. This unanticipated resolution started a fight, led by Mayor Thompson of Jackson, Mississippi, a former President of the NLC, and Mayor Fant of Shreveport, Louisiana. Thompson contended that the resolution, though cleverly worded to disguise such an intent, was really meant to give support to the Civil Rights Act. Outraged, the Southern mayors chided that organizational procedures had been manipulated to suppress expression of their views.

According to one staff member, the "Equal Opportunities" resolution passed the Resolutions Committee originally, largely because one Southern mayor, Herman W. Goldner of St. Petersburg, Florida, had been induced to support it. He and Mayor Cavanagh of Detroit were then its co-sponsors. Seven of the ten members of the Resolutions Committee were also members of either the USCM's Executive Committee or its Advisory Board. Their consensus had been arrived at in an Executive Committee meeting earlier that year. These seven, with foreknowledge of the content of Kennedy's speech, had decided on a strategy that involved keeping the resolution quiet; to circulate it in advance might give the opposition time to mobilize its forces. The resolution provided, in standard Conference vocabulary, that:

> WHEREAS, the President of the United States has honored the Conference of Mayors by appearing at its 30th Annual Conference to address the Mayors of the Country on a critical problem confronting the nation; and . . .

> WHEREAS, the President has appealed directly to the Mayors for help in finding a solution . . .

> NOW THEREFORE BE IT RESOLVED that the United States Conference of Mayors endorses proposals by the President that: (1) Bi-racial human relations committees be set up. (2) Care be taken that local ordinances are in accord with non-discriminatory practices. (3) Equal opportunities be provided for all people.[10]

At the last session of the Convention Mayor Lee (New Haven) who was presiding, used an old procedural gambit. He moved that all resolutions on the slate be considered in one motion, a procedure that required only a simple seconding and vote. The disputed proposal would be more easily slipped through if mayors with an interest in any one of the other resolutions would have to risk eventual defeat of their own by voting against consideration of the whole package. Despite this attempted appeal to self-interest and ignoring the inherent guarantee that there could be no identifiable tally for later political talk, the debate raged on—illuminating the severity of the problem of internal cohesion with spotlight intensity:

MAYOR MURRAY A. STOLLER, Roanoke: . . . you've turned this session into a rubber stamp session and I want to go very much on record as being against this entire procedure. . .I feel that these resolutions—when the history of their adoption is brought to the attention of the world, of the press—will be of such a nature that anyone could not possibly take them seriously.

PRESIDENT LEE: Your exception is noted for the record. . . . It is the opinion of the chair that the "ayes" have it and the motion is carried.

MAYOR SMITH: I would like to appeal the decision of the chair and call for a division of the house.

PRESIDENT LEE: Will all those in favor of the report of the Resolutions Committee please rise? We have one vote per city . . . I rule the adoption of the report.[11]

The battle was won. Once the procedural issue permitted the resolution to be included in the "bloc," the Executive Committee and the Executive Director now had the power to implement the resolution as they saw fit, to "conduct the affairs of the organization."

Since the USCM staff had wanted more than a simple resolution to commit the Conference to civil rights, Gunther had already met with William Taylor, the United States Civil Rights Commissioner, and John Feild, consultant to the Eleanor Roosevelt Foundation. Feild was "loaned" to the Conference to help determine what it feasibly could do. Feild designed the Community Relations Service concept, but agreed with Gunther that asking the USCM for more dues to support it "would be rough on the Southern group, who would have to get any increase in dues from their city councils." An elected Southern official just could not be expected to risk his political neck. The only way around the dilemma was to accept a Ford Foundation grant, but the Conference had never before accepted "outside money." To avoid raising this spectre, the grant decision was deliberately left to the USCM's Executive Committee to whom "foundation money" did not automatically imply "outside control." The necessary grant, a decision never referred to the membership at large, was obtained and accepted.

The Conference then hired Feild to set up a service that could help any city willing to set up its own community relations commission. The service has since been conducting frequent surveys of what cities are doing in the community relations field and sends these "Experience Reports," along with analyses of city, state, and federal civil rights laws to all member cities. As a form of inducement, flattering publicity is given to actions undertaken by mayors to ease racial tension through expanded equal opportunities in public and private employment.

According to Feild, once the program was established it became most useful to the very mayors who had opposed it. When a Southern mayor no longer had to vote for the program or ask his city councils to finance it—that is, when he no longer had to identify politically with the civil rights issue—he was free to use the Conference's services to help ease racial tensions within his constituency. Several cities that had resigned from the Conference because of ideological disagreement rejoined it to take advantage of the Community Relations Service.[12]

It is difficult to assess how much the growth of local Community Relations Commissions since 1963 has resulted from the activities of the Conference's Community Relations Service. Although the facts may have varying meanings, local commissions have increased in quantity from 112 in 1962 to 263 in 1965. By then, one-third of the member cities from the South had such commissions. In any event, here was an instance where, by avoiding an overt ideological crusade and manipulating the procedural arsenal instead, an important goal was achieved with general benefits. The Conference is likely to succed when it can provide a service for politicians that is not as readily available to them elsewhere and do so without stoking partisan political fires at the local level.

But perhaps less expected is that when the Conference successfully puts pressure on cities to create new governmental machinery, it in this way contributes to increased comparability of individual cities. This is of interest in the sense that similarity reduces the complexities involved in planning federal participation in urban areas, and certainly in the administration of federal programs.

Liberal-Conservative Cleavages

Conference members, already bifurcated by the passions of a North-South sectionalism which should have long since cooled to the temperature of anachronism, are beset as well by cleavages among liberal and conservatives. This type of political fissure could baffle most any observer unaccustomed to the vagaries of American politics; it sunders across even the guarded lines of sectionalism and of political party.

The USCM staff, thought to be inclined towards the "liberal" side of most issues, sometimes has a considerable problem assuaging conservative mayors. One staff professional cites the example of Mayor Bracken Lee of Salt Lake City, who calls the Conference "the gimme boys," and who "just doesn't believe in federal aid." Even more challenging perhaps is the 1964 joust with conservative Mayor Hasselburg, of Bloomfield, Michigan, who proposed that cities resolve to repay federal grants for urban renewal. A somewhat more pragmatic member gently reminded Hasselburg that "even conservative businessmen were in favor of urban renewal." Comforted by this reference to those in whose ideological company his self-image could remain intact, the mayor quieted down. However, the organizational cleavages which accompany the liberal-conservative syndrome are all too abundant in the annual reports of USCM proceedings. On the other hand, since this particular malady has its greatest temperature rise in the presence of a reporter or a TV camera, the Convention proceedings do reveal a somewhat artificially heightened fervor.

Still, the primary loyalty of members is to their own constituencies. Although most large cities are politically heterogeneous enough to allow considerable flexibility for mayoral maneuver, a mayor does lend support to one over another of the multiple factions and interests within his electorate when he takes a firm stand on any given issue. If his special governing coalition has a particular ideological coloration, he will either have already assumed it or must play the chameleon. The situation raises a mayor's political stakes in any choice to identify with issues which might label him on either a "liberal" or a "conservative" side of a controversy. For this reason, USCM policy of printing discussions at its major meeting, while intended to offer an opportunity for mayors to "play to their home audiences," has at the same time increased the liabilities for dissenters of "going along," and therefore has costs for group cohesion.

The leadership faces strong and occasionally unmanageable opposition from a passionate minority engaged in this ritual when it attempts to manage a political issue that has ideological overtones. Typical of the oratorical fireworks provoked by liberal-conservative division is the flare-up during the 1966 meeting set off over the school prayer issue by a conservative mayor's insistence that the Conference resolve:

> WHEREAS, Senator Everett M. Dirksen and others have proposed, in Senate Joint Resolution 148, an Amendment to the United States Constitution 'to permit voluntary participation in prayer in public schools,"
>
> NOW THEREFORE BE IT RESOLVED that the U.S. Conference of mayors supports this proposal.[13]

The Amendment mentioned had been introduced in Congress by the honey-toned Senator Dirksen, leading conservatives in a strategy to reverse the Supreme Court decision that customary morning prayers held in public schools violated the First Amendment. It had provoked heated rebuttal and counter-strategy by liberals who generally welcomed the Court's ruling. When the proposal to support the conservative position was introduced into the USCM, it elicited similar response. Mayors disposed towards temperance did battle by parliamentary maneuvers; those disposed towards drama volleyed with the full range of "Americanisms" and traditionally untouchable political sanctities.

The USCM's Resolutions Committee, composed mostly of liberal mayors, voted with only one dissent to recommend to the membership that this Conference Resolution Number 21 not be adopted. Mayor Stevens, of Wichita, Kansas, insisted that although the Resolution on the Dirksen proposal was not among the recommendations of the Resolutions Committee, he wished to speak on it. Another conservative mayor seconded the motion to open discussion and the Chairman was obliged, despite his reluctance, to permit debate that he knew would become a pyrotechnical display. Mayor Herman W. Goldner of St. Petersburg, rose to "suggest that the resolution is an extremely dangerous one . . . I think the division of opinion . . . raised by floor considerations . . . would not be meritorious."

Mayor Stevens rejoined with the warning, of which he seemed to have a special pipe-line knowledge, that God was listening to every word being uttered and that since "God is very much alive, He might appreciate having the USCM act on the proposed Resolution to counter the attempts around the country to convince our people that God is dead." Resolution 21, Stevens insisted, should therefore be unanimously adopted! At this point Mayor Goldner, risking the accusation of idolatry, was more moved by considerations of parliamentary procedure than by how God might judge the discussion. He tried his feeble best to turn the eyes of the conferees earthward by a simple request for a ruling by the chair, on his conviction that "the motion was to bring the matter before the house. It was not a motion for adoption."

USCM President Blaisdell gratefully acknowledged this move, and with greatest dispatch attempted to lead the mayors out of the morass of their own words. However, the move for tabling the motion to bring the resolution before the meeting was narrowly defeated, and the controversy continued to rage.

Mayor E. Dent Lackey of Niagara Falls, New York, submitted that "this is not a spoon-fed group of men. . .to withhold such a resolution from the consideration of this body is undemocratic." Committee Chairman Mayor Maier of Milwaukee, retorted that "we are acting as a legislative body . . . If the procedure is undemocratic, then procedures in legislative bodies thoughout the United States—including Congress—are undemocratic,"

Mayor Goldner persisted that the subject be brought to a vote. President Blaisdell again tried to head it off by insisting that the motion before the house was that this resolution be rejected. Goldner, however, insisted that procedures were secondary because the point of the motion was that "our children must be taught to pray. . ." Mayor Elliott Roosevelt of Miami Beach, voicing the thoughts of many, insinuated that the mayors were embroiled in talking for political purposes at home and noted that "the time has come to abide by our constitutional government."

Once again Blaisdell ruled, and again in vain, that it had been moved and seconded that the resolution be rejected. Mayor Stanford R. Brookshire of Charlotte, South Carolina, then made a substitute motion urging that "we ought to consider the reason most of our forebears came to America—to worship God anywhere, any time, in their own way. We ought to have that privilege. . ." President Blaisdell interjected, "Mr. Mayor, your motion is out of order." Vice Mayor Abe Cohen of Lynchburg, Virginia, ignored this reminder on the "rules of the game," and pledged his own ethnicity to the fray: "I'm Jewish and when I went to school we had prayers at opening and closing and I see no objection to it happening again."

In the end, the liberal leadership lost control to a passionately ideological conservative minority and Resolution 21 was adopted. The vignette illustrates how discussions within the USCM sometimes take on the quality of emotional political oratory rather than considered debate on the merits of an issue and are sprinkled with conspicuous appeal to democratic "rules of the game." It also points up several other characteristics found among groups of elected public officials. First, according to orthodox interest group theory, the active minority, or leadership, of an interest group exerts a kind of oligarchic control. Second, this active minority contributes to the greater cohesion of the group, which it is able to do because of a general apathy and lack of comparable leadership skills on the part of other members.[14]

The internal dynamics of the USCM do not fully support these propositions. In the first place, its leadership has not exerted oligarchic control. There is too frequent a turnover of leaders at elections, and members are not willing to be led. Their relations with government and with the press are not dependent, as in most interest groups, on access granted by the organization's leadership. Second, when leaders (both staff and big-city Executive Committee members) do attempt to exert strong controls over the full membership, it provokes revolt and dissension rather than compliance and cohesion. Third, the Conference does not reveal the usual internal pattern of leader-follower relations, members are not "generally more apathetic" than leaders, and each individual has leadership skills that rival those of the formal "leadership" of the group.

The school prayer case shows that the passionate minority which controlled was not the kind of minority which in traditional organization theory usually prevails. Clearly those who, in the parlance of group theory, were the "active minority," those with the greatest continuity and intensity of group involvement, lost. A "passionate minority" here, in contrast, was *ad hoc* and ideological.

Finally, the school prayer resolution is symptomatic of an unfortunate but perhaps necessarily diffuse public focus which may be characteristic of a group of elected public officials. Part of the group's yearly policy package includes resolutions incorporated only in deference to a particular mayor's specialized interests or political needs. Clarity of purpose and dedication to well defined goals are to this extent sacrificed. USCM policy resolutions from 1959 to 1969 reveal the amount of time wasted on issues not primarily "urban" or not intended for staff implementation, as, for example, in statements addressed to state legislatures instead of to the federal government, the real target of Conference activity.

The widespread tendency to simplify and categorize issues by labeling them as "liberal" or "conservative" usually obstructs rather than facilitates political action, especially on those aspects of an issue not susceptible to liberal-conservative distinctions. In the USCM, to describe a proposal as one which will "separate the liberals from the conservatives," is to polarize the mayors and thereby prevent the Conference from taking any public stand. If the issue is really substantive, rather than emotional (as was the school prayer case) the USCM can exercise surprising ingenuity in closing the political fissures of liberal-conservative differences.

One of the greatest strengths of the organization, in fact, lies in its ability to reconcile internal conflicts and to work around the deadlock induced by demagogic labels when the stakes are high. A case in point, and a great contrast with the Dirksen donnybrook, was the USCM's handling of the controversy surrounding the clause in the 1964 federal anti-poverty legislation which called for "maximum feasible participation" by the poor. In some localities, this clause induced a conflict so severe and so intractable as to require solution at the federal level.[15]

The Economic Opportunity Act of 1964 provided for direction and control by local neighborhood units in the administration of community-centered poverty programs. This was to be both a procedural breakthrough and a substantive experiment. Community Action Agencies could be private organizations while receiving funds from the federal government, a sharp departure from the standard practice of dispensing public funds only through public bodies. Participation in these agencies by the poor themselves was to be encouraged by the Office of Economic Opportunity as authorized under "maximum feasible participation."

The USCM had firmly endorsed President Johnson's war on poverty and the Community Action Program when it took this form initially, In 1964 it referred specifically to the Act's "plan to conduct all-out attacks on poverty by building on local initiated community action programs."[16] The Conference had also urged that local government channel the funds and coordinate the projects. As a united organization it took the stance that local officials should retain a final power of approval. At the time the USCM took this public stand, the question of where control over the community action programs should rest had not yet become a liberal-versus-conservative issue. The mayors' position was based on "principles of public administration," "government responsibility for public programs within its jurisdiction," and a politician's natural antipathy toward building up organizations that might challenge his political control. Five prominent (and liberal) members of USCM testified to this effect in Congress.[17]

Once subsequent developments pinned a "conservative" button on the attitude that local government should have approval power over community poverty projects, the previously neutral and accepted concept that federal funds should be dispersed through a public agency came to imply "discrimination against the poor." Under such conditions, the USCM could no longer assert a public position. Paradoxically, mayors holding the opinions expressed as official USCM positions prior to their identification as "conservative views," were the "liberal group" within the organization. Conservatives and Republicans supported intra-city community control of independent community action programs which would mobilize the poor against the inertia of "entrenched bureaucracies." In reality, the issue was only confused by the use of the conservative and liberal pigeonholes.

When Representative Edith Green of Oregon sponsored an amendment to the Economic Opportunity Act which would give local officials the control over the Community Action Program which the mayors had thought appropriate, the USCM nevertheless took no public position. Its previous consensus had been based on the "governmental" issue of mayoral responsibility for the public programs within his jurisdiction; once redefined along liberal-conservative lines, the mayors began to align themselves accordingly, and their public rhetoric reverberated with the spotless ideological purity which, once sparked, usually leaves the USCM tongue-tied with neutrality.

This time, however, the group's staff realized that the mayors faced a challenge which superseded ideology, program commitment and constituency desire. It prepared to do double battle— first with its members, split asunder on the spectrum of ideology, and second, hopefully backed by the membership now unified, with the federal government

The threat posed was the idea that federal funding of private groups which had no connection with local government, yet were authorized by OEO to carry out community action programs "within city limits," was contrary to the interest of local government. As a social policy, the ideas of promoting political activity among the poor and enabling them to organize in their own behalf to "fight city hall" came mainly from President Kennedy's Task Force on Juvenile Delinquency. The intent was to supplant feelings of powerlessness and alienation that were thought to cause anti-social behavior with feelings of political efficacy by building up small private groups within poverty areas which would become capable of controlling their own communities.[18]

"Maximum feasible participation" and non-publically controlled (but publically funded) CAA's can thus be considered as attempts to encourage social change both for and by deprived segments of society and to raise their relative political, social and economic status. Most liberal mayors would—in the abstract—support both the policy and its intended results, the more so because a large part of their own constituencies (the urban poor) would be beneficiaries.

However, several factions in Congress had begun to encourage the independent local groups to organize as political opposition to their own mayors. As separate entities, the Community Action Agencies were forming clusters of discontent throughout the already strife-torn urban areas. Even more important, these poverty program groups could not be held accountable to anyone—official or electorate. Yet despite this, it would be the mayors who would be blamed for any mishap. Worse still, they could become channels through which the federal government could exercise control over the local polity by the power of its purse-strings, and assist in toppling any city official who happened to be out of grace.

Once this invitation for chaos was made clear, the mayors coalesced around the conviction that control by local government of its own domain was at stake. Ideological appeal and constituency benefits faded even more rapidly when the mayors discovered that the *Community Action Program Workbook* officially recommended political activity by the poor through their federally funded agencies. "Local government as an interest group," this time with interests of its own, joined forces with one another in a professional association, with the USCM as vanguard.

The Conference, now protecting its raison d'etre—the viability of local government—invaded with its full reserve of political artillery. First, its prestigious Executive Committee contacted OEO, insisting that before making any community action grants, it obtain the approval of the citywide agency. Next, the mayors formed a committee under Mayor Daley (who else can deliver the votes of Illinois for a Democratic President) which expressed their collective wrath directly to Vice President Humphrey. Humphrey assured the committee that the recommendations of the OEO workbook for promoting political activity among the poor would not be implemented.

It was not a coincidence that the Fall of 1965 saw a new issue of OEO guidelines which severely restricted the independent financing of community-action programs.[19]

In short, local government won. The urban lobby this time acted not for urban programs or for social change, but for a separate interest of local government itself. Elected public officials, individually or collectively, have a right given by the governed to govern in their interest. In this case, the mandate of the governed was used by the governors to protect their own interest in governing.

Big City-Smaller City Cleavage

The divergent interests of big-city mayors and small-city mayors is another natural occasion for political cleavage.

A statement released to the press at the 1969 USCM convention by the mayor of Lafayette, Indiana, expressed the feelings of many mayors:

> . . . this committee does not have proper representation of cities with less than 100,000 . . . If we are going to remain a Conference of Mayors, those small communities should have equal rights and should expect to have their views supported by this Organization as do the larger commmunities.

The fact is that cities of different size do have different needs. Another mayor, a member of the Executive Committee, stated:

> The biggest problem of the USCM is the large vs. small city

split . . . I'm interested in urban renewal . . . I can build public housing and urban renewal at the same time, and relocate those displaced by the urban renewal right into the public housing. The biggest cities can't do this; they have no land for public housing.

The conflict between the small and large cities is evident in the struggle over President Kennedy's proposal to set up a Department of Urban Affairs. It might appear that this was simply a case of elevating the "urban interest" in the public view, meriting wholehearted approval from an urban lobby. Yet there was contention. Smaller cities objected out of fear that such a Department would favor the big cities. Also troublesome were the basic questions of what constitutes the urban interest and how is it best represented? The persistent issue of the degree of federal involvement and controls was another divisive element. Mayor Goldner of St. Petersburg argued that:

> direct relationship between municipalities and the federal government . . . defeats and depresses the individual intiative . . . of the local municipalities . . . creation of a Cabinet post for urban affairs would tend to weaken this self-determination and vigor on the part of cities.

Mayor Daley commented on the matter of size of federal controls:

> If any Mayor states . . . regardless of the size of his city . . . that he and his people can take care of all the problems arising in that locality, I have never seen it. The problems that confront the large and the small cities know no boundary lines . . . and there was never any intent, surely by the creation of the Department of Commerce, or Labor, or of the Interior to take away any powers from the small communities.

Mayor George E. McNally of Mobile countered by recalling when his city "dared to question the allocation of public housing," the federal government retaliated by closing off funds for Mobile's public housing authority. "I think this is just one example of what could happen," he said, "if we put the centralization of power in the federal government."

In the outcome, the resolution of support for setting up a Cabinet department passed by unrecorded vote under the very strong leadership exerted by Mayor Celebreeze who was presiding. Its language was traditional, with due tribute to the diverse political views and familiar postures of a membership dedicated to the American, democratic, "rules of the game." The consensual nature of the resolution is evident from its language—alternating between clarity and deliberate ambiguity. It reads in part:

> the complexities of modern life compel the interdependence and cooperation of all governmental units to cope with common problems . . .

> WHEREAS, joint federal-state-city resources, programs and efforts must be utilized fully if solutions to the problems are to be reached, and WHEREAS, the nation relies first on the cities . . . the vast centers of American life—to provide the initiative, dynamics and leadership necessary for attainment of domestic objectives, and . . . WHEREAS, the traditional American principles of local autonomy, home rule, self-determination and fair legislative and administrative representation at state and national levels are endangered not by intergovernmental collaboration but—too often—by failure of state governments to acknowledge the rights and needs of the cities . . . NOW THEREFORE BE IT RESOLVED that the United States Conference of Mayors:

> Reaffirms its support of federal-state-city cooperation and

> asks once again for establishment of a Cabinet post to deal with the problems of the cities.

Supporters of the bill were subsequently at issue over whether the new agency (HUD) would be formed by elevating the Administrator of the Housing and Home Finance Agency to Cabinet level, or whether it would involve a transfer of programs from other departments as well. This, however, was never brought before the Conference itself. Large-city mayors wanted a strong, multi-faceted department; others wanted none at all. One of the legislative strategists for the 1962 Administration bill suggested that the Conference "just supported the bill at the hearings."

It seems probable that the Conference staff accepted a compromise version of an Urban Affairs department to avoid another disastrous confrontation which might have developed if they had demanded more. USCM would not let itself alienate the executive agencies with which it had close relations or the interest groups for whose support it usually negotiated on housing programs. It was clear that USCM allies had different political stakes in the establishment of the Cabinet Department, so the USCM sidestepped strong opposition by adopting a resolution acceptable to the broadest range of its supporters. It was sensitive, as one speaker put it, to those

> who wish to maintain the special status housing has in the Federal Government. In recent years, with the assistance of these groups, housing legislation has been enacted almost yearly to aid home purchases and financing. The Housing and Home Finance Agency, and its constituents . . . *are by and large reluctant to face up to the proposition that housing is but a part of the larger problem of urban development.*

The Conference also noted "the concern of existing federal departments and agencies that they might lose jurisdiction over programs and responsibilities." Given these considerations, the Conference reasoned that:

> The "housing" group could be given some assurances that their views and problems would be given sympathetic consideration by the new department, or that the Under Secretary would be a "housing" man, but they can be expected to prefer the status quo. On the other hand, the fears and concerns of the exponents of existing agencies can be effectively placated if they can be given some assurances that their favored programs would not be transferred. Accordingly . . . it would seem preferable that the proposed Department of Urban Affairs not be contemplated in terms of transferring such

programs as the highway construction, airport construction, hospital construction, water pollution control, or school construction in impacted areas to such a new Department.

The point is that the USCM wanted such a Cabinet department. It recognized the need for expanding the formal representation of urban interests, other than housing, in the federal bureaucracy. Yet its basic task was to manage possible conflicts and to arrive at a compromise acceptable to opponents yet compatible with its own support. It was a delicate undertaking but if successful would result in passage of the legislation which Congress had defeated on several occasions. Its approach was strictly pragmatic. The politics of consensus was deployed rather than a knock-down confrontation which would have splintered the coalition that brought HUD safely through the legislature.

Once the Conference overcame internal divisions, it set out to build the support coalition that pushed the bill through Congress. It can now justifiably identify itself as HUD's "clientele" group and refer to HUD as "our baby." Here was an example of large cities influencing the federal government to redress the political imbalances of rural- and suburban-dominated legislatures. Government institutions, in line with Truman's thesis, had responded.

It may reasonably be asked why the smaller cities put up with the frequent victories of the large-city membership? After all, it is their votes that often make victories possible. And, why do the big cities want the smaller cities at all?

The answer rests in the simple, perhaps obvious truth that for the implementation of policies, the big cities need the added political leverage provided by a broader base of presumed popular support, that is, the consent of a larger number of cities. And smaller cities, who depend for much of what they need on the day-by-day services of the USCM, accept the price of a reasonable exertion of big-city influence. A fair trade. The politics of consensus works because it gets things done. If in the total process the essential character of the large metropolis is only dimly in the background, if philosophy must be blurred by political reality —that is a fact of life and a mayor is, above all, a political animal.

The relationship between the HUD establishment and its clientele group reveals greater complexity than conventional organization theory implies. By and large group theory suggests that it is the interest group that pressures the government until institutions adapt. Here the interest groups had vacillated over exactly what it was they wanted. The federal government was initiator as well as reactor to the constituency concerns of the "urban" officials. The President, therefore, not only responded to interest group pressure to adjust relations among competing interests, but also to what he considered to be his major single constituency, the largest cities.

Efforts to raise an agency to department status can, according to organization theory, usually be interpreted as a desire for independence from the President, rather than as a desire for integrated programs; reorganization is requested for purposes of better access to government. The HUD-USCM case was quite different. The Conference has always had a very close relationship with the President. There is clearly a "situation of mutual support" because of overlapping constituencies, and the Conference has never wanted to be more independent. The USCM did not need to look to the reorganization for better access to government. On the contrary, there was the possibility that the institution might interfere or intervene in its relations with the President, Congress, member mayors, and other executive agencies. An urban affairs department, it was feared, might diminish the Conference's role as a kind of unofficial secretariat for the HHFA.

Nevertheless, these variations from conventional group theory should be considered only as elaborations of the pattern, perhaps identifiable as special characteristics of governmental groups. The overall situation, however, indicates the usual process whereby a group within government pressured another group, which reacted in predictable fashion.

Conclusion

The fact that the Conference is an inter-governmental lobby whose membership consists of the highest elected public officials of large cities is a variable which affects its structure, its leadership practices and its organizational procedures. Some aspects of USCM behavior derive from the fact that the mayors are elected rather than appointed officials, some from the fact that they represent large cities rather than small cities; some from the fact that they represent cities rather than states or Congressional districts, and some simply from the fact that they are officials.

Primary loyalty of members to the policies of their individual constituencies results in natural and unpreventable cleavages within the USCM. These cleavages correspond to the current political or ideological cleavages of the national political system, and are determined by forces external to the organization. The cleavages change according to the distribution of ideological inclination and the political party affiliation of members.

This fluidity is important in evaluating the role of an inter-governmental lobby as an instrument of social change. On one hand, congruence with current national political cleavages within the group severely limit it as an instrument of change because it becomes an automatic mirror of the status quo, not a "mobilization of bias." On the other hand, turnover at elections keeps the group responsive to the most recent demands for reform, as indicated by the electorate. Moreover, as an inter-governmental lobby the USCM has a great number and higher level of access points to government. If the members use their political leverage on those federal officials to whom they can be of electoral assistance, the lobby will have a very high potential for effecting change. The kinds of changes it may attempt, however, can be those "of interest to government as government," or of interest to elected local officials as well as those "of urban interest." The urban lobby, as seen in the Community Action Agency case, is truly an inter-governmental lobby in that it presents the interests of one level of government to another on matters pertaining to the *idea* of governing (authority commensurate with responsibility and control in its administrative jurisdiction).

It is significant, however, that an interest group of elected public officials does not seem to have the capacity for unified and conspicuous self-presentation. In short, the group *qua* group loses some of its representational character, and amassing the political power of the mayors becomes difficult. This affects the urban policy subsystem as a whole in that one of its major support groups minimizes its own visibility to the public. Although it does manage to bring its members together, it can sometimes appear as

a "nongroup" to governmental actors in the subsystem. The difficulties of decision-making within the Conference thus become part
of the general difficulties of federal urban decision-making. The
range of interests, decisions, and constituencies is so broad that it
encompasses, and thus reflects, most of the pre-existing cleavages
in the nation.

In the 1930s', and 1940's the Conference contributed greatly
to the urban policy subsystem by fostering communication among
groups, among cities, and between these and the federal government. Today, a "national urban policy" requires a set of attitudes
shared by actors in the subsystem, and the mayors of the large
urban centers to which such policy would apply must experience
these shared attitudes.

In a group so involved with federalism, in which local constituency attitudes and local issues, regardless of their relevance,
shape members' points of view on the national questions with
which the USCM is concerned, shared attitudes are difficult to
bring out, even when they do exist. Even when constituency attitudes are not relevant to an issue, mayors tend to "play to the
home audience," diminishing group cohesion. In the language of
group theory, cleavages based on overlapping membership, and the
high probability that "potential groups" within the membership
will coalesce to take issue on most subjects that become public
knowledge (rather than remaining quiescent, as is more usual)
illustrate some of the problems with evolving an urban policy.
These problems of cohesion within the USCM highlight the
reasons for the general looseness of the urban policy subsystem—
its complicated involvement with federalism, localism on non-
urban issues, and the conflicting commitments of the participants.

Yet, despite the difficulties, the USCM has persisted to project
some measure of a reasonably articulate system to represent urban
interests in Washington. A mechanism to produce maximum attainable consensus has evolved. Distracting confrontations on too
many diverse demands are nimbly avoided. The multi-centered
nature of the system enables one group to compensate for the
incapacities of another. The truth is that the USCM has been
able to apply a high quality of political skill to make up for the
inherent weaknesses. Its political skill in managing internal conflicts despite their intensity within the organization is an important

reason for the USCM to be considered here as a pivotal group. In fact, its internal processes of aggregating consent resemble more the kind of processes that usually go on among groups rather than within them. Its special forte equips it all the better to arrange alliances.

The Community Relations Service arranged just such an alliance between Northern and Southern mayors, and indicates that the USCM has been an influence in forming the attitudes of its members in addition to articulating those which already exist. The group can apparently go beyond facilitating consensus; it extracts one when the urban interest requires.

The role of the Conference in the establishment of HUD is similarly informative. Cabinet-level rank for the urban interest escalated the importance of the urban subsystem and provided a focus for leadership around which urban groups could rally. It ratified in an institutionalized, formal way the kind of direct federal-city relations for which the Conference had always worked, and acknowledged the cities as the "third partner" of federalism. This was achieved largely through sensitivity to the productive effects of compromise. The large city mayors may have gotten less than they had wanted; nevertheless, for the USCM itself, *HUD became a vehicle by which to "kick upstairs" the problems of the representation of those urban interests on which the group could not unite its members.* The group itself thus helped to bring into being another member of the urban decision-making complex that could be an important force in structuring the coalition necessary for action in federal urban legislation.

Government acting on government does differ from ordinary interests acting on government. It has more access to vital pressure points, but less cohesion. Relations with federal officials are much more complicated than those of an ordinary clientele group. And unlike with ordinary interest groups, it does not necessary follow that the less its cohesion, the less influence it will have on government. Its centrifugal elements do not prevent the Conference from having substantial impact, and as a HUD Assistant Secretary emphasized, "We would not go very far without consulting them [the Conference]." A solid residue of mutually advantageous values remains.

On the other hand, one must conclude that a membership of

elected public officials is dysfunctional for the internal cohesion of an organization. Successful lobbying *by* mayors depends on successful lobbying for coherence and consensus *among* mayors. Some of the reasons that its internal cleavages do not completely splinter the Conference and thus render it ineffectual are to be found in an analysis of its formal organizational setup, its compensatory integrative mechanisms, and its informal leadership controls.

An urban lobbyist must demonstrate the ability to generate support by building consensual coalitions among many urban interest groups. Coalition formation is a common enough political strategy, but one which usually implies trading support among different, though not conflicting interests (farmers and truckers for instance). In urban lobbying, however, these coalitions involve groups which, paradoxically, are more likely to have contradictory interests (urban renewal *vs.* housing, small cities for highways, large cities for mass transit). Consensus, in short, can be structured. How this can be done is therefore of particular importance to the process of urban lobbying.

CHAPTER V

Structuring Consensus

THE Conference is a loose coalition of urban interests, capable at any moment of splintering into total ineffectiveness. To prevent this, formal and informal mechanisms exist to manage inner dissention, and insofar as possible to keep disintegrating tendencies in check.

Conference membership policy is the first expression of these consensus-structuring mechanisms. The USCM is open to all cities of over 50,000 that are willing to join; in 1970 it has a membership of 435 cities whose added population represents a considerable percentage of the total electorate. While this diversity contributes to lower cohesion, the strength in numbers tends to compensate for it. Each city has one vote regardless of size, which tends to balance the weight of the large-city mayors by the sheer numerical preponderance of the smaller-city mayors. The broad membership policy vastly increases organizational access to and influence on Congress. The mayor of the largest city in almost every Senatorial and Congressional district belongs to the USCM, and can contact the legislators whose constituencies he shares on behalf of Conference goals.

Still, there are complaints that the Conference favors the big cities. There is a general tendency to regard the Conference as representative of the large cities, although many small-city mayors are in positions of USCM leadership. Whom, then, does it represent? Who are its beneficiaries?

Virtually all of the nation's large cities having a population of

135

over 200,000 are members. One-third of the 312 cities with a population of 50,000 or over, a total of 102, are also members. Surprisingly, 27 percent of cities with populations between 100,000
and 200,000 are not members.*

There is also another significant element beyond that of population size. The larger cities have, as a rule, more non-whites, more
foreign-born, more non-propertied, more blue collar workers—
the traditional ingredients for more liberal voting habits—than
do the smaller cities. The smaller cities are by comparison more
conservative.

Viewed in its broadest perspective, the USCM membership
policy of balancing large with small cities is partly a response to
rivalry with NLC, partly a reflection of the need for more funds,
and partly a function of the need for allies. However, ultimately,
the Conference is thought of as expressive of the attitudes of the
nation's largest cities and as leaning slightly left of center on most
issues. There is a reluctance to drive for an expanded membership
from those large cities not yet affiliated with the USCM: they
contain many ideological dissenters of the right; they are either
politically conservative in general, or opposed to USCM civil
rights policies. In some cases, it also happens that a newly-elected
mayor does not want to be identified with what he has come to
think of as the "political club" of his predecessor.

According to the data, then, the Conference does represent
the largest cities, in the sense that all the "giant" ones belong.
However, their strength is greatly diluted because of the quantity
of smaller cities with equal voting power.

Although USCM membership policies are intended to minimize
dissent while maintaining the representative qualities conferred by
diversity and numbers, one might argue for an alternative practice
to eliminate more of its cleavages, sharpen its focus, and heighten
its policy-making capacities. Since the urban problems and the
political outlook of the largest cities seem to differ in perspective
from that of the smaller ones, why not decrease the membership
to include only the 50 to 100 largest cities. Under such a policy
the USCM could speak unambiguously for the giant metropolis'

---

* See Appendix VII for membership chart.

and leave it to the National League of Cities to express the views of smaller urban concentrations.

The Conference's decision to broaden rather than to restrict its membership reflects its conviction that achieving consensus from an ideologically diverse constituency, regardless of the difficulties this entails, results in more potential action by the formal political institutions. The alternative course toward a more rapid and facile internal consensus among large cities might pose critical issues more sharply; however, it is argued that this would simply transfer fundamental-consensus building from an internal to an external effort, by, for example, increasing polarization between USCM an NLC. When inter-group deadlock among the urban lobbies themselves occurred, disagreements would have to be reconciled within Congress or the executive branch. The ultimate "mix" of urban legislation would be formulated by people who less understood the implications, and under circumstances which neither group would be able to control. Still worse, perhaps too many separate "confrontations" might confuse Congress, prevent a coalition of support, and make action on any urban legislation impossible.

The USCM is convinced that its choice enables it to practice the art of the possible—consensus politics. Confrontation, to this school of political behavior, is more akin to war than to domestic priorities. After striking its primary bargains within its own ranks, it then turns to achieving agreement between the USCM and the NLC. In that way, demands made on Congress and the Administration have broad-based support in advance. Also, by trying to achieve a balance between ideology and numbers (having left out those cities whose intense dissent would be highlighted by their large populations), the Conference is able to cover two fronts. Its blend of large and smaller megalopoles can enlist the interest of the President for whom cities are obviously an important voting constituency. And it maximizes access to the Senate by including as many cities in a Senator's state as possible.

Of course this policy exacts its price, and the Conference expends considerable energy trying to avoid balkanization. Its risks, on one hand, splintering into powerless ideological factions as a result of its attempt to represent an "interest" that is too broad to be handled by a single group. On the other hand, even given cohesion, it must still avert the diffusion of influence that might be implied by the vagueness of representing cities—an aggregation of concerns too diverse to be considered an "interest." Once again, although this problem is inherent in the idea of an urban interest, it becomes even further complicated when it involves numbers of cities as well as numbers of interests. Nevertheless, by its early decision on membership, the Conference made its choice for the politics of consensus in preference to the politics of confrontation.

To survive with this choice, its internal dynamics must perform in at least three respects: It must offer strong leadership; it must hold out rewards for participation which will be great enough to encourage continued membership irrespective of policy differences; it must provide strong integrative and socializing mechanisms to reduce occasions for overt conflict.

Leadership Controls: The Active Minority

The constitutional structure of the Conference and the informal leadership practices of its active minority reveal some of the ways by which an urban lobby can structure control.

During its early years * the Conference was tightly controlled by its Executive Director, Paul Betters, and by its President, Mayor Fiorello LaGuardia of New York. LaGuardia provided the policy leadership and the link with President Roosevelt, and Betters provided the contacts and expertise of a skilled lobbyist.

> Paul Betters had a little group of big-city mayors as a pressure group. He was close to President Roosevelt. The Executive Committee met often; during their meetings, F.D.R. would drop in, and the meeting went "off the record." Or, the President would invite the Executive Committee over to the White House, and it was all off the record. It has never been clear what went on, but it was obvious that the Conference was an important cog in the F.D.R. organization.[1]

* In 1932, there were 100 members; in 1953, 300; and in 1969, 435.

A staff member recalls that "they had a very loose way of operating but there was no demand for democracy. The guys were happy and they usually had a big social blowout at the meetings at the Waldorf. The dues schedule was peculiar too. One mayor might pay $10,000 when, according to the dues schedule, he only needed to pay $250."

This suggests that the Conference was in some respects run by Betters initially as a private lobby for those cities willing to pay for his services.[2] When Betters joined the armed services during World War II, LaGuardia "just moved in." There were, as before, no working committees and no formal rules.

It was when Betters returned from the service that a clash developed between the two strong personalities of LaGuardia and Betters. In one letter about wage stabilization that LaGuardia wrote Betters, something of the sharpness of the conflict is revealed. "I wish," LaGuardia wrote, "you would leave matters of policy alone. You are getting this wage matter into a terrible mess. I have asked you just to compile queries and refer them to me."[3]

LaGuardia's twelve-year hold on the organization was finally broken in 1944, when a group of mayors raised money privately to give him a banquet "upon his retirement"—and the gift of an automobile. This time-honored way of disposing of a bothersome personality by a publicized honor caught LaGuardia completely by surprise. Since then, no Conference President has served for more than two years.

The Constitution of the Conference is a short, loosely drawn document which permits a great deal of flexibility. Effective control rests in the Executive Committee and there are no restrictive guidelines as to circumstances when decisions must be referred to a balloting of the entire membership. The Executive Committee has, by writ, total power: to change the population basis for membership, to fix membership dues and service fees on the basis of a city's population, to fill vacancies on the Advisory Board and on the Executive Committee itself, to conduct the affairs of the organization in the year between its annual meetings, to refer only such topics as it chooses on which it may wish an expression of opinion from the full membership, to make honorary appointments, to determine the time, place and program of the annual meetings; and, not least, to appoint the Executive Director, who in turn has magisterial powers.

The Constitution provides that the USCM Executive Committee consist of a president, a vice president, the immediate past president, chairman of the Advisory Board, and nine men elected at the annual convention. Although technically they hold office for one year only, there is no limit to the number of terms they may serve. An Advisory Board of fifteen to twenty-two members is named on the basis of regional and population considerations. Finally, the Constitution specifies that the "Executive Director shall transact the necessary routine and financial business of the organization as may be determined by the Executive Committee and Advisory Board." Direction of the organization, therefore, rests in the hands of the Executive Committee and the Executive Director, with, in some slight measure, the Advisory Board.

A number of procedural customs and practices not in the Constitution strengthen the established control mechanisms. Some of these practices occasionally come under attack. They are justified, however, as central to a continuity of policy and as practical procedures needed to arrive at a result, considering the diversity of interest of the membership.

The Executive Committee and Advisory Board must, constitutionally, be designated at the annual convention; but this has come to be a rubber stamp procedure. The convention is asked to approve the complete slate submitted by a Nominating Committee that has itself been appointed by the Executive Director with the advice of the current Executive Committee. It usually also includes at least one member each of the Executive Committee and of the Advisory Board. The recommendation of the Nominating Committee must be voted by the Conference as a whole. The device of a single vote on the entire slate—take it or leave it—practically assures its passage. "One year, twenty-seven California cities threatened to quit," a staff man tells. "I said: 'Los Angeles pays $4,000 dues and has one vote. You pay far less and among you, you have twenty-seven votes. I'll take Los Angeles!' They changed their minds."

Group Integrative Mechanisms

Control at the level of the Executive Committee is the Conference's method of assuring continuity of policy and a hard-core working group that becomes socialized and integrated into group norms. The Nominating Committee, conferring with the President, Vice President, and Executive Director, chooses both the Advisory Board and the next Executive Committee. The Chairman of this Advisory Board becomes the next Vice President of the Conference and, the following year, President. He sits on the Executive Committee as well as the Advisory Board. Since continued leadership of the Conference is dependent on success at elections, members of the Executive Committee who are seniors in service are those, who, like the chairmen of the committees of Congress, have tenure—safe seats. This policy assures that members will slowly be socialized into the normal operations of the organization and gives some control to those who can act on controversial positions because their reputation at the polls is established. According to the Conference staff, the effect of this instrument for continuity and coherence is considerable. "Once in, by the time they have any role of consequence, they all think the same. For example, at the 1962 meeting, Mayor Goldner was against the one-city–one-vote principle. By 1963, he was neutral. By 1964, he was its staunchest supporter."

Mayor Goldner, long a dissident, became a member of the Advisory Board in a customary procedure of "incorporating the opposition," that is, of submitting a potential "troublemaker" to the constant influences of the dominant official and staff viewpoints. It is a device that the Executive Committee can use indefinitely by virtue of its power to add to its own membership. It was probably in mind when the Executive Committee brought in Mayor Maltester of San Leandro, California, in 1966 without prior submission of his name for membership approval. The Committee justified its decision by the observation that "it would be unwise not to include a member from California at this time." [4] In fact, Maltester was elected President of the Conference in 1969.

California cities, as a group, had been mavericks. The con-

troversial Mayor Samuel Yorty of Los Angeles was drawn into
the Advisory Board in 1962, although Yorty, first elected in 1961,
had had little time to become active in the USCM. Yorty is a
political personality with substantial personal contacts and high
visibility. A former state assemblyman and United States Congressman, he starred, in 1966, in a series of 90-minute commercial
television programs called "The Sam Yorty Show." In a similar
waiver of rules for similar reasons, Mayor John Lindsay of New
York was also placed on the Advisory Board during his first year
of office, as were Mayors Shelley and Alioto of San Francisco.

Vacancies on the Executive Committee resulting from death,
election defeat, or resignation, are filled by the Nominating Committee from the Advisory Board on the advice of the Executive
Director. This gives John Gunther strong political muscle and
subjects him to enormous pressures.[5] Since he depends on the
mayors to cooperate in implementing Conference policy, his
power of appointment must be judiciously exercised as a system
of fair recognition; he dare not be capricious or arbitrary. For
the Executive Committee, he must consider those who will best
testify in Congress, carry out assignments for the Conference and
get their Congressman to support particular legislation. An Executive Committee member must, as a staff man puts it, "come around
often." Actually the mayors lobby each other and USCM staff
for positions on Conference committees. This process is an intensive one and takes place not only at annual conventions, but all
year long.

The Executive Director's authority gives him latitude to press
for support of what he considers "appropriate legislation." This
includes both pursuit of Conference policies determined by its
formal resolutions and acting on new issues. It is he who usually
decides which federal activities are important to the mayors and
informs them accordingly. In practice, this means that to a substantial degree, interest group staff rather than interest group
members define the urban interest for the cities and to the federal
government.

Upon examination it becomes clear that the Advisory Board
has not functioned as prescribed in the USCM constitution. Its
only really active role as a body is to plan the annual meeting
program and to serve as a reservoir for Executive Committee

membership. Thus, even those who emerge as leaders must serve a "leader's apprenticeship" before attaining higher organizational office. The constitutional provision that members of the Advisory Board shall be chosen "on the basis of regional, population, and similar considerations" is flexibly interpreted. In a memorandum to the Executive Committee in 1966, Gunther pointed out that this criterion must be kept in mind, but must not be frozen into a hard-and-fast rule. The reference to regional and population basis for appointment to the Advisory Board is intended, he maintained, "to express desirable guidelines and not to set forth a formula for distribution of positions on that board."

The advisory capacity of the Advisory Board, and the criteria for its members, appear to be largely a rhetorical obeisance to the "democratic rules of the game" which call for broad-based leadership and regional representation. With its actual freedom of interpretation, the Advisory Board becomes a cornucopia of "prizes for good behavior" available for discreet use by the leadership. There must be enough to entice (and absorb) the occasional maverick, and the leadership must not be left without recourse. Thus it is Conference practice to have the number of mayors on the Advisory Board actually below the constitutional limit of twenty-two. This encourages members to compete for Advisory Board positions and can be a dependable incentive to elicit cooperation.

Even the voting procedure at the annual convention, in spite of the one-city one-vote rule, seems to have been susceptible to manipulation. The constitution does not provide for a quorum. Instead of operating under Robert's Rules of Order, the Conference makes its own parliamentary procedures. Roll call votes are not permitted, and voting is by a show of hands, by standing, or by voice. Votes are counted but not recorded. Another integrative mechanism of the Conference, this procedure is comparable to the function of voice, division, or teller votes in Congress. When votes become simply a majority instead of a personal statement, members are less likely to feel compelled to "vote the ideology" or to "show the folks back home."

Voting at the USCM meetings is considered important by member mayors. Many want credit for having sponsored an idea, others want to see "who will line up with whom." In some ways these votes can be interpreted as expressions of personal political support, possibly for a future endeavor, or even as early indications of party solidarity on a new issue. It is therefore not surprising that there have been attempts to "stack" the voting sessions.

At one time, difficulties arose because some mayors brought along delegations of their special assistants and other city personnel to the annual meeting. Mayors were on their honor to let only one person vote for the delegation, but it was an honor system subject to abuse. Large cities with large delegations bring to bear the sheer weight of numbers.

A fully legitimate method by which a state with many large cities can sharply influence action is by making sure that the entire state delegation of its mayors attends the sessions and stays on through the last day. In 1965, the Mayor of Burlington was the only mayor from Vermont. He observed that "there are ninety-six delegates here from California, and they can control the Conference."

In 1965 the Conference attempted, at Gunther's suggestion, to correct this condition by adopting a "credential card" method of voting. This had its complication because those qualified to vote had to sit in a separate section from those who were not; and a mayor generally is enough of a primadonna to want to be wherever he wants to be—and damn the rules! Gunther contended that it is useless to move the voting up to an earlier day because for the busy mayors this would automatically make that day the last one of the sessions.

Another mechanism of control by Conference leadership is the practice of calling for the submission of resolutions several months before the annual meeting. A resolution that does not have the recommendation of the Resolutions Committee needs a two-thirds vote, as against a simple majority for the others. Since 1966, the resolutions have to be submitted two weeks in advance of the meetings. Late resolutions may also be considered, but again, only by a two-thirds vote. This too is a custom often breached. As already indicated, it does not prevent the Resolutions Committee from including controversial resolutions that have not yet been seen by the membership.

Rewards for active participation in the Conference, themselves socializing devices, are another aspect of the internal dynamics connected with the political nature of the membership. Compliance with Conference policy is motivated in good part by a wish to be on the Advisory Board, and, in due course, on the Executive Committee. To share in the control of policy, to have access to highly-placed federal officials, to be appointed to a President's blue-ribbon commission, to have access to off-the-record information on federal programs, in short to be "in," is tempting to any political office holder.

The strong control which the Executive Committee exercises thus serves a double function—uniting a multi-factional group and offering a reward for the willingness to be "united." Membership on this committee is an asset which a mayor can present to his constituents, especially in a campaign for another office. Mayor Cavanagh of Detroit, for example, exerted strong and successful pressure on Gunther and on the Nominating Committee to place him on the Executive Committee so that he could advertise this position during his bid for the Democratic Senatorial nomination against G. Mennen Williams in 1966. Cavanagh became President of both the Conference and the National League of Cities and stressed this. Although some mayors resented Cavanagh's tactics, Gunther calmed them with the implied promise that "mayors are expected to make political mileage out of their participation in the Conference. That is their reward for working hard." In fact, the organization itself gains further status from the use of its name by a popular candidate.

On the other hand, if the campaign is a mayoralty race, exploitation of an important post in the Conference for individual political purposes has elements that can do injury to the group. When an incumbent Conference officer loses an election, the winner who replaces him as mayor is often reluctant to join. A Conference staff member explains:

> This happened, for example, in Oakland, California. Cliff Richell was the Vice President of the Conference. In his campaign literature, he played it up big. The guy running against him won. We congratulated him, and offered him membership. But he said, 'I'm not interested in Cliff Richell's

club.' However, he soon started coming 'round to meetings. The reasons that mayors are active in the Conference is that it does something for them.

The Conference does attempt to control the exent to which it is flaunted politically. It has a publications director who, according to another staff member, "was hired for the explicit purpose of keeping the name of the Conference out of the newspapers and to promote the publicity of the *individual* mayors who have worked especially hard." Ideological divisions affecting the conference as a whole are minimized, thus it is easier for mayors of different political persuasions to participate. "A lot of mayors disagree with this policy because they want the Conference position made public. These are mostly the ones who want to use it for political purposes. But Gunther likes the idea of low visibility. He believes that more can be done that way."

An especially attractive reward for active participation is dangled in the form of a possible appointment by the Executive Committee to a federal advisory committee, to special commissions requested by the President, or to select groups sent to represent the Conference at conventions of political parties. Federal officials usually work through the Conference whenever mayors are needed on governmental projects. By a kind of gentlemanly understanding, the Executive Committee can enable an individual mayor to play a more conspicuous part in the arena of national politics.

The services that the Conference performs for its members must also be ranked high among the rewards for participation. It sends mayors daily information sheets on Congressional and Administration activities which might be of interest to cities. These reports have a major utility since in addition to comprehensively touching on all relevant subjects, they underscore the highlights in what might otherwise appear as an overload of information. Subtle or "hidden items" with foreseeable, but not immediately obvious consequences are bold-printed in an effort to give meaning and direction to the enormity of paperwork that usually passes between levels of government.

The USCM sends the mayors copies of pending Congressional bills affecting cities, amendments as they are introduced, and testimony from hearings, all with accompanying explanations.

Mayors questioned indicated that since legislation has become so complicated and its practical meanings so difficult to decode, the USCM is of great help in keeping them abreast of developments and in raising signals for action appropriate to a mayor's self-interest. As bills are passed, members are notified and the legislation is explained from a mayor's frame of reference. Especially important are the regulations and reports of executive departments and agencies that are sent out. Administrative guidelines do not as a rule get much public attention but have crucial bearing on the implementation of federal-urban policy in individual cities. Changes in procedures and allowable practices may have far-reaching political consequences to which mayors should be alerted.

The Conference also helps the mayors in their applications for available federal grants and instructs them as to how they might qualify for others with which they are not familiar.

USCM staff briefs members who want to testify before Congress to ensure that they represent the consensus of the group. It arranges for a mayor to meet with federal officials and with other mayors so that they can share experiences and compare problems. Members cited these last two functions as particularly useful. The staff serves as an "idea workshop." A mayor interested in solving a particular city problem can get information on how other member cities have dealt with it. Here again, the Conference may serve as an agent for lessening the diversities among cities which complicate any attempt at a "federal urban policy." As part of this effort towards informed cities with rationalized and comparable systems of public administration, it supplies mayors with researched reports such as its studies on: *Municipal and Intergovernmental Finance* (1953), *Economic Opportunity in Cities* (1966), *Poverty, Race and the Cities* (1966), and *The Mayor and Federal Aid* (1968).

Labelling this internal education system as "research" is related to the "official nature" of the membership and serves as a dissent-reducing technique. Although the research reports have an obvious policy bias, they never overtly advocate a particular solution; they are presented only as "simple reporting." The Conference staff explained that "mayors are better able to act on a report than on a suggestion carrying any inference that they are being told what to do. Membership sensitivity thus dictates that when dealing with internal politics, the Conference employ "indirect, soft-sell lobbying" and statistics rather than exhortation of its members. Factual material presented in "reference book" form gains acceptability by appearing as apolitical and non-ideological. It is an integrative mechanism in that it is a control for dealing with a group of chief executives accustomed more to giving orders and advice than to taking them.

A fairly recent service performed by the USCM for its members is that of holding training seminars for city officials on coordination of federal-city aid programs at the local level. This service could well turn out to be one of the USCM's most important contributions to federal-city relations in the 1970's.

Major legislation which will channel more funds to cities (Housing Act of 1968, Amendments to Social Security Act, Medicare, Economic Opportunity Act, Urban Mass Transit, etc.) has already been passed. The problem viewed from the Washington end of the subsystem is mainly one of funding, which lies in the domain of the Appropriations Committees. These committees are already being "encouraged" in a highly concentrated and organized way. However, the preliminary research which exists indicates that available funds are not being maximally and most efficiently utilized at the *local* level. Individual cities have not developed integrated systems for the application, processing, collecting, distributing and monitoring of federal aid to keep up with federal capability to dispense it. The establishment by each city of a special staff office for federal aid coordination, as is being encouraged and programmed by USCM training seminars, may well result in "found" federal monies.

According to the Conference, the first task of each recommended City Development and Coordination Office should be what is ostensibly a simple one. It should compile information on the following:

A—Programs for activities in which each agency is now engaged and federal aid is received, either directly or through the state.

B—Programs for activities in which each agency is now engaged and which qualify for federal aid, but for which no federal aid is received because the state is not participating.

> C—Programs for activities in which each agency is now engaged and which qualify for federal aid, but for which no federal aid is received because on application has been made therefor.
>
> D—Programs involving desirable activities in which an agency is not now engaged for which federal aid is available.[6]

It may seem surprising that cities do not keep this information as a matter of course; in reality, however, attempts at getting it involve a major political, administrative, and intellectual *tour de force*.

First, there are complex and sometimes inconsistent planning requirements attached to many grant programs. State and local governments must prepare both specific functional and broad comprehensive plans based on different standards and data. On the other hand, sometimes direct federal action is taken *without* regard for local plans. Although there is great need for inter-agency coordination among federal field offices, the federal agencies are not organized to cooperate effectively at the regional level. In 1968 there were over two hundred direct federal-city aid programs enmeshed in over four hundred separate appropriations which operated through twenty-one federal departments and agencies. These departments and agencies have in addition some one hundred fifty major bureaus and offices in Washington, and over four hundred regional and sub-regional offices in the field.[7]

The only centralized consolidated information on federal aid available to states and localities was first published in 1967 by OEO. Moreover, the state governments which include even more offices and agencies, administer over 75 percent of federal grant-in-aid funds.

Although several of the major programs of the 1960's were, in part, designed to bring order out of administrative disorder, they sometimes resulted in political chaos. The *de facto* complications arising from the "maximum community participation" or "decentralized" programs in the Economic Opportunity Act are well known. In some programs, loans and grants for public works and development facilities may be made to private organizations as well as to governmental agencies. One of the reasons for this arrangement was because the mayor, although the chief political official of his city, was never responsible for *all* public service programs with anti-poverty effects. The major unit for administering the Social Security Act and Aid to Dependent Children, for example, is the county. Although Community Action Agencies under OEO were designed to be administered by private agencies in order to avoid problems of jurisdiction, there was no discussion of the effect of this arrangement on the normal pattern of administering grants through local governments.

Job Corps and Vista are administered directly by OEO, with the state governors empowered to disapprove programs. The Neighborhood Youth Corps is administered by the Labor Department, although contracts are made with both state and local public and private agencies (with a Governor's veto subject to overrule by OEO). The Adult Basic Education and Work Experience Program is administered by HEW through state agencies according to specific program plans, and then by grants to localities. Not only are programs ostensibly for the same purpose administered by different federal agencies; they are also authorized and funded by different Congressional committees. Transportation programs, for example, are partly under the jurisdiction of the Public Works Committee.

Any analysis of federal aid received and receivable by a city involves so many different agencies with so many different programs in their planning requirements, matching grant requirements, time span, and uncertainties of funding by Congress that it is no wonder that the job has not been done. However, it is for exactly this reason that new management system must be developed. Their result may be a greater concentration of urban lobbying at the state level, or even the intra-city level, to ensure the most efficient use of federal programs.

USCM—*The Continuous Lobby*

The staff does virtually all the work of the Conference and looks after the long-range goals and policies of the organization. As one testimony to its importance, by far the greatest part of USCM budget is allocated for staff salaries. Since its establishment, the Conference has had only three Executive Directors.

Paul Betters served from 1932 until his death in 1956; Harry Betters until 1962; and now John Gunther, who formerly served as a general counsel to the organization. This stability has been a major factor in policy continuity. In 1960, the organization added an associate director. Hugh Mields (who, as mentioned, came to the Conference from previous positions with the HHFA, NAHRO, and the NLC), held this position from 1960 to 1967. Mrs. Janet Kohn replaced him until 1969, after which the merging of staffs between USCM and NLC made an associate director unnecessary. The structure of this staff merger provides the two groups, still separate as to memberships, with increased service and policy-making potential. The joint operating units being co-sponsored are a Center for Policy Analysis, an Office of Public Affairs, a Center for Program Implementation, a Man-in-Washington Service, and an Office of General Services. The Center for Policy Analysis will hold continuing seminars for top city officials on key urban issues, publish a series of papers to provide comprehensive analysis of those issues, conduct training programs for policy-oriented urban generalists, and inaugurate a new Labor-Management Program. Moreover, it will

> initiate long-range inquiry analyzing problems and issues that have yet to reach the level of legislation or even public debate. It will conduct congressional seminars on urban problems, contract for research on specific studies of interest to cities, including the application of new technology and new management tools to urban programs, and be responsible for the improvement of continuing liaison with internal organizations on the subject of urban development.[8]

The Office of Public Affairs will function as staff to both parent organizations in the areas of public information, community relations, public relations counsel, and public affairs programmed activities. The office will provide media liaison on behalf of cities in order to develop increased public understanding of the urban issues, city problems, and their solutions. It will be the communicating link functioning on behalf of the total range of operations in the League and the Conference by developing public interest in support of their municipal policies. It will also be available to cities for public affairs counsel on the subject of increased public relations activities in individual cities.

The Center for Program Implementation will design new programs to strengthen the capability and productivity of cities and state municipal leagues. Some of the programs to be developed include a service center to respond specifically to smaller cities; new ghetto and youth program services; detailed projections in restructuring local governments, and urban practitioners creativity sessions. In addition to these, the Center will also be responsible for continued liaison between metropolitan councils of government and the National Association of Counties, and for administering specific programs such as the Model Cities Service Center, the Federal Aids Coordinators Service, and the Urban Observatory Program.

The Office of General Services has been established to provide administrative and logistical support for the joint operations.

Finally, the Man in Washington Service will continue to provide staff offices in the nation's capital for individual cities, enabling them to identify and make the best use of federal assistance programs as well as keep Congressional delegations well informed of cities' interests.[9]

The USCM's necessity for a permanent Washington-based staff with wide authority to act is indicated by the "public official" nature of the organization. For maximum group cohesion the daily grind of Conference tasks must be carried out by political neutrals —those whose political preferences remain a private matter. More important, the consensus of those interviewed was that "politicians are short-term guys and the staff enables the Conference to have long-range goals." Obviously, mayor members do not have time to carry out detailed Washington work. For this reason, too, Conference committees have mayors as official members but need— and have—"working staffs."

The importance of these working staff committees cannot be over-emphasized. It is through them that consensus is obtained from other participants in the urban policy system for the pursuit of mutual goals. Members of these working subgroups are a mixture of the mayor's assistants in charge of a city's urban development programs; representatives of other interest groups, such as NAHRO, the NHC, Urban America, the Urban Coalition; Conference staff members; and outside consultants who have expertise in urban affairs and housing.[10]

It is through the permanent staff that other participants are drawn into the pursuit of goals of the urban policy system. These subgroups, such as the Community Development Committee and the Human Resources Committee, are where the real policy-implementing dynamics of the organization are concentrated. They analyze and criticize the legislative programs of urban interest groups, of the Administration, and of Congress. They generate new program ideas, identify the important urban issues, and recommended action to the mayors and the staff. It is they who constantly touch base with key legislators, Congressional staff, and Administration personalities. The working subcommittees are the instrumentalities by which overlapping group memberships—a potential for disunity in theories of interest group behavior—can instead function reasonably harmoniously within the urban subsystem.

Based on its year's work, the subgroup of the Community Development Committee submits a package of their resolutions to the Conference staff and eventually to the Resolutions Committee. The resolutions, the outcome of such preliminary processes, project the real business of the Conference in its increasing attempt to move towards an integrated organizational attack on the elements of the urban crisis. Policy initiatives are often timed to coincide with the debate on those issues in Congress and within the Executive. Legislative proposals are reviewed with the staffs of the Housing Subcommittee of the House, of the Banking and Currency Committee of the Senate, and of the relevant agencies of HUD. It is customary for the staffs of Congressmen from urban districts, of Congressional Committees, and of the executive agencies to attend the meetings of the working subgroup of the Community Development Committee. In this way they can both guide and be guided. The final proposals of the subgroup are then circulated to other urban interest groups. In this way the working subcommittees form what can be compared with an agency's "Planning, Programming and Budgeting System" within the interest group network of the urban policy-making subsystem. They provide the threads for the web of shared attitudes and interrelations as participants move from one into another position within the total subsystem. They are at once nuclei, catalysts, and finally, expediters in the process of aggregating consent.

Thus mayors themselves do not participate directly in this sequence of events. This has the advantage of making possible a filtering out of the political cleavages in the Conference membership, and the assignment of responsibility for policy implementation to upper level bureaucrats who are concerned with substance rather than rhetoric. They themselves are endowed with a "passion for anonymity." Proposals submitted by such a politically neutral group are more acceptable to Conference members than are resolutions suggested by rival mayors competing for public attention and applause. It is this group of invisible but dedicated men and women who, in the last analysis, structure the attainable consensus.

In driving for that consensus, these personnel-forces work with parallel subcommittees from other interest groups—the NHC, NAHRO, and the Urban Coalition. A Joint Ad Hoc Committee on Workable Programs of NAHRO and the USCM finds room also for representatives from federal agencies. Testimony to the unifying capacities of these diverse-membership subcommittees is the comment of a high HUD official that "it's hard to tell which urban group a particular idea came from. These working subcommittees that I've attended come up with things they all have a hand in." The sharing of ideas and experiences on the working subgroups reaches into the development administrations of the major cities through interaction among city administrators, and between them and federal government officials.

These well-staffed working subcommittees are another function of the nature of USCM membership. Committee staff workers are not, and could not be, paid out of the Conference's modest budget.* They perform this service as part of their jobs with the individual city government. Thus the ostensibly restrictive budget of the Conference is deceptive; the practice of staffing the Conference from the personnel of member cities helps to overcome a potential financial limitation. Since the members are cities, the

---

* The average annual budget for USCM was about $127,000 during the 1960's. However, in 1969 there was an increase of total revenue to $156,500, and it operated at a $5,000 deficit in 1970. The 1970 census will change the dues schedule and possibly raise the operating budget.

Conference is financed out of local public funds. Dues are based on population, and revenues increase only with every ten-year census. The dues schedule itself would be difficult to alter because each mayor would have to clear an increase with his city council, a body with which most large-city mayors have quite enough budgeting difficulties. Were it not for the ability to use city staffs, the problems involved in increasing revenues might seriously cripple the organization.

In evaluating the program capabilities of the USCM, one must ask whether the staff and the active minority are exerting the maximum effort to lead the mayors in generating innovative ideas and in focusing on an "urban issue context" that could meet the demands for an "urban policy" to the extent that any such policy can be shaped.

It is in the area of the USCM's policy-producing capabilities that a reappraisal of the internal dynamics of the Conference is most warranted and that opportunities for future leadership are greatest. Interviews with both mayors and staff indicate that USCM staff considers itself "a creature of the mayors"—more the cities' voice than the cities' guide. The predisposition of the organization has always been to consider as appropriate a pattern of persuasion, influence, and authority that flows from the membership upwards to the staff, rather than downwards from the staff to the membership. This frame of reference is not inappropriate for a lobbying group, since directors are traditionally creatures of the membership and, like the Conference staff, hired by the Executive Committee. The present director, John Gunther, considers the role of responding to the mayors as his main one.

But the point is that the Conference could conceivably play a much stronger role in helping to evolve a strategy—in the sense of a grand design—for federal-urban policy. Despite its newly-organized secretariat, it acts more as a vehicle of support than as a group in hot pursuit of something it has defined for itself as an over-riding goal. Certainly a greater effort could be made to "lobby the mayors," to make them more aware of their own responsibilities for formulating the kind of federal-urban strategies they demand of the federal government. Mayors should be asked to bear this goal in mind as having priority over their use of the organization for more limited concerns.

More staff initiative would not be a completely new concept. It was there in the 1930's. There were several occasions also during the 1960's when programs were in fact products of the USCM staff. Staff work on the Clear Air Act and the successful passage of an amendment to urban development legislation authorizing regional councils of government to receive federal grants (the 701 G Amendment) are examples of such initiative. The mayors showed no particular interest in them but the USCM staff saw long-term values and went ahead. In both cases the staff showed great foresight. The "environment problem" is now a popular political issue and the mayors will get credit for a vision really manifested by the staff of their professional group. The regional councils of government may conceivably become vehicles whereby federally assisted housing can be dispersed throughout a metropolitan area and help relieve the central city. But these are exceptional instances of staff enterprise; there is need for much more program pioneering.

Mayors themselves, even those on the Executive Committee, may not be averse to a stronger exercise of direction from the staff. Several, in fact, expressed interest in having the organization expand its function in the network of urban groups into that of a policy-making vanguard. Mayors from even the largest cities, who, it is generally felt, must be handled with kid gloves, indicated that they would welcome more forceful staff work. They themselves, they say "don't have the time or the long-range perspective to generate comprehensive policy goals." They acknowledge that "since the urban crisis is getting so complicated, someone has to do it. Our staff doesn't seem to feel it has the mandate for this, and doesn't try hard enough to control us, even though we know we can be difficult."

Some mayors complained that while they were remiss with last-minute amendments to the staff's resolutions, the reason was that "no package was really pushed, presided over and 'sold' by the Conference staff." Similarly, another remarked, "This week, the annual Convention should have been the high point of the staff's year, but they just melted into the background and let the mayors, who sometimes hadn't even seen the packet of resolutions before, just take over."

There are sure to be risks when resolutions are not coordinated in advance. Staff resolutions for 1969 contained two recommendations. One was an endorsement for the national housing goals and for the principle of involving private enterprise in construction as formulated in 1968 urban development legislation. The other was an endorsement of a tax reform program that would have withdrawn the tax incentives to private builders necessary for meeting the goals of this national housing policy.

These two were plainly mutually contradictory, and they constitute evidence that either they had not been thought through fully enough before submission or that the staff supinely presented options on which the mayors were to make a determination without having it clearly before them that these resolutions were in conflict. "No wonder," said one of the mayors, "that individuals who spot these things can so easily take over." Although it is still too early to judge, it may be hoped that the new NLC-USCM joint secretariat will take on responsibilities for attempting to remedy this condition.

The staff may not relish the risks involved in producing directives towards a more comprehensive program. It can, though, take some steps towards sharpening the thrust of the organization by at least eliminating those resolutions that are not at all relevant to urban problems, or those addressed to state legislators and other bodies that the Conference has no intention of following up. There are, in fact, occasions when such resolutions further strain relations between the mayors and the governors, and at a time when more abrasiveness can ill be afforded.

Since the late 1960's, the Conference has had a greater opportunity than ever before to influence the federal government. This opportunity derives in part from a Bureau of the Budget Circular which freed its staff from dependence on the policy resolutions of its members as its main mandate for leadership, and in part by the establishment of the Advisory Commission in Intergovernmental Relation (ACIR).*

When the basic public housing and urban renewal legislation was authorized in the 1930's and 1940's, Local Public Authorities and Local Housing Authorities were set up in cities to utilize

---

* ACIR was established in 1960. Bureau of the Budget Circular A-85 appeared in 1967.

the programs.[11] These bodies were purposely created to appear non-political. Mayors had only power of appointment (generally for fixed or overlapping terms) and did not control them. They were under the jurisdiction of local redevelopment officials whose interest-group representative was NAHRO, not the USCM. The mayors at first paid little attention to the LHAs and LPAs.

In the 1950's, things began to change. The USCM and the NLC had noticed that the forward-looking social approach to urban renewal programs by Mayors Lee of New Haven and Lawrence of Pittsburgh had possible political leverage. Armed with this insight they encouraged other mayors to "think urban" and to become more involved with LPAs and LHAs. President Kennedy came to use the cities increasingly in his liaison with Congress. When HUD was established, President Johnson named Mayor Hummel of Tucson and Professor Robert Wood of MIT, both city-oriented in different ways, Assistant Secretaries.

According to their colleagues, both Wood and Hummel felt that the federal government should shift its attention from "special authorities" (LPAs and LHAs) to general local government. Urban problems, it was maintained, should not be attacked in "tiny fragments," and HUD should not work with factions as opposed to a political jurisdiction in its totality. From HUD's point of view, this meant a shift in its main clientele group from NAHRO to mayors, who better represented general local government. This was not surprising. Hummel, as a past president of NLC, was familiar with NLC and USCM, and knew how to work through them. Wood, on the other hand, preferred to work directly with mayors as chief executives of local governments. Both strategies were simultaneously to broaden the scope of HUD's clientele.

This increased attention to "general government groups" actually began with the ACIR. It had been established to improve the effectiveness of the American federal system through increased cooperation between the national, state, and local levels of government. ACIR is made up of three private citizens, three Congressmen, three Senators, three Executive officials, four governors, three state legislators, three county officials, and four mayors. The mayors, two of whom must be from cities of under 500,000 population, are "appointed by the President from a panel submitted jointly by the NLC and the USCM." [12] Thus, the act establishing ACIR in effect called for ever closer relations between the NLC and the USCM and made the Conference, via four of its leaders and its duty to appoint and consult, officially a part of the executive branch.

With the institutionalizing of the USCM into government the Conference staff could now have a stronger voice in federal urban policy, one less dependent on the varying moods of its general membership and upon the often impulsive triggering of its resolutions procedures. The ACIR was a legally established umbrella under which to bring together representatives of all levels of government to consider common problems, the administration of federal aid programs, and the need for new legislation.

The Bureau of the Budget also became interested in the concept of dealing with general government groups. HUD set up meetings with BOB to discuss ways of further educating this agency to appreciate the general government point of view. As a staff arm of the President, BOB would have a natural talent for understanding and working with chief executives. It was organized to function with an eye for how details would fit into a general program. Since it had grown to be the place where agencies' legislative proposals were made complementary with a President's overall program, it would be an ideal institution for a similar kind of "administrative clearance" of regulations affecting intergovernmental programs.

At the request of the President, the Bureau of the Budget informed executive departments and agencies that regulations and rulings affecting the local interpretation of program administration must be cleared through relevant organizations. Procedures for informing local government associations of proposed new or revised regulations were prescribed:

> The issuing agency will provide to the ACIR a copy and a summary of the proposed regulation . . . The ACIR will promptly transmit copies . . . to . . . the following local government associations: . . . International City Managers' Association, National Association of Counties, National League of Cities, and United States Conference of Mayors. [13]

In this action the staff of the Conference was given another institutionalized role in the policy process of the executive branch and a corresponding opportunity to exert a greater measure of direction and influence on mayors and their programs. It remains to be seen what use the urban lobbies will make of this new instrument.

Conclusion

Since the internal dynamics of the USCM accentuate the skillful ways by which the procedures of an organization can be tailored to meet the most intricate of political circumstances, these internal dynamics merit intellectual attention even of themselves. Here however, the mechanisms by which dissension is reduced and political cleavages compensated for enable the urban interest to be elevated and elaborated from the specific and the particular to the general and the national.

Consent is structured within the USCM; given its diverse political makeup, in contrast with those groups clustered around a single, or functional purpose which are therefore like-minded to begin with, the study of the internal processes of the USCM becomes a lesson on how consent and accommodation is structured throughout the urban policy subsystem as a whole.

Systems theorist David Easton has pointed out that "a major response mechanism through which political systems typically avert any serious decline in the level of support for an existing regime is to be found in the processes of political socialization." [14] Since support within and among the urban lobbies is fraught with the dangers of fragmentation, any socialization mechanisms by which the urban groups can integrate their members into their own behavioral norms and stabilize their relations with other groups acquires major importance. The choices involved in structuring consensus begin at very early stages of concern—from a group's membership policies, in its constitutional structure, through its leadership practices, and by its overlapping subcommittees.

These working subcommittees are among the most important of urban lobbying devices—in terms of political management, urban interest aggregation, inter- and intra-group agreement, sources for new ideas, and structures for obtaining agreement throughout the entire urban policy subsystem. Illustrating this point, the Community Development subcommittee of the USCM serves as a kind of "little legislature for the urban interests," and includes representatives from all the different private and institutional actors. The ways in which this subgroup in effect co-opts other individuals and groups are to some extent comparable to the process by which a regulatory commission is co-opted by the clientele it regulates.

The membership policy of the USCM, although intentionally a part of its strategies of accommodation, is perhaps no longer functional for the best representation of large-city urban interests. Now that USCM and NLC have merged their staff operations, perhaps a better strategy would be to have the membership of both groups be more highly differentiated. The largest cities ought to be clearly and unambiguously represented through the USCM, and the smaller ones through NLC. The reasons for having both kinds of cities in both organizations which obtained before the merger—for allies, consent-building, broad-based membership to cover Congress—are no longer as persuasive. The joint staff could work out the appropriate coverage, alliances, and agreements. This arrangement would allow the largest cities to have a clear identity and a representative body undiluted by smaller members' claims at times when sharpness of focus and urgency of demands made this desirable. The need for clarity as to who is demanding what may be greater now that the number of "giant" cities is on the decline. In any event, the problem of internal policy-making is so great within the USCM that eliminating a major source of dissent and consequent compromise of real needs might well be worth the risk. In other words, there may be too *much* desire by USCM to avoid "confrontation;" it compromises too much, and at the expense of the policy-productive capacity of large cities, the focal point of urban crisis.

The crisis in urban policy-making and policy-making machinery at the federal level is in part a crisis of coordination and communciation. The new BOB procedures for consultation with local officials through USCM and NLC are another step in alleviating one aspect of this "crisis." It is by attention to such small things as appropriate and complementary administrative rules and regulations that any urban policy at the federal level can be effectuated.

The ACIR further coordinates other institutional actors (both governmental and non-governmental) to fill a gap in policy-making machinery by bringing together representatives of all levels of government and to provide another important linkage center for the people involved in different aspects of the subsystem. The significance of this last function is evident from the interrelations of ACIR members both as individuals and as representatives of other participating groups and institutions in the urban policy subsystem.[16]

The attention the executive branch has given to general government groups in the 1960's increases the possibilities for policy influence by the generalist urban lobby groups in the decision-making process. Consequently it also enhances the potential of the intergovernmental lobby as an instrument of social change by implanting in the national executive those whose electoral fortunes and responses to programs are tied almost completely to happenings on the local level. The establishment of HUD, most of whose programs are of the direct federal-city type, gave an institutional "home" to the direct federal-city relations encouraged for so long by so many urban interest groups, and provided the organizations with a prestigious target for alliance-building activities. The nature of each group's alliance-building activities, or its relations with other participants in the subsystem and with HUD, are important because capabilities of issue subsystems vary according to the complementarity of the strategies adopted by its members. Moreover, the impact of an individual organization depends in part upon the strategies of persuasion it adopts.

The methods of interest articulation employed by and available to the USCM are variables which define its role in a policy subsystem. In turn, its role is a referrent by which the roles of others are defined. Which of its strategies are a function of a public official membership, which are available to urban groups in general, and to what extent do USCM political strategies complement those of its allies in urban interest representation? What is the relation between strategies adopted and policies produced? These questions must now be examined.

CHAPTER VI

Strategies in
the Political Arena

THE strategies of ordinary interest groups usually center around the Congressional Committee and Admininstrative agency that have jurisdiction over their particular concern. These groups have the advantage of being able to direct their energies at institutions organized according to function, and thus into channels already established and at targets almost immediately obvious. The influence pattern which develops resembles a triangle—a bureau, a committee, and a clientele group. J. Lieper Freeman illustrates this kind of policy-making triad between the Bureau of Indian Affairs (in the Department of the Interior), the Congressional sub-committees on Indian Affairs (of the Committees on Interior and Insular Affairs), and the American Indian Federation.

The lobbying strategies of urban public interest groups involve more complex patterns. First, they must impose what might be called geographical concerns on a functionally organized federal government, since the urban lobbies represent functional interests specifically related to geographic areas (cities). Second, urban strategies, in addition to aiming at urban problems, must be directed to the special area of inter-governmental relations. Merging a primary urban policy interest with a secondary "government relating to government interest, urban lobbies compete with many special function groups for attention in many places. These groups and places include Congressional committees, agencies, and county, state, and federal governmental interests represented in institutionalized communications channels—the Subcommittee on Intergovernmental Relations, the ACIR, and the OIR.

Strategies for representing urban interests, therefore, involve
multiple and simultaneous tactics and targets which are further
complicated by the political affiliations and ambitions of mayors
and others who are part of the urban lobbying subsystem. Thus
urban lobbies work through their mayors and through personal
contacts and political relations, through city Congressional delegations, through state delegations if the state is highly urbanized,
through key legislative Committee members and agency heads,
through the President and his staff, and to some extent, through
political parties' national platform committees and legislative
caucuses.

The necessity for complex, multiple strategies mean the tasks
of urban lobbying must be divided among several groups. Each
one is expected to bring some special asset to the urban policy
subsystem. The NLC, for example, provides broad-based support
by its very large membership, its influence on Congressmen and
Senators with smaller city constituencies and on those who are
generally conservative. The NLC is welcomed in Congressional
Committees that are not particularly urban-oriented and was
therefore the urban lobby focus in the Public Works Committee
on Air and Water Pollution, and in the Judiciary Committee's
passage of the Safe Streets Act of 1968. NLC also has better relations with state governmental officials and with the Republican
party than has the USCM.

In contrast, the USCM has better relations with the Democratic party, with federal executives, and with the more urban-
oriented Congressional committees. It can provide a more concentrated and forceful political thrust versus broader support upon
the more liberal Senators and Congressmen and on those with
larger-city constituencies. There is a symbiotic relationship between
the two main generalist urban lobbies; a focus on the strategies of
the USCM will illustrate the interdependence and specialization
of roles.

Nolo Contendere; the Strategies of Non-Action,
Elitism and Presidential Support

As with all groups in the governmental process, the role of the USCM emerges as a function of its internal politics on its external strategies. Having already noted its internal dynamics, the limits of its strategies are more readily understandable. It was foreseeable that the Conference could—and can—have no open policy commitments on highly controversial political issues. The political elitism characteristic of big-city mayors, and their conviction that the largest cities have the greatest political impact, have not surprisingly led to a strategy of separatism vis-a-vis the NLC. Finally, the Conference cannot openly oppose the policies of federal officials whose support individual mayors rely upon in their election campaigns or with whom they share a mutual constituency.

Nor can the Conference afford to oppose the policies of the President of the United States. On one hand, a President usually courts political support of the big cities; on the other, the mayors are dependent on the President for vital support of crucial urban programs. Moreover, the political fortunes of the mayors depend a great deal on the President, whose access to a mayor's constituency via the mass media and whose contacts with local party officials give him considerable leverage.

The policies of the Conference on controversial issues is for the leadership to exercise strong and skillful controls to avoid internal dissention. On some issues, no public position is taken at all. The tendency to avoid taking a visible stand on highly controversial issues affects the Conference's role in the urban alliance, its relations with other actors, and the extent to which it can pursue agreed-upon policies. The Conference may in fact work behind the scenes on controversial issues on which it has stifled open debate; but it is the overt policies and public postures that at once limit and define its role in the urban system. Open and active support is more useful to Congress, federal agencies, the President, and other interest groups simply because a controversial issue is, by definition, one that needs visible and active coalition-building.

United support by the network of urban groups therefore becomes very significant. On the other hand, the fact that intergovernmental lobbies of elected public officials may sometimes be unable to undertake highly visible activities may simply change the location in the policy process at which decision-making is concentrated. If, for example, a group is unable to openly advocate relevant measures before formal introduction of a bill, a Congressional Committee may delegate its stage of the bargaining process to an *ad hoc* collection of experts over which the Committee (through its staff or its members) may still exert a dominant influence. This purposely keeps a low public profile. The staff of the "elected official" lobby may participate significantly, but without jeopardizing the political interest of its members. Under different circumstances, similar activities incident to the passage of a piece of legislation after it has been introduced would take the form of public hearings, or "closed" committee meetings. The point is that the strategies of an intergovernmental lobby of elected public officials affect the stages and location of decision-making.

Some of the legislative issues defined as controversial in the 1960's were rent supplements, civilian review boards, open housing, and mass transit. The Conference took no official position on any of these. All those questioned, other than members of the Conference staff, considered the USCM as "generally conservative" and unable to take an active part in "controversial issues."[1]

According to Patrick Healy, Executive Director of the NLC, "both organizations have problems with controversial issues. For example, neither debated open housing or rent supplements." The League, generally considered the more conservative of the two organizations, opposed civilian review boards while the Conference took no position at all.[2] When review boards are supported by mayors of large cities, it is generally in response to pressure from minority groups, and this support is considered "liberal" policy. According to one Conference staff member, many of these mayors wanted the Conference to pass a resolution supporting review boards. The Conference staff could then follow up this resolution by initiating comparative studies and "how to" suggestions. The USCM's more conservative elements intervened, and in the end no position was taken. The liberal element was only able to prevent the Conference from following the League's negative stand. Mayors would therefore pursue their own policies without coming into an open conflict with the Conference. The Conference intimates in its public statements that controversy isn't shunned at the annual sessions, where full and free discussion is encouraged. But by tradition, resolutions are limited to subjects in which cities have universal interests and on which the mayors can generally agree.[3]

But side-stepping controversy, however warranted and skill-full, can still strain relations with some officials. From time to time Senators and Congressmen from regions with big-city constituencies sponsor or support advanced and therefore controversial legislation for which they want an official expression of Conference support. When it is not forthcoming the legislator waxes indignant. Several Congressional aides and committee staff people have complained that "we couldn't get the USCM to support federal money for colleges because a public issue splits them." But here an adroit tactic can be used: the USCM will be asked to give way to a specially organized *ad hoc* pressure group chiefly from USCM members, who then come out in support of the bill. Such *ad hoc* groups are most effective.

The most specific complaints were made about the Conference's failure to enter the rent supplement battle. Under this program, low-income families from undesirable neighborhoods would be able to relocate to housing built by private developers, and the federal government would supplement the rent. Low-income housing would be dispersed throughout a metropolitan area and prevent the tendency for the poor to get caught in a ghetto cycle. The program was controversial because it would change the social make-up of a community, especially since originally it did not give local communities a veto over the location of privately built rent supplement units. The program would get around the usual suburban objection to public housing projects by permitting families displaced by urban renewal to live in existing suburban housing, with the government making up the difference in rent.

The conclusion to be drawn from the USCM's failure to take a stand on the rent supplements is that the nature of its membership limits its ability to face controversial issues head on. The strategy of "nolo contendre" inhibits the capacity to come forth with positive programs. Yet involvement in controversy might serve to further alienate conservative and rural members of Congress who label the group a "liberal, big-city lobby." The votes of these Congressmen are also needed for city legislation.

The Conference attitude affects even agreed-upon policy. Civilian review boards, rent supplements, and open housing are very much connected with the Conference's current goals. The purpose of the USCM's Community Relations Service is to help establish city commissions to review and make recommendations about racial and minority problems. Civilian review boards have the corollary purpose of investigating complaints of police brutality. In a sense, then, review boards would have been complementary to community relations boards. Similarly, open housing and rent supplements can be seen as extensions of the Conference's commitments to urban renewal, public housing for low-income families, and an amelioration of ghetto conditions. Open housing laws were designated to encourage Negroes to move out of the ghettos. Rent supplements would permit easier relocation of families displaced by urban renewal and open up many more facilities for use as public housing.

Avoidance of open support, however, does not always mean avoidance of the issue. Sometimes it can be a way of facilitating activity, of enabling the USCM to concentrate on the practical aspects of a situation, or of recognizing that another group would be a more effective "prime mover" on a particular issue. The rent supplement program had been supported by the Conference until "someone succeeded in tacking on to it a Workable Program Requirement." This meant that city councils would have to become involved, and it was going to be too difficult to get approval for the federal building codes. This is only one of many examples of what may be the most characteristic attribute of Conference policy—a commitment to pragmatism rather than idealism.

The staff has made it clear that they are not interested in jumping on bandwagons in the name of idealism. Rather, they look at a program and ask, "Will it work?" "What will it do for New York, for Chicago, for Philadelphia, for Detroit?" This approach reflects the attitude of local mayors who are equally concerned with concrete, workable results.

The Conference's role on the issue of federal aid to mass

transit programs was misperceived by those to whom grandstand support visibility is what counts most. A Congressional aide with particular interest in the mass transit bill felt "let down" by the mayors; another explained what the USCM eventually did on the mass transit legislation: "The Conference," he said, "is wary about pushing mass transit because they're worried about crossing swords with the governors, who are interested in the highway programs, not transit. The problem is that there is no mass transit lobby, and there is a strong highway lobby. The Conference must form the nucleus of a transit lobby . . . but they don't seem to be banging any doors down."

The mass transit issue confronted the USCM with several dilemmas. It was an issue to which the USCM wanted to give high priority, but it was also one which divided the large- from the smaller-city mayors. Since mass transit was associated with the Democratic party, it might divide USCM membership along partisan lines as well if highly visible activities were undertaken. Moreover, as the Congressional aide had the insight to foresee, it *could* bring the mayors into head-on collision with the governors. Finally, the stakes of functional interests such as railroads, automotive, and highway groups had to be reckoned with. A successful strategy had to balance all of these considerations, and at the same time avoid giving a "vested interest" stigma to a legislative campaign by large cities for a program of which they would be the primary beneficiaries.

Although public support was sacrificed, the USCM did find a strategy by which to avoid most of the other conflicts discussed. The staff had authority to act because the USCM had passed resolutions supporting mass transit in 1962 and 1963. Thereupon, following consultation with Banking and Currency Committee staff and with Laurence Henderson as "front man," a private non-profit corporation, the Urban Passenger Transit Association (UPTA), was formed to see the legislation through. Hugh Mields, then associate director of the USCM, was its President, Alan Pritchard of NLC its Secretary-Treasurer, Henderson its Executive Vice President. John Gunther, Executive Director of the USCM, was on the Board of Directors. UPTA was funded by the USCM, the railroad groups, and other organizations interested in mass transit. Its members, in addition to NLC and USCM, were the Pennsylvania Railroad, transit equipment manufacturing companies, transit unions, and the Railroad Progress Institute. According to both Mields and John Barriere (then chief of staff of the housing sub-committee of the House Banking and Currency Committee), the USCM "carried this operation," which succeeded in mobilizing support for mass transit, and in delivering forty indispensible Republican votes in Congress. Collision with state-oriented interests was avoided, consensus among the functional interests was created, and, most important, the legislation passed in 1964.

The multiple combinations of ways the USCM can use the political leverage of its mayors becomes evident. The mass transit bill called for pressure on Republican Congressmen by Republican mayors. The Corporation formed (UPTA) enabled the USCM to dilute the partisan implications of the bill by combining with the functional interests (railroads, unions, etc.) in constituencies shared by mayors and Congressmen that would give them both, regardless of party, good justification for supporting the legislation. The USCM could push its Republican mayors to push their Republican Congressmen, and political pressure could be applied by a highly motivated convinced railroad and union group which stood ready to assist.

It is not always true that the optimum communications channel to a Congressman or Senator is through a mayor of the same state and party. Interparty conflicts and differences of ideological wings, competition among elected officials from the same state for higher office, will determine the Congressman's best contact channel. The USCM keeps track of all these relationships and acts out of the totality of its data. Its resources for using strategic people go well beyond those with Conference affiliation.

Failure of a Merger: A strategy of Separatism by a Political Elite

The large-city mayors consider themselves a political elite. That their personalities and self-images affect organizational behavior becomes clear from the history of the frequent proposals to merge the Conference with the NLC.

The USCM and the NLC are the "core" interest group actors

in the urban policy subsystem because of their commitment to "general urban policy," in contrast with the more functionally limited interests of the NHC and NAHRO. Since the mid-1950's, the purposes, functions, and policies of the two organizations have become increasingly similar.

It might seem, then, that a merger would be mutually advantageous, especially as it would demonstrate the solidarity of the urban interest to the federal government. The Conference, however, has always balked at every proposal to that effect. In 1967, for example, when both organizations appointed committees to hold joint discussions on cooperative relations, the attitude of the Conference was that "the USCM is not persuaded that those purposes are somehow served now by dissolving itself as a consistent, continuing force over those thirty-four years for a better urban life. Competition between organizations whose aims touch at points can be healthy . . . and a joint voice on these points need not be confusing." [4] In contrast, it was the NLC which emphasized that "one unified National Municipal Policy should be established by the cities of the United States and a statement of major municipal goals created to focus the power of municipalities on the solution of critical problems they have in common . . . To have more than one organization serving as spokesman for the nation's cities on national urban policy matters tends to fragment a total, unified effort and could at times be divisive." [5]

Both Gunther and Healy were in favor of a merger. But the mayors themselves, although suggesting greater use of interlocking directorships by electing mayors to both Executive Committees simultaneously, were determined to keep the two organizations separate. According to Gunther, their reasons were that they wanted to maintain their elite status and the "large city" image their name conveyed. "The mayors of big cities," Gunther elaborated, "won't go to a meeting of so many thousands of people. They're 'clubbish.' Nor will they permit policy to be made by both mayors and state league directors and they would object to a dilution of their voting power. It's bad enough that New York City has only one vote at the present Conference meetings."

The rejection of unification maintained the multi-centered shape of the interest group branch of the urban policy subsystem. The strategy of separatism continued the division of labor with the USCM specializing as "elite" group representing large cities, and the NLC retaining the subsystem's role of a "democratic" group representing smaller cities and providing broad-based, mass membership support. The compromise between elitism and pragmatism, however, was the merger of their staffs as a common secretariat.

"Don't Embarrass the President": *A Strategy of Support*

Although Conference strategy has alternately focused on the President, Congress, and various administrative agencies, it has had a special relationship with the President that is independent of either individual strategic decisions or Conference goals. This special relationship has been one of the moving forces behind the Conference. It remains to be seen whether this will survive the Nixon Administration's focus on state governments for a larger role in the federal-state-city relationship.

Whether the relationship changes or not, the major urban interest groups will still continue to be of special importance for a President. It is up to the mayors to carry out the Presidential programs in their cities, so in a way, they are responsible for the programs' success. With urban programs now of national concern, a Presidential commitment to the cities is necessary, whether or not his electoral strategy hinges on their support as in past administrations. Certainly a Democratic President in particular has to carry the largest cities, the traditional Democratic strongholds. Likewise, the mayors need the President's support, making the relationship mutual.

The popularization of the Presidency, largely through television appearances, has put the President in a powerful position to give publicity to a local candidate. He can appeal directly to a city for support of a policy—even over the head of a recalcitrant mayor. The decline of the big-city political machine has made the President's position as head of the party and holder of its purse strings a more important source of potential support. Mayors, then, think twice before openly opposing policies advocated by the President. The President, conversely, is the most effective leader the Conference could hope for in support of any given program.

Staff members of the Banking and Currency Committees are aware of the oscillations in the USCM relationship with the President. When Democrats are in power, the Conference works with the Administration. "Bills then come down here as Administration bills, with the deals the Conference has been able to make already worked into them. The Conference works much more closely with Congress and its Committee staffs when the Republicans are in the White House." The Banking and Currency committee has had perhaps the widest experience of all who are involved in urban legislation. Ironically, the Democrats in Congress feel left out when their own party is in power and "come into their own" only when a Republican is in the White House.

In order to oppose an Administration program successfully, the Conference has to have the support of the League. Although the Conference can seek the support of Senators from highly urbanized states, the League has better contacts in the House, many of whose members are conservative and come from small towns. Thus, on an Administration measure, the Conference has difficulty in putting together the necessary opposition single-handedly. Supporting the President on urban proposals can sometimes elicit the same effects as opposition, because the President may make concessions to the Conference in return for its backing. Moreover, it saves the mayors from the possibility that the President will go directly to the people, by launching a campaign on their constituencies to push for support. As one Congressional staff member who has worked with the Conference through several different Administrations put it, "When the Conference opposes the Administration, it can't get anywhere. When it goes along to support it, it is very useful."

The Conference has other potential difficulties. When a mayor is uncertain of his constituency's reaction to a Presidential policy, his safest decision is to go along. Otherwise, he risks the loss of Presidential support or, less directly, the support of his Senator or Congressman who, in turn, does support the Administration. The political relationship between mayors and the President thus restrains the Conference from taking general anti-Administration stands and from open opposition to a particular measure, except in rare instances. One example will illustrate the dilemmas that can

arise. In 1966, President Johnson sought the Conference's support
for his Vietnam policies. Some mayors had become skeptical of
American policy, especially as the war was diverting money away
from the cities.

Twice a year, the USCM's Executive Committee meets to appraise the "State of the Union," and to determine the Conference's priorities. The President usually requests support for his
objectives, one of which was support for his conduct in Vietnam.
Early in 1966, the Conference staff prepared a "Draft Statement
on National Policy" which was critical of the war and incorporated several of the demands for more money that the President
had specifically asked the Conference not to push for. The statement also questioned the President's defense policies by asking
"Are we—as a nation—allocating our national resources on a
sound and reasonable scale of priorities?"[6] Answering in the
negative, the statement went on to say that greater priority should
be given to domestic urban programs, and that the President
should restore cuts in the local community action agency funds.
Perhaps the most interesting part of this draft was the section
commenting on the Demonstration Cities Act of 1966:

> The Demonstration Cities Act of 1966 will be a hollow
> mockery of any rebirth of our cities without adequate funds
> and an expanded scale of operations and planning. We question
> the approval of $575 million for planning for space explora-
> tion beyond the moon at a time when there are blatant, known
> needs to meet human suffering on the planet we already oc-
> cupy. This seems to us a distortion of national priorities that
> cannot any longer be tolerated. At the very least, this money
> should be re-allocated to urban development without delay.

The Executive Committee decided the Conference should not
present such a strong statement, so a second draft was prepared.
This merely stated that "there is immediate need to expand the
planning phase of the program (Demonstration Cities) to permit
any eligible city to participate. Sufficient funds for this purpose
should be provided this year."

The final statement, endorsed in June 1966, said that ". . .
WHEREAS, the Conference repeatedly has pledged its support

to the President of the United States for any measures necessary to repel aggression . . . we salute the valor of our fighting men in Vietnam . . ." The Conference gave the support requested (albeit for the men, not the war policy) and much diluted its own demands, simply asserting that pressing domestic needs should not be overlooked.[7] Except for a few clearly anti-Johnson mayors, most felt their political fortunes were too closely intertwined with the President's to flatly deny his request.

The same kind of fate befell an attempt by the liberal mayors to oppose the ABM in 1969. The ABM resolution did not come from the Executive Committee; it was introduced without prior announcement by the mayor of Chicago. The resolution was headed off because the White House learned of the plan in advance and quietly alerted a number of mayors to fight any resolutions embarrassing the Administration.[8] The *New York Times* reported:

> Jerome P. Cavanagh of Detroit came to the annual meeting of the United States Conference of Mayors yesterday with a strong resolution that would have put the organization on record as opposed to the Safeguard antiballistic missile system now being debated in Washington, with the funds saved to be diverted directly to the cities. . . .
> Richard J. Daley of Chicago submitted instead with Mayor Cavanagh's support, a more generally worded resolution designed to attract less opposition. But the Resolutions Committee adopted an even milder substitute that simply included the military among several budgets that the mayors believe could be reduced.[9]

The finale of the "Anti-ABM Resolution" (or Anti-Nixon, as it was interpreted) did not mention the ABM. Instead, buried in a general resolution was a statement that the USCM considered it "Imperative that the national government re-examine the federal budget . . . to transfer funds from programs that can be deferred to programs which fill the essential needs of people for education, housing, employment, health care, and a decent environment." [10]

The resolution was ultimately amended to include a commendation of the Administration's "efforts to achieve peace." The

President was not directly challenged, and since criticism of expenditures was extended to so many programs, no one could take offense. Moreover, at the final business meeting, the resolution was further amended to give the President the support he wanted by resolving that the USCM would "stand with the President in presenting a united country in the negotiations toward peace in Paris."

The President had the satisfaction of seeing the resolution diluted, but other federal officials who opposed the ABM ignored this literal dilution and heralded the intended spirit. In addressing the Convention, these officials "thanked' the mayors for proposing that the nation's resources be redirected from defense to the cities. Congressman Thomas Ashley (D., Ohio), chairman of the House Subcommittee on Urban Problems, remarked, ". . . in my view the imperatives that confront our cities today *require the multi-billion dollar shift of Federal funds from* defense and space programs to urban needs, as called for in one of the more controversial resolutions that you have adopted." [11] Similarly, Secretary Romney said he "appreciated the resolution asking for tighter control over the defense budget." [12] The dilution of wording notwithstanding, the political messages were understood.

Yet the unpleasant job of raising a direct challenge to the President was left for other groups. Therefore, although the USCM's original purpose had been to challenge the federal government, it abandoned this strategy and, in the opinion of some, abdicated its role at a time when such a challenge was most needed for the "rebirth of American cities." The alternate strategy may best be summed up by Mayor Daley, whose motto is reported to be: "Don't embarrass the President!" It was in pursuit of this that Daley substituted a less beligerent anti-ABM resolution. On the other hand, Congress "reads between the lines," and the resolution mentioning military programs was interpreted as support for those Senators who were building a coalition to defeat the ABM and to put a stop to the spiraling military budget. It was not really necessary for the USCM to speak with maximum force on defense spending because sibling groups in the urban policy system were raising the same issue at the same time. It is interesting though perhaps incidental to note that within six months of the time that these groups began to focus their criticism directly at defense spending, the Secretary of Defense announced a substantial budget cut.

The ABM issue is indicative of mayoral and general governmental strategy in one other respect—the politicalization of issues. As in all parts of the political system, "signals" are sent from one faction to another. The alignment of the mayors is important, of course, for the outcome of the substance of legislation. It is equally vital, however, as a signal indicating along what lines an issue will be divided: Democratic-Republican; Liberal-Conservative; North-South, and so on. The line-up will be a major factor in subsequent strategy; but it will have much broader implications as well, reaching those political observers throughout the nation who take their cues from it. The political alignment, then, will determine the public position of officials and candidates far down the line, signaling the possible consequences of their association with personalities and issues.

Convincing the Feds: Strategies of Persuasion

The political sensitivity of the members of the United States Conference of Mayors led indirectly to the formation of two new organizations, Urban America and the Urban Coalition.

Several mayors, along with some members of the Conference and NLC staffs, felt that a new "urban coalition" was needed to deal with controversial subjects. Such a group could spearhead opposition to Administration proposals without being accused of the "vested interest" stigma attached to the Conference and the League.

Early in 1966, John Feild of the USCM felt that President Johnson had lost the consensus which elected him. There was growing opposition to the Vietnam war, and his domestic alliances were crumbling. Feild projected that the new Congress would be more conservative and less likely to act favorably on appropriations for city programs. Moreover, Johnson had decided not to raise taxes to counteract inflation, a decision which hurt the cities by reducing the amount of money spent on programs for the poor. A series of meetings with urban group leaders and with Stephen Currier of the Taconic Foundation eventually led to the creation of Urban America.

The new organization, formed from a merger of the American Planning and Civic Association and the Action Council for Better Cities, combines business, labor, civil rights groups, city planners, housing groups, private individuals and mayors. It is a coalition group which brings the private sector into the urban subsystem, and is expected to come up with new programs, analyze old ones, and become a focal point for dealing with civil rights problems in cities. However, it does no lobbying and does not pass policy resolutions. It distributes a national economic report each September—before the President's budget message—with recommendations of national economic policy and evaluations of the effects of existing economic policy on cities.[13]

It was hoped that the new coalition, free of the "big-city" stigma, would reach rural and small-city Congressmen. In addition, it was to conduct a massive campaign to educate the public on urban problems, an area not covered by either the NLC or the USCM. Its most important roles are its policy and research functions and its States Action Center, which assists governors on urban problems. Its Urban Policy Center reports on matters of public policy relating to cities, with emphasis on future organization patterns, problems of urban government, and the relationship between government and business regarding urban matters. These reports are more controversial and prescriptive than those of the USCM. In the past two years it has published reports on the needs of the youth movement in the urban ghettos (a somewhat touchy subject for mayors), on the crisis conditions of cities, and a provocative discussion of "unbudgeted billions that go through the tax system's back door.[14] It also published, together with the Urban Coalition, an assessment of the nation's response to the crisis described by the National Advisory Commission on Civil Disorder.

Urban America is an organization through which the Conference can speak indirectly when such strategy seems appropriate. *The New City*, published July 1969, is about new towns, a concept which generated much controversy in the Conference. It was prepared by Urban America and co-sponsored by the USCM and the National Committee on Urban Growth Policy. The effect was to lessen the controversy the book would have provoked from an organization with a specific constituency. The Urban Coalition came into being to fill the gap in the urban policy subsystem created by the specialized focus or political limitations of the other participants. Both Urban America and the USCM helped to form the Coalition. New groups, in other words, did not arise as rivals in the urban policy subsystem, but were deliberately created by existing participants. In its 1968 annual report, Urban America proudly announced that the Urban Coalition had come into being at a meeting in Urban America's board room ". . . The Conference of Mayors and the National League of Cities joined the effort to shape such a coalition. . . ."

The Urban Coalition's primary role is to provide material and services in urban crisis situations. During the 1967 riots in the nation's capital, the Washington, D. C., Urban Coalition formed an emergency council.

> Within an hour of its creation, the Emergency Committee had made contact with all the public and volunteer groups involved in the collection and distribution of food and clothing and had drawn a master plan for a flow of goods to inner-city stores not burned out, as well as to the established centers.[15]

The Urban Coalition also has a policy function and, perhaps more important, a coalition lobbying function. Although Urban America brings together similar business, labor, civil rights, church, and political leaders, it does so more for public relations and educational purposes; Urban Coalition brings them together in a lobbying capacity. Several mayors as well as some NLC and USCM staffers expressed the opinion that Urban Coalition could be a more effective lobby than either the USCM or the NLC because of its broad functional base. However, one member of the Urban Coalition's Executive Committee told this author that the organization was having great difficulties with internal dissention, and tended to have no more influence than did its individual functionally organized members.

William Slayton, Executive Vice President of Urban America, has noted that his organization, unlike the others, does not

. . . have a specific constituency—namely mayors and the cities
—as they do. The Urban Coalition, which we (Urban America) were quite instrumental in creating, differs from Urban
America in that its effort is in bringing together the spokesmen
of major segments of American society to see if those segments cannot speak with one voice on the urban conditions
and the programs necessary to improve the urban condition.
Their concern is with more immediate approaches to the
urban crisis; our concern is with somewhat longer-term
solutions.[16]

Urban America and the Urban Coalition were formed by the
urban subsystem in response to pressures which existing groups
could not cope with. The system lacked the appropriate machinery
to deal with sharply defined, ideologically compacted and emo-
tionally inflamed problems such as those growing out of the Vietnam war, "white backlash," and cutbacks in federal urban spending. The League was too conservative. The USCM, having to
mute controversy and tread softly on crucial civil rights issues,
was not equipped to carry on large-scale public education programs and, as representative of a political rather than a functional
constituency, had to deal with short rather than long-term issues.
New groups were designed to counteract the effects of these limiting characteristics.

Strategies of Persuasion: Tactics, Targets, and Types
General Tactics

Within the limits imposed upon it by factors already indicated,
the Conference can exert a surprising tactical versatility: different
methods of communicating with federal officials, the planned distribution of research findings and copies of Conference resolutions
to carefully chosen targets, an avalanche of testimony at Congressional hearings, a wide range of methods for mobilizing grass
roots pressures upon strategic Congressmen. The staff is in un-
ending contact, by telephone, letter, or personal visits, with
Congressmen, Congressional committee staffs, administrative
agencies, and members of the President's staff. Federal officials are

invited to speak at the Conference's annual meetings. A yearly award is given for "distinguished public service." Letters and resolutions are made public when an official is cited for "good work." It drafts bills and offers its suggestions on legislation and program implementation. It holds annual dinners for Congressmen and their staffs. In its *U.S. Municipal News* and *Federal-City News*, it publishes information on municipal developments as well as news and editorials of Conference activity. It regularly prints *City Problems*, which reports on the speeches, workshops, resolutions, and discussions at the annual meetings.

The Conference also has sponsored new organizations, such as the United States Conference of City Health Officers, National Institute of Municipal Law Officers, National Institute of Government Purchasing, and National Institute of Municipal Clerks. In addition, it is associated with the International Union of Local Authorities and the Inter-American Municipal Organization. It has a network of support-giving affiliates which, along with other urban interest groups, form targets for coalition-building activities by the Conference. One of the USCM's most important strategies is to provide federal officials with feedback on federal programs in urban areas and to present suggestions for changes on the basis of first-hand experience.

There are certain strategies that are shunned by the Conference. It avoids using the general communications media and public relations campaigns. It does not endorse candidates, publish Congressmen's voting records, or contribute money to election campaigns. It avoids these tactics in order to escape political entanglements which could immobilize it.

There is another strategy, however, apparently not utilized to full advantage by the USCM which would avoid such negative implications. This is the practice of working through large city Congressional delegations. Mayor Daley of Chicago utilizes this most skillfully. The dean of Chicago's Congressional delegation is Dan Rostenkowski, a ranking member of the Ways and Means Committee and chairman of the Democratic Caucus. Daley retains Hugh Mields, whose connections throughout the urban network are well known, as a special consultant on federal urban programs. Mields works directly with Rostenkowski and with David Stahl, who handles Chicago's federal-urban programs at the local level.

Under Daley's guidance, these three work together to determine
program priorities, to keep the city's delegation informed and
active in lobbying fellow Congressmen at expedient pressure
points, and to calculate where and when pressure from Daley himself would be most effective. During the course of interviews, this
author has repeatedly been told of the powerful lobbying effects
and almost awesome tentacles of the Chicago Congressional
delegation.

It is true, of course, that the cohesion and power of Daley's
delegation stems partly from Daley's tight party control, partly
from its size, and partly from the strategic location of its members.
New York City's Congressional delegation, for example, has a
different relationship with Mayor Lindsay. It reflects the New
York situation of four-party politics with serious fragmentation
within the two major parties. But perhaps a situation in which a
Congressional delegation is so splintered or where some of its
members are prospective political rivals of their own mayor is
suitable for greater staff direction from the NLC and the USCM.
Even a politically neutral staff could then try to organize the
Congressional delegates themselves or tap some of its mayoral
members to do so.

Public Official Capacity of Members as
a Political Resource

The different strategies the Conference uses must be seen in
the context of the political muscle it is able to exercise.

> . . . power of any kind cannot be reached by a political interest
> group, or its leaders, without access to one or more key points
> of decision in the government. Access, therefore, becomes the
> facilitating intermediate objective of political interest groups.
> . . . Perhaps the most basic factor affecting access is the position
> of the group or its spokesman in the social structure.[17]

The USCM takes advantage of its members' access to the federal government and presents itself as the "voice of the mayors."
Each mayor also has his own particular contacts, thereby increas-

ing the number of points of access for the organization as a whole. "If we have a mayor going to see the President on his own, we (Conference staff) tell him, 'When you see the President, ask him to do this!' This is especially effective when the mayor is someone like Mayor Barr, who is also a Democratic National Committeeman."

Other members of the subsystem perceive the Conference as a liaison to local government. An assistant to Vice President Humphrey noted: "We consider the Conference a short cut to the mayors, not as an interest group. Talking about our relations with the Conference is like talking about the relations between one level of government and another." Similarly, a Congressional staff member said, "The Conference is considered the arm of local government and, as such, is treated as 'government' rather than a voluntary organization."

The League, the Conference's closest ally, also acknowledges the superior access gained by the Conference's membership. "If it is known that 'the mayors want this,' that makes something important even though it might have been the League which was really pushing it," a spokesman said. The Conference itself accentuates its elite qualities in its statement of self-definition: "It is not a political club, a mass organization of office holders, a privately-endowed civic association, or a special interest lobby." [18]

The Conference staff, too, gains easier access:

The staff goes to lunch with the Democrats in the House and Senate and a mayor who has come to testify—like Daley, for example. Then, when the staff goes back to a Congressman later, he'll remember that this man was with Mayor Daley, and he'll be anxious to be accommodating. They (Congressmen) do not think of us as just another trade association.

Another Conference staff member said that one way to measure an organization's access is by the willingness of agency heads and Congressmen to accept phone calls from the organization. "If I worked for a church or trade group, they'd switch me to an assistant. Because I represent mayors, they'll talk to me and maybe, at the same time, tell my mayors to get on the stick about this or that."

One of the essential differences between a group of government officials, such as the USCM, and other voluntary groups is that the former has a kind of *ipso facto* legitimacy—a natural relation to the "social good." Their participation in the governmental process is expected rather than suspected. The nature of Conference membership is a political resource by giving the organization a high degree of access to federal officials; it also gives it influence, once access is gained, by surrounding its claims with an aspect of legitimacy.

The Conference represents mayors, and through them, the urban population. Its claim to legitimacy is validated by the fact that the mayors are elected by those they represent. "When the Conference speaks, it speaks as grass roots spokesmen for elected officials who are most directly representative of the overwhelming majority of the nation's citizens." [19] Similarly, a Conference lobbyist noted, "We try to take advantage of the 'public interest' aspect of our group. We make people feel that we are government, and, as such, we must 'do right.' "

Such representative claims of the Conference are taken into account by the federal government as well. President Truman, for example, said that he "viewed the Conference as a group of elected executives responsible to large populations." [20] President Eisenhower pointed out in a message to the Conference's annual meeting, that "your people are the elected officials who are closest to our people . . ." [21]

USCM influence is pervasive also because federal officials realize the mayors are spokesmen for a population to which they, too, are ultimately answerable.

> The very designation 'official' is a formal recognition . . . that a designated individual . . . has the right and the power to make and enforce authoritative decisions . . . The right is usually granted only for a specified period of time; therefore, all officials are more or less vulnerable. This vulnerability is the main key to understanding their behavior as decision-makers . . . Elected officials want to be re-elected; this usually means they must please their constituents and satisfy those persons who might support or oppose them in election campaigns. [22]

The mayor of a large city in a Congressman's district can influence his city during the Congressman's election campaign. A mayor is also a potential threat to a Congressman in that he may run for the Congressman's seat in a future election. The leverage inherent in this relationship adds to the Conference's reservoir of political resources.

The nature of the USCM's membership creates three other, more indirect effects. First, it permits the group to lobby while still maintaining its tax exemption. Most interest groups that have tax-exempt status, such as Urban America and NAHRO, are limited by the Internal Revenue Code in the amount they can spend on influencing legislation.[23] The Conference, however, is financed out of public funds, which gives it the status of an individual city.[24]

Second, mayors have a common frame of reference with other elected public officials. This is a great asset. According to a Conference lobbyist, ". . . the fact that the mayors are politicians provides a very meaningful relationship when the Conference is trying to communicate with other politicians. They (federal politicians) wouldn't agree with an appointed official; elected politicians raise more meaningful issues with each other." Evidence of this may be seen at Congressional hearings, where "only mayors, rather than Conference staff, testify before Congress, because mayors speak the same legislative language as their fellow elected officials." [25]

Third, the cities which the mayors represent have political leverage through their purchasing power. In 1937, Executive Director Paul Betters, initiated the practice of comparing prices of materials purchased by various municipalities. The Conference would then file complaints with the Federal Trade Commission when it could show proof of collusion in bidding for city business. In fact, said Betters, "We had been the chief client of the FTC during that year." [26] The Conference has also sought legislation which would permit local governments to purchase materials at prices paid by the federal government by including such a provision in its supplies contracts. Since the government buys enormous quantities and usually can get lower prices, such an arrangement would be of great advantage to the cities.

An elected public official membership, then, is a valuable political resource with respect to access, legitimacy, political influence, permission to lobby, rapport with national politicians, and influence over business derived from the economic power of cities. These resources give the "political push" to the organization's strategies.

The Conference and Political Parties

Any Conference strategy directed at political parties must necessarily include both major parties to ensure impartiality. According to Gunther, the Conference "says the same things at both conventions," and sends representatives to both Democratic and Republican platform committees to stress their views. In 1960 the Democratic Platform came out with an urban plank largely through the efforts of the people sent to lobby for it—Hugh Mields and Ed Logue. In 1959, Mields of the USCM worked closely with Logue (then in New Haven) on the Democratic Task Force on Urban problems. Mields also had a close relationship with James Sundquist, Secretary to the Democratic Committee in 1960. The Committee itself was chaired by Chester Bowles, previously Governor of Connecticut and Ambassador to India. Logue had worked for Bowles in both places. Thus, according to a participant, "Between Logue's connection with the chairman (of the Platform Committee) and Mields' relationship with Sundquist (its Secretary), we managed to get an urban plank in the 1960 Platform."

Yet the Conference, without violating its non-partisan policies, does become involved in national election campaigns, helping to organize the mayors for campaign participation. In 1960, for example, it helped organize "Mayors for Kennedy" as well as "Mayors for Nixon." It will even write speeches on urban issues for candidates; and, in addition, furnish the candidates with information on the personality and particular interests of a given mayor.

The Conference staff also indicated, however, that the organization must be careful not to permit a party to use USCM meetings to launch its candidate. Just before the annual meeting in

1958, for example, individual mayors were telephoned and invited to a reception for Senator John F. Kennedy given by Mayor Hynes of Boston. When Conference staff members asked Hynes where he got the money for the reception, he replied, "I have a friend named Joe (Kennedy)." Clearly, this kind of activity, even though non-official, puts the Conference in an embarrassing situation with its Republican mayors.

Presentation of Research Results and Information

> Most lobbyists consider research results to be integral components of their presentations. . . . Research has become honorific in modern American society . . .[27]

The Conference frequently uses research results to support its positions. This data is usually in the form of surveys and statistical tabulations compiled from questionnaires sent to member cities. The NLC and NAHRO usually join the USCM in compiling the material and in presenting it to Congress and the Administration. Since the information is gathered independently by so many different sources, and since it indicates the needs and opinions of individual cities rather than of the Conference *per se*, it is regarded as a legitimate representation of the urban position. Many federal officials lack the channels to get this information from cities themselves, so that the research activities of the Conference provide them with a useful service.

One typical survey will serve to illustrate the strategic use of this research resource. In 1966, the Conference did a study on urban renewal jointly with NAHRO and the League and presented the findings to the Urban Renewal Administration and to Congress. The survey concluded that

> . . . 363 cities could effectively utilize over $5.4 billion in federal grants to plan and execute urban renewal projects during the current three years, or more than twice the $2.2 billion authorized by the Congress for fiscal years 1967–68–69 for all cities in the United States. This puts the average annual rate

of demand for the 363 cities at $1.8 billion. The largest Congressional authorization for one year thus far has been $750 million for fiscal 1969.[28]

These results, of course, were intended to convince the federal government to budget more urban renewal money.* The breakdown of information was useful to indicate which cities were using urban renewal money, to what extent, and what applications were pending. Congressional aides agreed that Conference reports are useful to Congressmen, especially to those from rural areas who need a frame of reference for viewing city problems. Congressmen from urban areas also find valuable information in the reports, such as data on the costs of water pollution programs in individual cities. It is significant that this Urban Renewal Survey was reproduced in full by Congress and included in the official hearings on the 1966 housing legislation.[29]

The Conference is sometimes asked to provide research for use by Congress. The research topic, in such cases, is determined by the Congressman or Congressional committee requesting it. Conference strategy thus includes lending its communications and research facilities to those members of the subsystem whose policies it supports, and who support Conference objectives.

Research provided federal officials is not always formal. Frequently they write to the Conference to ask what the cities are doing to implement a given policy or program. Relevant information from data supplied by the cities is then compiled and presented.

Direct Personal Communication

It is characteristic of the Conference's strategy that it has little public visibility and as a rule deals directly with the federal official involved on a given issue. These dealings may take place via face-to-face meetings, phone calls, or letters, and they are used both to press the Conference's own programs and to present complaints about existing federal policies, rules or regulations.

* See Appendix VI.

The Conference's Executive Committee usually meets with the President each January to present ideas for urban programs for the coming year. When the Conference has complaints about programs, it tries to talk with administrative agencies on a staff level first.

> If there's something we don't like, we deal first with the technician who has written it. If that doesn't work, we go to the assistant secretary of the department. If he says that 'the decision was made from higher up,' we go to the department head. If he won't change things, we tell him that we won't 'go along,' and we try to get someone from the Bureau of the Budget, or a Presidential assistant on our side . . . Sometimes we can get a confrontation of the Presidential assistant, the Cabinet head, and ourselves. This may not change policy, but it can change the way the policy is administered.

An interesting example of the Conference's relations with federal leaders occurred in 1969, when Vice President Spiro Agnew addressed the annual convention. Agnew's prepared speech, copies of which were distributed in advance, dealt with extending the income tax surcharge. He wanted the mayors to support the measure then pending in Congress. The mayors, however, were preoccupied with another matter—that federal money for crime control granted by the Safe Streets Act was not getting to the cities. As always, the Conference had wanted a direct federal-city program, but this time had lost the battle, and the Safe Streets money went through the states before being allocated to cities. Neither the Conference staff nor the individual mayors had been able to impress upon the federal government the fact that the cities were just not getting the money, and that something was wrong. In response to the widespread agitation of the mayors on this issue, Agnew met with a group of them before his luncheon speech. The mayors evidently made their point, for Agnew disregarded his prepared speech and spoke extemporaneously, assuring the mayors that he would trace the roots of the problem.

Conversely, there are times when the frequency and extent of personal contact between the Conference and federal officials permits the Conference to play a useful public relations role for the federal government. Vice President Humphrey's telephone call to Gunther, in April 1967, is one such instance. A mayor had been making vigorous complaints to his Senator that the "federal people" were putting too much pressure on him. The Senator relayed the complaints to the Vice President. Humphrey contacted both the Cabinet officer involved and Gunther to learn more about the situation in that city and to work out a solution. His call to Gunther was to ask him to reach the mayor and smooth things over, while avoiding unfavorable publicity. Gunther knew just what to do.

Testimony in Congress

The Conference does a great deal of testifying before Congressional committees to put the mayors' position "on the record." This is a common interest group strategy. The Conference, however, handles Congressional testimony in a distinctive way to take advantage of its unique membership. As noted, the staff does not testify; only mayors appear before Congressional committees, and they testify in a double capacity—as elected public officials of a particular city and as representatives of the Conference. The approach is multi-barrelled because more than one mayor testifies in this dual capacity at the same hearing.

In choosing its representatives, the Conference takes into consideration the make-up of the Congressional committee and the relations between committee members and individual mayors. Mayors are briefed before testifying, and often material to be presented is checked out with Congressional committee staff members. Prior to the June 1966 hearings on the federal role in urban affairs before Senator Ribicoff's Subcommittee on Executive Reorganization, "We briefed every mayor very carefully the night before they were to testify. Jerry Sonosky (a member of the staff of Ribicoff's subcommittee) was there too, and we went over all the materials."

Grass Roots Campaigns and Closed Campaigns

Conference staffers, Congressional aides, committee staff members, and other interest groups interviewed all agreed that the single most important political resource of the Conference was its ability to influence Congress through Congressmen's mayors. The Conference can therefore mobilize massive campaigns for a piece of legislation because it has a ready-made campaign leader in the district of each strategic Congressman. Depending on the importance of the legislation, the Conference may write, telephone or wire the appropriate mayors, requesting them to contact their Congressman and Senators. The Conference also asks mayors to induce city councils, local administrative agencies, interest groups, trade unions, individual citizens, businesses, and churches in their cities to pass resolutions or write letters. The Conference therefore has the resources with which to get the individual city governments themselves involved in a campaign.

The Conference can also utilize its membership to determine which group or individuals in the Congressman's constituency has the most influence on him. It can wage a grass-roots campaign without spending organizational funds; its individual members can carry the burden by virtue of their office. These efforts may take the form of a closed campaign which builds a wide base of support from below and carefully selects its participants in order not to alert the opposition. This participant-minimizing strategy was used with considerable ingenuity in the campaign to persuade the federal government to withhold city income taxes of federal employees, undertaken in January and February, 1967.[30]

For years, the Conference had been urging Congress to authorize such legislation. Not all cities have local income taxes, but for those that do, it costs a great deal of money to collect them. Employee failure to allow for city taxes results in delinquent payments. Moreover, since the city provides the federal government with the service of withholding *its* taxes, the feeling was that there should be reciprocity.

Gunther wanted to get this legislation before the 90th Congress. He felt that if it could be done without public hearings, it would arouse less opposition and pass without much fanfare. He met with Wilbur Mills, Chairman of the House Ways and Means Committee, and then arranged for Mills to meet with a small group of mayors whose cities stood to gain the most from the bill. Mills said, "Well, if there won't be a lot of fuss made about it, then I'll try to get it through. Have all those in favor of the legislation let me know quietly. But I want all support to be in by February 17th."

Since most of the background for the legislation was already on record from past hearings, Mills agreed not to hold further hearings. The Treasury Department also favored such legislation, but the Conference alone bore the burden of generating support for it. Mills had insisted on evidence from the constituencies of those on his committee that the legislation was desired. Gunther first called Healy of the League to arrange a joint letter of support to be sent directly to Mills. The purpose was to show the solidarity of the "city lobbies." Then he wrote to the mayors of cities with municipal taxes, telling them that Mills

> agreed that he would be willing to report a bill out of his committee without further hearings if sufficient evidence of support were forthcoming from the cities affected by February 17th. . . . Therefore, it is urgent that you as mayors write to Chairman Mills advising him of your support. In addition, you should urge interested federal employee unions also to go on record.[31]

Gunther made a point of writing only to those mayors who were known to endorse the legislation. He knew that "cities like Camden, New Jersey, for example, would probably oppose the legislation. It won't permit a city income tax and would be angry to have federal employers withholding taxes."

The mayors reacted quickly. By February 17th, Mills had received letters of support from all the mayors on Gunther's list. Some had persuaded their city councils to pass supporting resolutions, which were also forwarded. The mayors urged local unions of federal employees to write to Mills. Walter Backrach, Mayor of Cincinnati, got letters from the local chapters of the National Association of Letter Carriers, the National Association of Post Office Mail Handlers, the National Federation of Post Office Motor Vehicle Employees, and the National Association of Special Delivery Messengers, and submitted them along with his own letter of support.[32] On February 17th, all written statements received by the Ways and Means Committee were published as a single committee document. The campaign had been quiet, efficient, satisfactory, and deliberately "closed," involving only a few members of the urban policy subsystem, the Ways and Means Committee, carefully selected individual mayors, and unions of federal employees. According to Gunther, the strategy was made possible only because the Conference membership was able to provide the highly controlled, quiet political push requested.

Conclusion

When a political issue needs the prestige and attention that endorsement from a united group of large-city mayors can give it, the USCM's failure to take an official position on controversial issues and its reluctance to antagonize the President dilute its effectiveness. Similarly, when the Conference is hamstrung by internal dissention it cannot create a bandwagon effect, even though its members have the political resources to do so.

The USCM has not been immobilized by lack of a clear mandate from its members. As has been shown in the case of local government control of Community Action Programs and in the case of mass transit, quiet work behind the scenes still goes on and is effective, despite the absence of noisy challenge. Moreover, as had been shown in the tax withholding case, low-key tactics and access to the more important strategic decision points 'may be an even more appropriate mode of action.

Once the Conference unequivocally supports an issue, its contributions to the urban subsystem are particularly great. It has greater flexibility and a wider range of strategies than most other groups.

Perhaps the most interesting strategy of the USCM is its disposition to form other urban groups to fill functions for which it considers itself less capable or less appropriate. This constitutes a self-conscious expansion of the urban policy subsystem undertaken by its members to "cover the field" and compensate for their own limitations. Although such a multi-centered group structure might produce some confusion in Congress or in the Administration as to "who is saying what for whom," a many-sided group system may be the most desirable arrangement for representing urban interests. It may be less susceptible to being isolated, contained, or co-opted by governmental participants, and it may have greater policy-generating capabilities and political impact than a single major group. The division of labor, functions, and multiple representation which exists in a subsystem with an elite large-city lobby (USCM), a broader-based smaller-city lobby (NLC), specialized groups (NHC and NAHRO), a long-range research and planning coalition (Urban America), and a shorter-range policy-lobby coalition (Urban Coalition) may prove to be absolutely necessary for an interest that is so diffuse. In addition, since it appears that these groups have been working more and more closely together rather than developing rival claims, the policy-making capacity of the urban subsystem seems to be increasing. Since Urban America and the Urban Coalition are quite new, however, it is too soon to tell how broad a spectrum of urban interests will be included in the system that grew up around housing and urban renewal. The attempt by the urban groups to reconcile ideological factionalism both within and among groups before letting conflicting demands filter into the formal political machinery seems to be a reasonable way of preventing the kind of confusion and conflict that would make action by the federal government impossible.

The strategy of creating another organization at the point where existing groups run into some kind of impasse could, of course, reach a point of diminishing returns. Consensus cannot be obtained by creating more and more organizations; the diversity may become too great for an alliance.

Successful representation of urban interests in the future depends also on the leadership capacities of HUD and the extent to which it can unify its clientele groups.

As will be seen by the case of the campaign for Model Cities appropriations, the Conference has considerable skill and capacity for mobilizing support, and now has an important and cooperative relationship with HUD. It has acted as a lobbying front for the arm of the government that is officially charged with responsibility for urban programs. The Conference, in fact, has had considerable impact on the programs administered by HUD, namely the housing and urban development programs to which the USCM has been historically committed. It seems appropriate, therefore, to focus on what these commitments are, and how they have affected public policy.

CHAPTER VII

Major Commitment:
Housing and Urban Development

DURING the ten years 1960-1970, there were a number of substantive areas to which the generalist urban lobby groups directed their main attention: Direct federal-city aid for housing and urban development, mass transit, air and water pollution control, several poverty and civil rights programs, and public health and welfare (including hospital construction) measures. Another high-priority issue has been and is the taxfree status of municipal bonds.[1]

Although it is difficult to pinpoint the exact contributions of the participants in the total process, it is clear that NLC and USCM have both made important policy contributions in all these areas. The origins of legislation have become increasingly difficult to trace; these groups act sometimes alone and sometimes in concert with others. Contributions are sometimes on the level of "high policy," other times on the level of small alterations. One can, however, get a more accurate sense of the effects of lobbying on federal urban policy by making an attempt to circumscribe the inputs of a particular group. An effort has been made to do this with the USCM by a process of comparing interview data, drafts of legislation, minutes of meetings, and unpublished records. In any such evaluation, however, one must bear in mind that the impact of a lobbying group derives from a combination of abilities and processes—originating an idea, becoming its major sponsor in Congress, changing its administrative aspects in the federal bureaucracy, or building coalitions to exert additional influence. Adjustments of existing legislation are considered policy-additive (or policy-making) despite the expectations of "comprehensive policy changes."

Several elements account for the degree of USCM success: the amount of public clamor that the members make about the issue involved, the amount of effort the Conference staff makes, the nature and number of allies the organization can rally, the length of time that the issue has been identified as a high priority urban issue and the legislative precedents it has, and the Congressional committee through which the legislation must pass.*

According to a chief strategist for the mass transit legislation of 1964,

> If that bill had had to go through the Commerce Committee, as an early version was slated to, instead of being pushed through the Banking and Currency Committee as an "urban development measure," we would never have gotten what we did.[2]

Perhaps the USCM's single most significant contribution to mass transit was that of steering the legislation to an urban-oriented committee. On the poverty program, one of the Conference's legislative strategists indicated that

> During the first years, we didn't get anything we wanted. The House Education and Labor Committee was run by Adam Clayton Powell, who stuck with the Administration.

---

* One can appraise USCM effectiveness on certain issues as follows:

> mass transit—medium to high
> air and water pollution control—medium to high
> poverty programs and civil rights—medium
> public health and welfare—low

These ratings were obtained by having both past and present staff members of the Conference rate each activity area in terms of their own opinion of the organization's goal attainment. The list of activity areas, on which the staff had indicated H (high), M (medium), or L (Low) was then checked against the opinions of some of the interviewees from Congress, from the Executive, and from other interest groups.

We had no experience with this committee, no inside help. But by the time the program was running, we knew we had to make friends there, and later we helped get the Green Amendment through.[3]

Apart from housing and urban renewal, most urban programs are relatively new, and, as far as the federal bureaucracy is concerned, in a state of flux. Mass transit, for example, has been moved from HUD to the newly created Department of Transportation. The Office of Economic Opportunity has been re-organized, personnel has changed, and some of its programs transferred to HEW. Air and water pollution control go through the Public Works Committees, whose jurisdiction over the programs has been a matter of contention among agencies within HEW. Neither of these programs had been directed toward large urban centers until the 1960's, when "Hugh Mields, the ubiquitous lobbyist for the United States Conference of Mayors, took up the clean air cause."[4]

The Conference has been most successful and its impact most directly traceable in the area of housing and urban development. Further, this is the oldest subject matter of federal-urban concern and action; it is the issue area in which the urban interest groups have had their greatest experience and effect. It comprises the problems that are perhaps most relevant to the urban crisis, and to which the USCM has given highest priority. Finally, since housing and urban development is a reasonably limited area, identifying relationships and long-range consequences becomes more manageable, as well as more interesting. The relations among the "middle level bureaucrats" of the Housing and Home Finance Agency (now HUD), the Banking and Currency Committees, and the core urban interest groups have had a persistent pattern of relations. Housing and urban development is thus the "core" issue area of current federal urban-oriented policy.

Macro-Policy: Public Housing, Urban Renewal, Low-Moderate-Income Housing

The housing and urban development policy of the federal government, now under the aegis of HUD, is made up of a variety of programs. Each has its own type of financing, some by direct grants, others funded out of government trust funds that bypass the annual appropriations process.

Different sections of the federal housing program also vary greatly in the constituencies they are designed to serve—mortgage bankers, savings and loan associations, construction trades, labor unions, real estate groups, farm groups, civil rights organizations, veterans, big-city groups, small-city interests, and so on. The number and variety of programs and interests served may be seen by the "panoramic view" of HUD's federal housing policy offered by the Senate description of 1967.*

Within this vast array there have been some "breakthroughs" or "macro-policy" programs—those which are truly innovative —while others are more appropriately termed "incremental variations." [5]

Public housing was initiated in the National Housing Act of 1937. Urban renewal was incorporated into Title I of the Housing Act of 1949. Low and moderate-income housing was written into the Housing Act of 1961 and in the home ownership provisions of the Housing and Urban Development Act of 1968. It is to these that the USCM had made its optimum contribution. By contrast, the Conference has not evidenced much interest in the FHA mortgage insurance programs or the mortgage credit operations of the FNMA (Fanny May).

The concepts of federally assisted public housing, urban renewal, and low- and moderate-income housing were shaped and advocated by the Conference, NAHRO, and the NHC. All of them labored together as one "working committee" which conceptualized, drafted, and circulated comprehensive program goals long before they appeared in the form of proposed legislation.

* See Appendix V.

Congressmen and Senators came to be interested in these measures (with a little "guidance" from the groups), after which they used the consultative and drafting services and the support of the "housing alliance" to manage the bills through the complex legislative process. In their initial stages, then, these were not Administration or Congressional programs; the thrust came from the prevailing coalition of urban interest groups.[6]

The important role played by the Conference-NLC-NAHRO alliance in bringing about the basic public housing legislation in the 1930's has already been discussed. Title I (urban renewal) of the Act of 1949 was another of the groups' major accomplishments, especially for USCM. Executive Director Paul Betters called it "the most important federal action ever taken with respect to municipal government in the United States. . .The act establishes national housing objectives and the policies to be followed in attaining them." [7] It is still referred to as guideline policy in subsequent legislation and by the core urban groups.[8]

To maintain a constant watch over the program, the Conference immediately formed a Technical Special Committee on Slum Clearance to study and review the rules and regulations which the Housing Administration would promulgate on the slum program prior to the actual adoption. "We want to be absolutely sure that the rules and regulations to be adopted and under which the cities will have to operate are practicable and workable." [9]

Relations between the Conference and the Urban Renewal Administration were very close, especially since the URA was amenable to USCM suggestions. The Conference noted that it was "gratified that Nathaniel Keith was appointed Administrator since we had recommended to the President that this be done." [10]

A decade or so later, these same groups (NLC, USCM, NHC, NAHRO) and their newer allies were calling for a similar, updated, federal commitment for the urban crisis of the 1960's. The basic public housing and slum clearance programs were enacted in 1949, but it was not until 1961 that those with incomes too high to qualify for low-rent housing, but too low to secure adequate housing privately, were provided for in federal housing policy.

The influence exerted by the USCM on the housing legislation of 1961 can be documented by comparing the Conference's 1961 Legislative recommendations on Housing and Urban Renewal, prepared by Hugh Mields, with the digest of principal provisions of the Housing Act of 1961.[11] According to John Gunther, Conference staff met with Lawrence O'Brien of the White House staff once a week to plot how the legislation should be handled in the House and the Senate.

Alterations in the various housing programs, as well as the continuing effort to keep them operational and funded, have come from the same sources. The Conference, the NLC, NAHRO, and the NHC are still working to keep these programs in shape. In 1963, for example, the USCM Community Development Committee was chaired by William Rafsky of NAHRO, and the key agenda item was to draft "A Program for Low Income Housing" assembled by NAHRO. The resulting suggestions for community development legislation were incorporated into Senator Joseph Clark's bill (S. 2031) dealing with urban renewal and low-rent housing. In a speech on the Senate floor on August 8, 1963, Clark acknowledged that

> The bill deals with the many needs the mayors of our cities and redevelopment officials across the country have found in attempting to save our urban communities from decay and strangulation. It has the full support from the U.S. Conference of Mayors, the National Association of Housing and Redevelopment Officials, and the National Housing Conference. Many of its provisions embrace recommendations from these organizations, as well as the American Municipal Association, NLC and the Advisory Commission on Intergovernmental Relations.

All the four interest groups consider public housing, urban renewal, and low- and moderate-income housing their special domain. What then distinguishes the USCM from the others?

Micro-Policy: Special Directions of the USCM
Within the Areas of Public Housing, Urban
Renewal Low-Moderate Income Housing

John Barriere, chief of staff of the House subcommittee on housing from 1949 to 1963, credits the USCM with the important "vote getting" function in Congress at a time when there was no White House staff to perform this task. The other urban groups didn't have the same kind of political clout. "The NHC, which was really the public housing lobby, just couldn't bring in the votes. The USCM could—and did."

In addition to its reputation as a major vote-getter, the Conference is identified as that group which prefers commercial renewal over residential renewal, clearance projects over rehabilitation projects, and grants over loans in all federally assisted projects.[12]

These preferences show a concern with financial and political problems of large cities and may be considered a direct reflection of the biases of the member mayors. The USCM is credited for having raised the percentage of federal money that can be used for commercial, as opposed to residential, renewal from 30 to 35 per cent in the 1964 legislation. This interest is based politically on the attempt by mayors to ally with central business districts in the late 1950's, and based financially on the fact that renewing commercial property (which offers greater tax yields), is one way to expand the local revenue base.

A high official of the Conference wrote to the President of the United States that the cities needed an

> *Increase in grant funds available for nonresidential urban renewal projects:* Many cities are finding that the areas they are clearing are no longer suitable for residential re-use but can be used to strengthen the industrial base of the community or to restore and revive the central business district.[31]

The trend toward gradually but continually pushing the percentage of funds for non-residential renewal higher and higher is evident in each succeeding housing bill. Thus, in 1954, although the amendments to the Housing Act of 1949 allocated more funds for public housing, the emphasis was modified by permitting "ten percent of grants-to-aid for areas not primarily residential or to be redeveloped as residential." [14] The Housing Act of 1961 again placed more emphasis on non-residential development, extending the allowable percentage to 30 percent. In 1964, as mentioned, it became 35 percent.

The Conference has not, however, strictly confined itself to commercial renewal, and in fact, would be politically unable to do so without alienating some important urban renewal allies. Another concept associated primarily with the USCM is that it would "rather clear than rehabilitate." Rehabilitation in some cities is either more expensive than clearance, or cannot substantially improve the old tenement type structures that are the greatest source of urban blight. Rehabilitation restricts the use of the property involved more than clearance does. The Conference, however, has not ignored rehabilitation measures, and was, in fact, one of the forces in changing the rehabilitation project in 1965 from a loan to a grant program.

With most programs initiated as matching funds, the USCM has been especially interested in raising the percentage of federal contribution and in pressing for outright funding by subsidy as opposed to FHA mortgage guarantees or interest subsidies. It also advocates block grants rather than categorical grants. Block grants are subject to greater management controls by local government and are therefore naturally considered more desirable by mayors. Most such federal fundings are "formula" grants, distributed only for the specific purpose of the law governing the grant. The Conference has pressed for a "limited block grant" approach which would at least, as recommended in a USCM paper in 1963, "cover a community's entire renewal operation and thus eliminate the necessities for the administration of local programs in a project-by-project basis and to support any changes in law required to achieve this objective." Typical of the Conference's general attitude as to how federal programs should be funded is the expression of its views in that same paper, that Congress should "increase the present two-thirds federal/ one-third local grant ratio to 80 percent federal/ 20 percent local, and increase the present 75 precent federal/ 25 percent local ratio to 90 percent federal/ 10 percent local."

Although the mayors did not get their increased federal contribution in 1961, they were able to partially compensate for this by liberalizing the interpretation of what constituted "local contributions." According to informed commentators, "an increasing laxness in the interpretation of public capital improvements as local contributions," has meant that "the local cash contribution has shrunk to approximately 14 percent." [15]

This is a typical example of the way the USCM is able to play off Congress against the Administration. What it could not get from Congress, it could, in effect, get from a liberal interpretation by the Administration.

All Conference demands on Congress with respect to public housing legislation derive their common thrust from the necessity to make the housing program of practical utility to the large cities. The Conference repeatedly tries to raise the legal limit on the cost per unit of public housing. The 1969 maximum of $20,000.00 per unit created severe difficulties for the large cities. As explained by Gunther:

> The present cost limits on public housing are so low that we large cities can't *build*, even where we have jurisdiction. And since we have to include land costs, we can't build public housing at all in the core cities, except for the elderly. We've been working constantly to raise the limit—at least in effect, by trying to get land costs *out* of the figuring costs. The problem really is, why should public housing be allowed even $20,000 per unit when the guy in the $21,000 house pays most of the taxes to *build* public housing.

According to Jason Nathan, in 1969 the Housing and Development Administrator of New York City and Chairman of the Conference's Community Development Committee, the same type of statutory cost limits effect low- and moderate-income housing. Remedying this situation remains a major item on the Conference agenda.

Lowering the family income minimum which keeps so many

of the poor out of public housing is another Conference priority. By the same token, it favors placing an income ceiling on people who live in public housing. In short, the USCM believes public housing should not be diverted from its original purpose to provide housing for the poor. It should not house "mixed socio-economic levels," as urged by several other groups and, in 1969, by Assistant Secretary Cox of HUD. Consistent with its position, the Conference has always resisted the Public Housing Administration guideline that public housing should be self-supporting and self-liquidating.

The directions in which the Conference has tried to push federal housing policy stem from its strong commitment to urban renewal, and from what might be called its proprietary interest in maintaining and developing this program above all others. It makes a continuing effort to press Congress for longer-term authorization for urban renewal, for liberalization of local non-cash credits, and for several years advance funding.[16] "Advance funding is our critical concept. The Administration knocked it out of the appropriations for fiscal 1971, and it has no strong HUD support either. Therefore the Conference must take a very strong position." [17]

A HUD official indicated that the recent liberalization of the amount and type of non-cash credits a city may apply to its share of federal matching grants was "entirely a result of the Conference's efforts."

Another aspect of the Conference's firm commitment to an urban renewal program is its staunch opposition to the Workable Program Requirement that was written into the Housing Act of 1954 at the suggestion of Eisenhower's Housing Task Force.[18] The Workable Program Requirement meant that federal aid for future urban renewal and low-rent public housing would be withheld unless a city first adopted an overall plan of action for community development—a plan which must go through local legislative bodies. This threatened control by the mayor, or involved the possibility of delays which might deny him visible credit. The essential elements of a Workable Program are

1. Plans for adopting or improving building and housing codes.

2. Provision of a master plan covering major land uses, thoroughfares, and other community facilities and capital improvements.

3. Neighborhood analyses that are not limited to defects in housing conditions.

4. Examination of needed improvements in its administrative organization.

5. Consideration of whether its financing plans are adequate for its community improvement program.

6. Preparation of plans for housing for families displaced by all forms of government activity.

7. Enlistment of citizen participation in urban renewal and similar programs.[19]

The original Workable Program certification is for one year, renewable after a "progress review" submitted by a community which shows effective action toward its goals as established by the program provisions.

The Workable Program Requirement has been considered by some as the remedy for early abuses, omissions, or patchwork implementation on the urban renewal program. Others consider it a method by which a mayor or a local housing authority can be forced to clear plans through the city council and thus subject a city's entire urban renewal program to veto, revision, or delay. Still others consider the program as the surburban method of keeping federally-assisted housing away, by simply not passing a Workable Program. Finally, some regard it as "the chief technical instrument used in guaranteeing that urban renewal will lead to the elimination and prevention of slums." [20]

To the Conference,

... those who were for it were those who were against urban renewal, and wanted to use it as a way to hamstring urban renewal. It's bad enough for the mayor to have to go to the city council to get public housing sites approved. To have to get a Workable Program for years ahead through also is impossibly difficult.

The Conference therefore devoted considerable effort to making this requirement less onerous for local government. The group has been unsuccessful in preventing the Workable Program Requirement from being a pre-requisite for federal aid in urban renewal, but it has persuaded HUD to approve two-year certification. According to the Under Secretary for Housing and Renewal Assistance, this would not have been done were it not for USCM pressure. The Conference has also urged Congress to make it possible for the Workable Program of any community to be approved without necessarily securing the approval of the local governing body.

One final feature which distinguishes the Conference in the field of urban development is that it seems to prefer more money for renewal than for demonstration programs. The Conference is traditionally suspicious that experimental programs may somehow result in a cut in urban renewal appropriations, and has consequently sought reassurance on this as a pre-condition for support of a new program.

The USCM let it be known, for example, that it would not endorse President Johnson's Model Cities Program without assurances that the program would not use urban renewal money. In fact, the Conference insisted that the President ask Congress for extra renewal money that year in return for its support of Model Cities.

A description of the Conference's trade-offs on the Model Cities Program illustrates the nature of the politics of consensus and the skills in conflict-management and coalition-formation. The USCM's central role was in the appropriations process for the Model Cities Bill.

Model Cities Bill

On January 26, 1966, President Johnson transmitted to Congress a message about his "Demonstration Cities" Program calling for a massive, concentrated, and coordinated effort to rebuild or restore entire neighborhoods.[21] The idea was to "demonstrate" what could be done through a full-scale attack on urban blight. Each city was to pay 20 percent and the federal government 80 percent of the costs of planning, developing, and administering the program.

> The area covered by a city demonstration program must be a large segment of the entire city area. An urban renewal project may be much smaller. A demonstration program involved an area which must rehouse a substantial number of the original occupants and must provide for a social, economic and racial mix. An urban renewal project, on the other hand, may result in complete relocation of the original occupants and new occupancy by a totally different social and economic class. An urban renewal project may or may not have the benefit of other federal aids while a city demonstration program would be expected to take advantage of all available aids, both federal and local.[22]

One would expect the USCM to find the program very attractive, but this was not the case. The Conference objected strenuously to a provision calling for the creation of "new communities," or "new towns." The objection came less from the staff than from mayors. The mayors were afraid this might discriminate against older central cities and promote further economic and social disparities between central cities and new growth areas. They wanted assurance that "new towns" would not lead to fringe area commercial development to the detriment of the central city's tax base, or further promote economic and social segregation and outward flight of the middle class taxpayer. Most important, they feared "new towns" would mean proliferation of more units of local governments, the leaders of which would compete with big-city mayors for federal and state funds. In its analysis of the 1966 Urban Development Act, the USCM therefore emphasized that it advocates

> legislation which encourages development of new communities within existing core cities and the transformation into new

cities of existing smaller communities . . . The Conference of Mayors would support new towns legislation on those terms. But it cannot support new towns legislation which has the potential of disparities and developing outlying areas at public expense and at the expense of established communities.[23]

The USCM had still other misgivings about the Model Cities Program. The funds proposed seemed inadequate to meet its goals. The President's proposal contemplated providing planning funds without operating funds—a measure which would raise expectations without providing the administrative capacity to fill them. Finally, as mentioned, the mayors feared the Model Cities Program would interfere with funds for general urban renewal.

According to Conference staff, the mayors wanted a "ghetto" bill to tackle the worst areas—"the 40 major ghettoes in 25 cities." The USCM did not regard new towns as an answer to the ghetto problem. New towns would have no governments, and developing governments for them would complicate the already tangled picture of local government. The attitude of the Conference was thus the result of the commitment of big-city mayors. They had pledged themselves to renewing areas to whose residents they were accountable, to protecting their tax base, to being able to execute as well as plan, and to prevent further fragmentation of authority throughout a metropolitan region.

This configuration of concerns is a good example of representation of "governmental interests" as such. It also illustrates an attempt by chief executives to preserve their capacities for governing and to keep attention focused on the urban crisis in their own jurisdictions. ". . . Even if new towns turned out to be wonderful places, they would still be almost powerless to affect our present urban problems . . . and as sirens of utopia, they might distract from our proper work." [24]

The areas for "our proper work," in the USCM's view, were not even eligible for grants under Johnson's program:

Problem areas can't become eligible for urban renewal unless they have zoning codes, building codes, and the like, that meet federal standards. Areas needing it most don't have these. The Demonstration Cities Program would admit only those already fulfilling the requirements for urban renewal funds—and leave out the worst areas.

In spite of this hearty opposition to the bill, the Conference became one of its staunchest supporters. How did this turn-about occur?

It was partly a result of strong and expertly applied pressure from the President, and of a process of consensus-building and compromise wherein the Conference, the NLC, and the President all got part of what they wanted.

The President's strategy was to play up the Conference's prestige by giving it a leading role in getting the bill passed. He also agreed to add a provision for extra urban renewal money. The President then persuaded the NLC to support the new towns provision, depriving the Conference of the ally it needed to form an effective coalition to oppose the bill. According to the League, its staff also originally took a dim view of the Demonstration Cities idea. Its opinion was based more on the rent supplements provisions than on new towns. The large-city mayors had by this time come to support the idea of having the federal government supplement rents of the poor, as they could then use the money to find housing on the private market. The smaller cities objected, for fear that large numbers of urban poor would rent in the suburbs and interfere with the "balance" of their neighborhoods. But they, too, were all for the promise of more funds. So both groups found something in the Model Cities Bill they wanted along with something they did not want.

By 1965, the League came around to giving the bill its support. The Conference, however, withheld its backing pending further examination. In February 1966, the organizations concluded a joint "preliminary analysis" of the Demonstration Cities bill. Both had several reservations about the amount of funds proposed, about the ambiguity of the program's goals, and about the provisions for administering it. The joint analysis contained no reference to the new towns provision.

Apparently there was considerable tension caused by the Conference's objections to the new towns idea. What was to be a joint statement on the Urban Development Act of 1966 was prepared in April. Included was an expression of the Conference's reservations, and the League refused to endorse it. The statement was then revised and issued as a pronouncement by the Conference only. According to Patrick Healy of NLC, "If the League had joined the Conference in opposing new towns, the provision would not have passed." This estimate must be qualified by the fact that Representative Wright Patman, Chairman of the House Banking and Currency Committee which had jurisdiction over the bill, was a staunch supporter of "new towns" and wanted political credit for its legislation. However, the point is that had NLC and USCM stood firmly together, Patman might have bargained with them on another point, or the two groups would have generated from elsewhere the support needed to effectively oppose new towns.

At the same time, the Administration could not afford to lose the support of the mayors, and through HUD, was itself bearing the brunt of the lobbying burden. Since, according to a drafter of the bill, one reason for the USCM's lukewarm attitude was that "it hadn't been consulted enough by the Administration, steps were taken to counteract the feelings of being 'left out.'" President Johnson and Vice President Humphrey met with the Executive Committee of the Conference. Sidney Spector of HUD, a key member of the Presidential task force pushing the bill, called John Gunther of the USCM, and asked him to head the "strategy meetings" to get the bill through Congress. The meetings were to include the "urban alliance" contacted by HUD. This "alliance" was a constellation of old friends of the housing agency, of the urban poor, and of labor, religious, civil rights, health, and welfare groups. Since HUD had already taken steps to alert all of them to the fact that their interests were at stake the Conference could hardly permit leadership of this "alliance" to fall to another organization. Under Gunther's direction, therefore, the groups, now collectively called the Urban Alliance, began a series of weekly meetings at the Statler Hotel in Washington.

At this point another factor swung the Conference staff over to full support of the Administration's bill. Key members of the subcommittee on housing felt that the bill would fail if brought to a vote on the House floor. Support seemed to be coming only from HUD. The subcommittee did not want to report out a bill for which no one would applaud. "Accordingly, at the direction of the chairman, Mr. Barrett, the subcommittee staff prepared a

revised bill designed to cause as little trouble as possible. It contained no new funds and no meaningful criteria." [25] Under the
threat of Barrett's substitute proposal, the USCM turned its attention to getting the best possible bill with the best possible financing. It felt that although the Administration measure did not
request sufficient funds, the Barrett bill was even worse. Further,
if the Banking and Currency Committee pressured the Administration, the Administration, might reduce the amount it requested
to get the Committee's support.

So mobilized and motivated, the Conference staff prepared
resolutions for its annual June meeting requesting larger sums.
The President again asked the Conference to accept his program
and again, his personal touch and surprise tactics were effective.
A group of mayors and Conference staff members were invited
to the White House to talk to Lady Bird Johnson about urban
beautification. Toward the end of the discussion, the President
unexpectedly walked in—

> When the last mayor finished talking, the President sat Lady
> Bird down, and launched forth on what a tough time 'we're
> going to have in getting appropriations.' He begged the mayors
> not to scare everyone with their talk of billions—they couldn't
> get many votes to increase the funding anyway. He requested
> that they just go along with his estimate and that even then,
> they'd have to really work to get even his amount.

The result was that the Conference Executive Committee with-
drew its resolutions requesting more money; instead, it told the
press that the Conference felt there was an urgent need to pass
the President's budget proposals. But for this gesture, the Conference exacted a promise by the Administration of extra urban
renewal money. It was here that the President compromised. He
sent a Secretary of HUD to the USCM convention.

> Mr. Weaver, Secretary of HUD, flew to Dallas and delivered
> a bell-ringing speech saying the Administration would fight
> to the end for $2.3-billion. Then—in a key but obscure
> passage—he hinted that the Administartion might be willing
> to ask for extra urban renewal money as well.[26]

The result of the meeting was that the Conference gave its full support to the President's Demonstration Cities bill and urged Congress to fund it adequately. Although the groups had shifted some of their objectives, they still maintained some of their pet caveats. The Conference also called on Congress "to make it clear in the legislation that the demonstration cities operation will not act to divert resources from such established under-takings as urban renewal." Moreover, it resolved that:

the Conference opposes demonstration cities legislation which provides for planning funds only. (Such) an approach would only encourage widespread local planning and raise expecta-tions. . .without any assurance that the projects so planned would actually receive the federal grants necessary to carry them out. . .[27]

The President's subsequent call for $600-million extra for urban renewal was a direct result of the Conference's activity, and probably a reward for its support. The Conference received several other concessions for its effort. The name of the program was changed from Demonstration Cities to Model Cities,[28] and according to a Senate aide, section 701 (planning) of the Housing Act of 1954 was amended at the Conference's suggestions. Al-though Congress cut the proposed supplementary urban renewal authorization to $250-million, the Conference had profited nicely. In fact, it was willing to provide the leadership for the legis-lative campaign to get full appropriations for the bill, which became law on November 4, 1966.

This case study of Conference support for the Model Cities Bill is a characteristic one. Where there is Conference opposition to an Administration's urban program, it is likely to be a direct result of the nature of the organization's membership. Conference opposition to "new towns" came from the individual mayors concern with the central city and from their fear of losing poli-tical credit for a new housing program if the program were to take the form of new communities outside a mayor's jurisdiction. The NLC, on the other hand, would be able to absorb the new towns as new members. Both groups were interested in expanding the supply of housing, and both were interested in the lower income housing that rent supplements and the new towns program would have provided. Each group embraced the program best suited to the interests of its members, and rejected the other, so that in the end, both new towns and rent supplements were included. Compromise between the USCM and the League also was effected by adding a clause which stressed "equal regard to the problems of small as well as large cities." [29] The Administration supported both programs as well as the extra urban renewal money because the President, too, needed the support of both groups.

On occasions when the USCM and the NLC can act together, they can play off Congress and the President against each other. They had the option, in the case of Model Cities, of backing either Congressman Barrett's bill or the Administration's. It seems likely that whichever version had their joint endorsement would have gone through. The substance of this major housing legislation was, therefore, more the result of a "primary bargain" struck between the USCM and the NLC (and a "secondary bargain" between these and other concerned interest groups), than between committees within Congress, or between Congress and the Executive branch. Because the support of the USCM and the NLC is, in effect, mandatory for the successful passage of a housing bill as well as for its implementation, Congress usually insists on consensus between them before holding hearings on housing legislation. These groups have more information from which to evaluate urban programs than any other source; consequently, they act as main linkage points between the cities and the federal government and between the President and Congress.

The resulting Housing and Urban Development Act of 1965 is thus the outcome of a mutual concession between two interest groups, mediated by the staff of HUD, by the Senate and Housing Subcommittees, and by Joseph Califano from President Johnson's office. The strategy used by the Conference to fund the Act once it approved the legislation is typical of the way it operates, and illustrates its growing cooperative relationship with HUD. In contrast to the closed campaign strategy used for the withholding of city income tax case, the strategy for getting maximum funding was wide open, directed at maximizing the number of participants.

The USCM's Model Cities campaign is interesting also in that it was undertaken at the request of HUD. Executive agencies cannot legally "lobby" for their own bills. The Department, therefore, communicating through its Congressional liaison, Sidney Spector, called on Gunther to lead the campaign. Together they decided to first enlist the support of the House Independent Offices and Housing Subcommittee, which had jurisdiction over the bill, and then to concentrate on the full Appropriations Committee. Since the Appropriations Committee does not hold open hearings, a public campaign to let the Congressmen hear from the "folks back home" was selected as the strategy suitable to this case. Gunther wrote to the 62 organizations which had been previously contacted by HUD to enlist their aid as an "Urban Alliance" in support of the bill. His task was to persuade the various groups to attend meetings and then to preside over them.

The first meeting of this Urban Alliance was held on February 24, 1967. From then on, it met in Washington every week. It was decided to concentrate on the "middle-of-the-roaders;" the opposition was appraised as too set to be moved, and in fact, might be further alienated by any overt pressure. The Democratic "middle," those who might be persuaded, were identified as Congressmen Pryor (D., Ark.), March (D., Va.), and Shipley (D., Ill.). The Conference provided information on the largest cities in their districts and on the relationship between them and their mayors. HUD was notified that Pryor's district had "good-sized urban renewal programs." In acting on this information, the Secretary of HUD decided to call Pryor himself. According to a member of HUD, "This was Pryor's first call from a Cabinet Secretary. He was impressed and pleased. I think we got his vote."

In order to involve the groups in the Urban Alliance more deeply in the struggle for appropriations and to give them a greater sense of participation, Gunther intentionally raised controversial issues in the meetings. The idea was to create an excuse for inviting the spokesman from HUD to clarify the issues. Clarification and discussion is not lobbying, so that Gunther's tactics enabled HUD to participate legitimately.

All groups were exhorted to submit resolutions calling for

full appropriations, to persuade other groups to do so, and to send out bulletins saying that the Model Cities Bill was doomed if full appropriations were not allocated. The Conference kept lists of all resolutions and all organizations favoring full appropriations. It also kept a list of editorial comments from local newspapers as a guide to cities which required special attention by their mayors. The mayors were asked to personally call Congressmen and to urge constituents to speak to their Congressmen during Easter recess. Mayors were also asked to persuade their cities to authorize the use of Model Cities funds, thereby indicating how great the requests for funds would be. The Conference, therefore, used to the greatest advantage the official position of its members to launch a highly visible campaign for full appropriations.

The Conference As Policy-Maker

The kind of incremental, compromise policy described above supports a widespread opinion that urban lobbies, especially NLC and USCM, fail as effective policy-makers in terms of developing innovative and comprehensive programs addressed to the "real needs of cities," and have instead "nickeled and dimed their way through legislation." [30] Several HUD officials commented that the Conference "was either complaining that a new proposal would not work or asking for more urban renewal money," so HUD turned to civil rights, labor, and church groups to "try to get some dramatic new policy into legislation." Other criticized both the USCM and NLC as "failing to produce policy to meet either the political needs of the President or the substantive needs of the cities," being "interested only in technical amendments to legislation," or as "those mischiefmakers who just jump in with short-sighted, special interests, rather than with the true interests of the urban community."

It seems to be inherent in the clash of urban interests which characterizes decision-making that the opposition is "lacking in policy-making capacity," while the proponents are "catering to real needs." The adjustment of the Model Cities Bill requested by the Conference is therefore considered sensible and far-sighted by some, and as bargaining for special interests by others. The rhetoric of claim and counterclaim is a constant in the dynamics of most multi-centered decision making.

HUD, as a new organization, had to become established as a policy leader, to develop in-house capacity for program evaluation, and to assure itself of a diversity of clientele groups. This led to a tendency to underconsult some of those groups accustomed to greater participation. All HUD officials and Banking and Currency staff members interviewed indicated that "the Conference feels threatened when other components of government go into policy and when the Conference is not consulted."

The USCM's feeling is understandable considering that it performed a number of staff functions for the HHFA before it was raised to Cabinet status. During the Weaver-Wood period, HUD was known to be somewhat cool toward interest groups and disinclined to consult them until it had already decided where it was going. According to Under Secretary Robert Wood, the staff of HUD got tired of all the complaints about "no consultations." In 1967, it called in the home builders, private investors, and public interest groups (including the Conference) and told them, "If you want real participation, give us policy, and we'll take it to the White House staff and Budget Bureau." In Wood's opinion, the private sector and the home builders (NAHB) did come through with real policy proposals—quantifying housing goals, for example, to 26-million units in 10 years—but the public interest groups, including USCM, had not. They had no cohesion and therefore produced only policy additives. Similarly, in 1969, a HUD official said that the Conference power has become a veto power rather than an innovative, policy power, both in its ability to withhold support from the President's program or Congressional bills and from its ability to block program implementation at the local level.

This impression of the USCM's policy-making capacity is also held by others in the urban policy subsystem and by member mayors of the Conference itself. According to a city lobbyist, "The main problem with the Conference is that it has no new legislative ideas; it is too conservative. Its main use for us is building lobbying conditions." Mayors interviewed at the USCM's annual convention in June 1969, thought that the outlook for a greater policy-making role in the future was not good, due to internal dissention.

Another important reason for these low estimates stems from the USCM's attitude toward controversial issues, already discussed. The tendency of the Conference to become more conservative is not surprising. As a well-established group, it has gained the access to the federal government it desired, and its relationships have become semi-institutionalized. It is slow to enter into new relationships for fear of disturbing older, dependable ones. The Conference's attitude toward Daniel P. Moynihan, head of President Nixon's Council on Urban Affairs, would seem to substantiate this. Moynihan was one of the few important urban policy officials who was not at the USCM's 1969 convention. The reasons given for his absence were: "He has no power," "his presence might make the Vice President or Secretary of HUD feel that we were going around them" "the presence of the Vice President, according to protocol, pre-empts the presence of Moynihan," and "it would not be politically wise for Moynihan to be here from his point of view."

Whatever the reasons, it appears strange that the one person given responsibility by the President for "general urban policy," for overseeing its application and coordination (as opposed to the program responsibility of HUD or the liaison-with-cities role of Vice President Agnew) was ignored. The tendency of groups to use their traditional relationships is not unusual, however. In this instance, the "non-invitation" may have reflected the Conference's assessment of Moynihan's real power position. The point is that they could have provided him with the political support which would then enhance his importance and give him a "clientele group." Moreover, Moynihan had the potential for becoming the vehicle through which urban groups, whose major relationship is with the Banking and Currency committees and with HUD, could establish more intensive relations with other Congressional committees and Executive agencies. This would be a way of expanding the kinds of issues the urban subsystem could deal with—through the auspices of a central figure like Moynihan rather than through further proliferation of interest groups.

In analyzing the behavior of interest groups in general, political scientists have discovered that almost all the older, established ones display this tendency toward conservatism. They can be considered liberal when the criterion for "liberal" is a positive attitude toward government activity, yet be conservative when the criterion is a positive attitude toward change.

> This is very largely due to the fact that, lacking any independent standards, all politicians depend upon those organized interests that already have access to government and to the media of communication. According to the second criterion of liberalism–conservatism (attitude towards change), all established interest groups are conservative.[31]

Conservatism on the part of the Conference, then, is not only a function of its internal dynamics and of political expediency, but also of interest group maturation.

Organizations which consider themselves major sources of policy input are likely to de-emphasize the policy-making role of others. It would be well, therefore, to look further before judging the capacity of the USCM as policy-maker.

As noted earlier, the Conference is most interested in public housing, urban renewal, and low- and moderate-income housing. Of these, it has put its highest priority on urban renewal. Consequently it is appropriate to choose the programs of the Renewal Assistance Administration (RAA) to determine the Conference's policy influence. The RAA carries out the following programs which, for analytical purposes, can be considered policy outcomes:

1. Urban renewal—loans and grants
2. General neighborhood renewal plans—grants
3. Community Renewal Programs—grants
4. Code enforcement projects—grants
5. Demolition projects—grants
6. Rehabilitation loans
7. Rehabilitation grants
8. Neighborhood facilities—grants
9. Open Space Land—(urban parks and central city)—grants
10. Urban beautification (central city)—grants [32]

To ascertain the influence of the USCM on these various programs, persons interviewed* were asked to "star" those programs on which they felt the USCM had acted in a policy-originating capacity, and to check those in which it had acted in a "major supporter" capacity. Transcripts of hearings and USCM working committee documents were checked for convergence with these opinions. It must be pointed out that when policy-initiating capacity is attributed to the Conference, it does not necessarily mean that the Conference has acted alone. Policy ideas usually emerge from the working subgroup of the Community Development Committee which, as noted earlier, can, through either formal or informal representation, include: NAHRO, NHC, NLC, the Urban Coalition, Congressional committee staff members, Senatorial and Congressional aides, and HUD officials. The suggestions coming from this working group thus already have wide support, and their exact origins are difficult to trace. The important point is that the Conference does have this kind of policy-generating machinery, and that other members of the subsystem recognize it as such.

Of the ten programs listed above, the Conference is given major policy responsibilty for seven, a kind of "joint authorship" for one more, and a major supporting role in two. Its effect on the urban renewal program has already been shown. Federal aid to cities for general neighborhood renewal plans and community renewal programs are considered part of the same program since they simply widen the scope of urban renewal. As a knowledgeable observer comments, "the Conference is the one that has sold continuity in the urban renewal idea." The USCM is credited for the 1965 programs of financial assistance to cities to enforce housing codes (considered in the 1950's to be a strictly local responsibility and a pre-condition to federal aid for urban renewal), and to demolish unsound structures which the locality has authority to demolish. The rehabilitation grant programs and the grant programs for neighborhood facilities were also attributed to the USCM and to NLC, despite the Conference's pre-

* Individuals from the Banking and Currency Committee, HUD, and urban interest groups.

ference for clearance. The Conference was considered only a "supporter" of the urban beautification program and of the rehabilitation loan program. Federal grants to help communities acquire land in urban areas for use as parks or "open spaces" was labeled a joint project between the USCM and Ardee Ames, in his capacity as legislative assistant to Senator Harrison Williams of New Jersey. But the Conference is credited for the "pilot" open space program of the 1950's. Moreover, the language of the amendment to Title VII of the 1961 Housing Act which outlined the open spaces program was drafted by the general counsel of the HHFA at the request of the USCM.[33]

It seems clear that the Conference has an impact on the policies of the Renewal Assistance Administration in either an initiating or supporting role in all of its programs. The programs, it is true, have been incremental—they may be thought of as adjustments to the basic urban renewal policy. The question is whether incremental programs are the result of the Conference, the urban policy subsystem itself, or of an inherent tendency towards gradualism within the American political system as a whole.

Macro-policy is a much more favored concept in current political rhetoric, and it is here that the Conference has been faulted the most. But it is worth bearing in mind that since recent demand for "urban policy" is so great, past output has been perhaps unduly derogated. It is necessary, therefore, to look even further before assessing the role of the USCM as policy-maker. What have been the major changes in the direction of policy in the 1960's? Has there been a change in the decision-making process that has altered the role of the Conference?

The distinguished urban analyst, Morton Schussheim of the University of Pennsylvania, has examined housing policy output during the Kennedy-Johnson years and determined seven innovative developments that could shape the future.[34] To distinguish macro-policy contributions, it may be useful to compare these trends with the general policy presentation of the Conference:

1) A revised official view of the central city and how to

save it. A belief that the core city can be salvaged by re-placing old real estate by new . . . a notion of the 1950's had been discarded.

Though many mayors and local renewal officials continue to cling to this approach, federal policy is now based on different premises. . . . Model Cities is the broader frame within which urban renewal may continue to be applied, but with less emphasis on clearance and more on rehabilitation of housing for present residents.

As has been shown, the Conference is still committed to the urban renewal approach, although it does not ignore other types of programs, and considers Model Cities an addition to, not the primary vehicle for, the urban renewal program. It seems to pre-fer clearance to rehabilitation.

2) An increasing insistence upon area-wide or metropolitan approaches in dealing with area-wide problems such as trans-portation, sewer and water systems, and land conservation and development.

The USCM has specifically participated in a metropolitan area approach to air and water pollution control.* It is also turning its attention to a metropolitan area approach to housing in an attempt to find a way to disperse federally assisted housing more evenly throughout metropolitan regions. While its activities in representing metropolitan regions have not been conspicuous, this is understandable. Its membership structure (representing cities as such), and its financial structure (each city appropriates funds out of its own treasury for membership), makes it difficult for the organization to put too much emphasis on this broader area.

A sharper focus on metropolitan areas as an approach to city problems might result in stronger relations between state and/or county governments and the federal government, a pos-sibility which poses a threat to the established pattern of federal-

---

* Discussed in another chapter.

city relations. It could reduce city control over programs and place political credit for federal projects elsewhere. In many cases, however, where an area-wide approach is in a mayor's interest, the USCM is becoming increasingly active.

3) Aids to private developers for planned sub-divisions and entire new communities were legislated.

Schussheim is here referring to "new towns," which the Conference opposed. Yet, one might ask, "In whose interests are these new developments?" New policy is not necessarily "objectively good," or unfailingly in the interest of the constituency it is designed to serve. The fact that the USCM has not put emphasis on these new directions does not mean it lacks policy-making capacity. The fact is that the concept of "new towns" is at odds with that of metropolitan area integration so that "general policy trends" which support both are contradictory.

4) Widening of housing options for lower income families.

5) Declaration of national housing targets in quantitative terms.

The Conference firmly supported both 4) and 5). It had a major innovative role in the low-income housing legislation of 1961, and a major supportive role with the NAHB in 5).[35]

6) The law of the land was set against housing discrimination by race.

7) Major steps have been taken to strengthen federal administrative and analytic capability. The establishment of a Department of Housing and Urban Development in 1965 will enable the Federal Government to develop more consistent policies. . .

The Conference took no public position on open housing, but has worked for this goal through its Community Relations Service. It was a major support for the establishment of HUD.

Of the seven new directions charted by Schussheim, only two

have not been in accord with the natural predispositions or open policy tendencies of the Conference. The others have been either accepted, although not always openly emphasized, or actively supported by the Conference; in the case of widening of housing options for lower-income families the Conference acted as a policy initiating force.

Having examined the position of the USCM with respect to innovative, macro-policy as well as on specific incremental programs, the conclusion must be that the record of the USCM is hardly as negative as has been suggested.

Policy By Intervening Elites; Trends in Goverment Decision-Making

A recent trend in governmental decision-making has made traditional urban interest groups' activities less identifiable. This lower profile may account for this discrepancy between opinions and facts about the USCM's policy role. In the 1960's, many of the most visible innovative ideas seem to have come from the White House staff or from Presidential task forces on housing and urban development. The Workable Program, a major innovation in urban renewal policy, came from the Eisenhower task force as far back as 1953; similarly, rent supplements and model cities came from the Johnson task forces of 1964 and 1965, on which the Conference was not represented. The "breakthrough" housing legislation of 1968, with its provisions for home-ownership by low- and moderate-income families is largely an adaptation of the suggestions made by the Kaiser Commission Report (The President's Commission on Urban Housing). The idea of incorporating incentives for metropolitan area cooperation into federal-city aid programs was given its greatest prominence in the recent Douglas Commission Report (The President's Commission on Urban Problems).

This increase of the task force phenomena has led Prof. Robert Wood to maintain that policy is increasingly being made by "intervening elites"—task forces, the White House staff, and policy centers outside the government. This implies that the theory stating public policy emerges from competition among a pluralist array of interest groups is outdated. Have interest groups been eclipsed by new kinds of decision-makers?

Many of those interviewed for this book did express the view that University policy centers, an increasing use of Presidential task forces and advisory committees, and the strengthening of agency administrative and analytic capacities through Planning, Programming, and Budgeting Systems have weakened or pre-empted the interest group's role in policy-making. High level policy seems to be considered the domain of Wood's "intervening elites."

The larger analytic capacity and program evaluation ability of governmental agencies, brought about by PPBS, probably has increased the capacity for and the tendency toward internal policy development. Coupled with the political need for a President to be a policy leader, this has meant that government itself can become more of an innovative force. The supposedly objective ordering of priorities inherent in the PPBS approach leaves less room for conventional interest groups in the in-house process of policy evaluation.

The extent to which use of PPBS has replaced or even significantly lessened the need for the conventional interest group in policy formation may be questioned. The role of PPBS is better understoood as an outcome of the increasing complexity of policy-making. New machinery has been called for to add new dimensions and facilitate choice. PPBS cannot replace the representation of interests—especially if one considers the aim of government to be maximization of public support that goes beyond the maximization of efficiency. Rather, PPBS experts are new participants in policy-making, supplementing but not eclipsing traditional groups. The pattern of relations between these newer elites and interest groups is a part of the urban policy-making subsystem that provides a fascinating glimpse into the process of of modern government.

The PPBS analysts have in effect become a new group with its own constituency—the campus intellectual, the reformer, the technocrat, the mathematician, the professors-in-government, the educated "liberal" and the believers in "comprehensive" programs "objectively" evaluated. In short, PPBS has brought new people into government, with different policy biases and interests. The traditional interest group, while it may not have the same capacity for handling and processing information, and while its method is generally incremental rather than comprehensive, continues to fill a need. This is the need for functional representation, for a source of ideas originating from the constituency to which they would be applied, and to provide the potential for feedback without which any cost-benefit analysis of social programs would be impossible.

Moreover, "policy by intervening elites" (of which PPBS is but one form) does not exclude the participation of interest groups themselves as "intervening elites." The USCM, for example, is usually represented on task forces and White House staff policy committees and maintains direct consultation with them. Sometimes it is the group itself which tries to precipitate the task force. In 1961, one of the Conference's priority items was to persuade the President to call a White House Conference on Urban Problems. Since some kind of participation is, in fact, more usual than not, the Conference was both surprised and resentful at being left out of the 1964 and 1965 task forces. Participation may take the form of infiltration of ideas, overlapping membership or through rotation of staff. Although the Conference was not part of the 1964 task force which came out with the rent supplements idea, for years it had urged an alternative to public housing that would put ghetto families into privately operated structures. This was the operational idea behind rent supplements.

Policy formulation by task forces may be viewed as a way of dramatizing some of the recommendations made by interest groups over a long period of Congressional resistance. The housing recommendations of the Douglas Commission in 1968, for example, contain many of the proposals long encouraged by the USCM. The Conference had advocated a plan to disperse low- and moderate-income housing throughout a metropolitan area—the objective of rent supplements. Moreover, the Douglas Commission's concept of using federal grants as incentives for metropolitan area cooperation, although given prominence by the Commission, had already been expressed in legislation. The USCM, in fact, is given credit for getting grant incentives for metropolitan area cooperation in both the water pollution control legislation of 1963 and in the Clean Air Act.[36] The fact is that there is considerable similarity between task force recommendations and USCM proposals.[37]

Overlaps of the kind that existed between the USCM's pet projects and the 1968 Kaiser Commission recommendations are particularly revealing because the Commission proposed removal of the Workable Program—a program opposed by the Conference from its inception.[38]

In terms of overlapping membership, Mayor Barr was a member of the 1968 task force at the same time he was President of the USCM. There was ongoing consultation between him and President of NAHB, AFL-CIO, and National Urban League, and members of the steering committee of the Urban Coalition and Urban America. At least one study for the Kaiser Commission was done by a consulting firm in which Hugh Mields, always a major figure in the NLC and the USCM, was a principal.[39] Mields himself was retained as a special consultant to the Kaiser task force for seven months. Similar overlap is found in the 1966 Task Force on Environmental Health, which includes both familiar names and familiar policy recommendations.*

John Feild went directly from the President's Committee on Equal Opportunity in Housing to become head of the Community Relations Service of the USCM. David Wallerstein of the USCM was "on loan" to an OEO task force in 1966. According to HUD Assistant Secretary Lawrence Cox, in 1970 the department is working with four task forces—on housing, renewal, codes, and the Workable Program—whose members are representatives from the USCM, the NLC, and NAHRO.

It would therefore be misleading to conclude that the Conference and the "intervening elites," are not interconnected. The USCM deserves to share in the credit for policy output attributed to the newer "task force" actors. The USCM certainly has not abdicted responsibility to them, as is suggested. On the contrary. Task forces consist not so much of new "intervening elites," as of members of the urban policy subsystem brought together as *ad hoc groups*. To quote from a 1961 Conference staff memo:

---

* Task Forces usually use the urban groups and key "urban" individuals as official consultants. See Appendix IV for examples and further overlap.

An anonymous task force to develop recommendations on urban development . . . has already been set up. We have no knowledge as to whether or not the action was formerly sanctioned by the President-elect himself . . . Its members are: Charles Wallman, representative of the Savings and Loan Associations of California and a member of Governor Brown's urban renewal advisory committee; Harry Held of the Bowery Savings Bank; Robert Wood of M.I.T.; John Barriere, Staff Director of the House Subcommittee on Housing and Joe MacMurray, formerly Staff Director of the Senate Subcommittee on Housing and Director of Housing for New York State under the Harriman Administration. Mr. MacMurray is chairman of the group and is considered an active candidate for the job of HHFA Administrator. . .The consensus on the part of most informed observers is that the group's background orientation is private interest.

Suggested Action to be taken:
NLC's President Hummel and U.S. Conference's President Dilworth should be urged on the behalf of their respective organization to seek an early meeting. . .with President-elect Kennedy to make their organization position known to the President-elect.[40]

The mayors subsequently did succeed in presenting their views on urban development. The point is that intervening elites are not, so to speak, "pure." Their membership is frequently drawn from other participants in the subsystem. The usual procedure, regardless of the actual membership of the task force, is to consult with, or to "clear" task force recommendations with appropriate interest groups. Staff members of the Kaiser Commission, for example, worked closely with the Director of the USCM, and "advance reports" were distributed to Gunther on most of the recommendations under consideration before the stage of final decision. This kind of "touching base" with those groups whose knowledge of the specific programs is greatest, is in some ways essential to the success of the task force. As Nathan Glazer points out, task forces, especially the "Presidential transition" task force tend not to select high civil servants who know most about the workings of government and the specific programs. . .Its civil servants are those who have already left government or who alternate between government and the universities, the research institutions, and foundations. Nor does it drain heavily from Congressmen and their assistants. . .But on the other hand, it does not move over into the direction of selecting men with the widest imagination . . . indifferent to the constraints of the political structure . . . moreover . . . the task force does its own work. It is not surrounded by assistants staff and specialists ready to answer questions or do research.[41]

In other words, the task forces need the expertise, research facilities and support of the older, traditional interest groups. Their present vogue may only mean that the decision-making process has taken on a different costume for an old role.

Once task forces have completed their reports, individual interest groups pick up the ball and act as organizations through which task force policy can be kept continuously before the public after the *ad hoc* committee has been dissolved. The USCM acted as a public relations vehicle for the National Advisory Commission on Civil Disorders by distributing a copy of the report to all member cities, and then aiding in the follow-up study, *One Year Later*, done by the Urban Coalition and Urban America. In addition to the "group linkages" to the task forces, the independent membership of task forces on urban affairs shows continuity. These two aspects thus suggest that task forces may be appropriately conceptualized as part of the regularized pattern of interaction in the urban policy subsystem rather than as "intervening elites." For example, Glazer points out that

a third element of continuity in . . . task forces . . . is to be found in the specific individuals who make them up, who seem to come from a common stock out of which a selection is drawn to offer advice for each administration, Republican or Democratic. Thus, the urban task force that met for President Johnson included a number of persons who had served four years before on the urban task force of Candidate and President-elect Kennedy; the urban task force that met recently for President-elect Nixon included a number of persons who had been members of the Johnson task force— and there were some who remembered back eight years to the Kennedy task force. Richard Goodwin, who played a role in the Kennedy task forces, put together the Johnson task forces—and, astonishingly enough, showed up as a member of one of the Nixon task forces.[42]

Presidential task forces, moreover, frequently include people either already part of HUD, or prospective appointees. The 1965 Presidential Task Force on Urban Problems is a good example of most of these overlaps. Its members were Robert Wood and Charles Haar, both of whom became HUD Assistant Secretaries within one year; William Rafsky, President of NAHRO; Walter Reuther (Urban Coalition), Whitney Young (Urban America and National Urban League); Edgar Kaiser (headed 1968 task force), Senator Ribicoff, Chairman of the Executive Reorganization Subcommittee of the Senate Government Operations Committee; Kermit Gordon of the Brookings Institution, and Ben Heiniman. This task force put together the Model Cities idea. Specifically the Model Cities Bill was under the jurisdiction of the Banking and Currency Committees, but Ribicoff's subcommittee held hearings entitled "the crisis in the cities," which brought out the positive aspects of the intended legislation, during the time Model Cities was running into difficulties in the Banking Committee's hearings. Task forces, in short, usually include the people who will be in strategic positions to support their own recommendations.

The suggestion that the federal government, more than any group, has become the more significant instrument of change on the macro-policy level may have some validity; however, once the general policy outlines have been set, the interest group still plays an important policy-adjusting role, and maintains close working relations with the middle-echelon bureaucrat, committee staffs, general counsels, and agency officials. It is at this level that much significant operational policy is made, because it is the middle echelon bureaucrat who controls the "nerves of government." [43]

Conclusion

As a participant in the policy-making process, the Conference set the level of debate for public policy on urban matters from its inception in 1933 until the early 1950's, and widened the federal agenda to include public housing, urban renewal, and low- and moderate-income housing. During this period it was a primary advocate of more money for cities, the major source of appeal for direct federal-city relations, and a generally moving force behind government action. It was a core participant in the basic urban legislation from which most subsequent programs have been derived. The USCM's policy output, therefore, seems to exceed its reputation. In response to a very general question, HUD officials felt the Conference's capacity for policy output to be low. Answers regarding its policy effect on specific programs, however, revealed that the Conference's effect on policy was quite high. The correlation between the Conference's expressed program goals and the actual operating programs of the Renewal Assistance Administration was, in fact, shown to be significant. Perhaps the discrepancy results from a changing concept of the term "policy," altered by the rhetoric of systems analysts and the "national policy" language of task forces, specialists, and coordinators.

Beginning in the late 1960's, urban problems became a highly visible public and national government issue, probably as a result of the widespread urban rioting and civil rights demonstrations. It was also during this period that the ideas of "comprehensive policy and program" envisioned by PPBS began to filter down from military application to potential use in domestic social programs, and the call for a national urban policy became part of the language of modern politics. HUD had been established in 1965, and was in the process of securing a position for itself in the policy-making process, as were Urban America and the Urban Coalition.

During the first stage of research for this book (1966-67), the Conference was given much more credit for a respectable role in the policy process. Interviewees were satisfied to accept the making of "policy" as gradual, incremental, and the outcome of small demands from many sources. During the second stage of intensive interviewing (1969), a mention of the word "policy" invoked such comments as, "We have no national urban or housing policy—we have only disjointed programs." Policy-making was defined in terms of what the respondents thought it should be—"broad," "sweeping," "comprehensive," "overall solutions to real problems." In other words, a distinction was made between macro-policy, which was a goal, and "micro-policy," which was a reality.[44]

The USCM's reputation as a policy-maker was judged on the basis of its capacity for the former, in terms of a dreamed of "national urban policy" in which it has never pretended to engage. This poses difficult problems of analysis. A helpful theoretical framework can be found in the approach of Professor Harold Wolman. Wolman distiguishes four stages in the policy process, each of which is treated as a subsystem of the housing policy system. These are 1) policy formulation, 2) substantive legislation, 3) appropriations, and 4) operations. "Each of these stages is necessary to successfully carry out a positive policy decision—each of them could, in effect, exercise a veto power over taking a particular positive action." [45]

In his analysis of the housing subsystem, Wolman found that as far as "macro-policy" was concerned, the national political and economic environment strikingly constrained the range of possibilities available. High interest rates and the priorities of the Vietnam War defined the nature of the problems for the housing subsystem, and "largely prescribed the manner with which it would be dealt." The Administration, White House task forces, and HUD played the primary role in proposing "major changes such as guaranteed income and employment programs," while Congress and interest groups dominated the substantive legislative stage and were found to be "quite important in more incremental distributive decisions." [46]

Wolman seems to be saying that to the extent that high level policy exists, it is formulated and made visible by the President, task forces, and HUD; but the traditional relationship between government and interest groups still makes substantive policy by exercising a veto and/or an enabling power over the policy formulation stage.

Policy formulation thus *does* include traditional interest groups, but sometimes less direct. Wolman's analysis clarifies the present role of the Conference by interpreting policy in stages, and provides some insight into the discrepancy between interview data and actual substantive impact on programs.

CHAPTER VIII

Urban Lobbying

THE New York Urban Coalition highlights city problems by urging New Yorkers to "Give a Damn." Urban lobbies have demanded the same from the federal government since their emergence in the 1930's. Working as allies they have been successful in bringing the problems of the cities into federal focus. But ironically, it may be that in 1970 some of the national attention is not so much due to efforts by urban lobbies but to the suspicions of many policy analysts that the urban crisis is getting worse. They have voiced these suspicions in the press and in professional journals, noting that metropolitan America is paralyzed by crime, poisoned by impure air and water, and threatened by housing shortages and transportation breakdowns.

These comments could have been written in the 1930's, when the urban interest groups first turned to lobbying for federal urban programs. Have the urban lobbies had no beneficial effect? Have the federal-urban programs themselves been irrelevant, or just insufficient, or worse, have they further aggravated the problems which they were supposed to solve? Or, perhaps neither urban interest groups nor federal programs could keep up with the rate and extent of deterioration of life in the cities. What has changed during the past 40 years?

To begin with, institutions and methods of dealing with urban problems have changed. Urban interests have extensive representation in Washington. Federal urban programs reflect

234

well-structured consent among urban public interest lobbies and newly-formed or newly "urbanized" governmental institutions. Urban inter-governmental lobbying has entrenched the practice of the "third" level of government (cities) pressuring the "first" level (federal) and bypassing the "second" level (state). This makes for complex patterns of decision making; it also provides policy-makers with extensive information and direct feedback. The machinery of an urban policy subsystem, developing for forty years and still in the process, shows at least the outlines of a flexible, fairly open, persistent and self-conscious interaction cycle. It is possible that urban inter-and intra-governmental lobbies are only in the early 1970's developing their full capacities for bringing about meaningful change through federal urban policies, especially since the establishment of executive branch affiliates to lend support is so recent. Still, it is possible to make some predictions by taking note of the attributes of the subsystem at its present stage and of the most important characteristics of its members.

The interest group members of the subsystem have evolved into a structure which is multi-centered rather than monolithic, indicative of the nature of the urban interest—broad, poorly defined, and needing spokesmen for all its facets. To present a united urban viewpoint in spite of internal cleavages has been a primary objective of its participants. The five principal groups in the system have been working together on urban issues since 1937. New organizations have been "creatures," in one way or another, of the original participants, and have joined their efforts to structure consensus. In the area of urban concerns, then, the hard core participants are constantly interacting. The linkages among them are identifiable, and they are concerned with the same policy agenda.

The generalist urban lobbies have represented the urban interest not only by persuading the federal government to incorporate the urban viewpoint in legislation, but also by asserting local government *itself* as an interest. In their efforts to bring urban poverty program agencies under local government control, and in their legal mandate from the Bureau of the Budget to participate in federal administrative regulations, their concerns have been with representing the city as an administrative entity. This stands somewhat apart from their efforts on behalf of urban social and economic problems.

Among the urban lobbies, the USCM brings special advantages to the urban interest network. Some derive from its role as liaison between cities and the federal government, dating from the outset of direct federal involvement in urban areas. This role has continued routinized relations between the Conference's staff and the national Administration. Others are spillover effects from its elected public official membership. Its mayors' command of political leverage by virtue of their overlapping constituencies with those of the President, Senators, and Congressmen; the group's utility to federal officials for program implementation and data supply; and the electoral support and public exposure the mayors can encourage, all induce greater federal responsiveness than might otherwise be forthcoming. Status, prestige and leverage, however, also have their drawbacks. They can at times dilute rather than enhance the organization's impact by making internal cohesion more fragile.

Basically, liabilities for lack of unity are generated from without, rather than from within the USCM. James Madison, in the *Federalist Papers*, saw government as the greatest of all reflections of human nature. In microcosm, the mayors mirror the diversities of a very large electorate, and the USCM thus represents the political complexion of the country at a given point in time. This is important when considering the inter-governmental lobby as an instrument of social change—if it reflects the status quo, can it also change it? Other interest groups have memberships and goals which change but little from year to year. The membership of the USCM, however, is constantly renewed at the polls and each election implies an instruction for new courses of action. This turnover keeps the group responsive to societal demands, in that an electoral victory would indicate a particular mayor is validly representing the needs of his city. The mayors are therefore in a position, at least potentially, to anticipate new trends and implement them through legislation.

If conclusions derived from the study of the USCM can be generalized, a membership of elected public officials, i.e. a "power elite," does make a difference in otherwise standard interest group behavior. Access is easier, influence is greater, legitimacy is assumed, cohesion is more difficult, and activities trigger wider reverberations at all levels of government. Statements on policy and goals are more carefully noted than would perhaps be the case with other groups, because they are signals as well as decisions. The political system is alerted to possible future alignments of parties, people and issues. These signals, as they are interpreted in varying ways by groups, candidates, incumbents, and party officials, can then become the basis for lobbying efforts of others on the mayors.

The activities of the collectivity of mayors in a pressure group are confined by certain limits. The range of urban issues is both wide and diverse, and elicits somewhat differing priorities of concern. For these reasons the existence of other urban clientele groups becomes crucial to urban interest representation.

Of the other urban lobbies, the National League of Cities is the most important. It contributes the "small city" support, balancing the "big city" bias of the USCM. NLC's larger and broader membership brings wider representation, and its reputation as more conservative than the USCM helps to remove a "liberal" stigma from any jointly supported legislation. Since membership in NLC by directors of state leagues of cities gives it more protection from the turbulence of every political maelstrom, it has traditionally had greater capacity for well studied policy positions and long-range planning. In combination, the two groups leave hardly a Senator or Congressman untouched by his constituency.

The Urban Coalition (which in 1970 absorbed Urban America), the National Housing Conference (NHC), and the National Association of Housing and Redevelopment Officials (NAHRO) add their own attributes and expertise of urban interest representation to the subsystem. However, it appears that urban interest groups which have not primarily been lobbies have felt hindered, regardless of their actual participation. The Urban Coalition compensated for this almost immediately by forming a subsidiary group just for lobbying. NAHRO in 1970 is in the process of following suit. The NHC has always been a lobby, concentrating on housing. Although frequently joined by others, it is this "inner circle" which usually coalesces for a multi-group presentation of demand and support for federal urban programs.

They invariably choose multi-group presentation of urban problems because of their conviction that consensus is indispensable for politically meaningful and lasting results. They are willing to undertake the large amount of preparatory work this consensus requires. Agreement on priorities has been reached, divergent ideas made orderly, the ambiguities of the urban interest clarified, and joint lobbying strategies devised before a proposal is presented to government.

Government, in turn, performs some of the roles ascribed to it by group theorists as well as some which are not. As it does not have to adjust competing claims by urban interest groups, it mediates the often heated contest between these urban interests and their opposition. It presides over attempts by the opposing coalitions to expand and parade their support, while also offering proposals of its own. Certainly government is not a passive registrar of pre-struck bargains or a neutral arbitrator, as its role is sometimes described by analysts of the relations between government and interest groups. Programs introduced by in-house governmental units become catalysts for action by the urban lobbies whose response then provokes reaction by government. One must conclude that group theory is still very much alive as a tool for analyzing and understanding decision-making about federal urban policies.

Political systems theory, too, offers a frame of reference which helps overcome analytical difficulties posed by artificial, misleading, or legalistic concepts of institutional boundaries. It is useful for clarifying complex group interaction within the federal urban policy subsystem, especially the informal yet vital relations which are often hard to detect. Its members include "regular" interest groups as well as officials, institutions, or agents of national, state, or local government. The activities and relations among Congressional committees, executive agencies, offices of local government, formal task forces, and the Presidency, are more easily understood if these units are conceived as "governmental groups" in a policy subsystem held together by a wide variety of ties differing in kind and intensity. The USCM fits a "semi-governmental" category, as do other private groups with public official membership. It is the link between the Washington urban policy-making subsystem and the cities' own decision-making subsystems, which makes it a pivotal group in the precariously balanced formation.

The formation holds its shape either through common goals or through frequently coinciding, if not identical, political stakes. To illustrate: to the USCM, direct aid to cities is a major goal. It can be more easily accomplished to the extent that it is or can be made to appear as of benefit to others, e.g. to administrators by promising possibilities for more agencies under their control or more leverage with Congress. Similarly, if a President felt direct federal aid to cities might identify *him* more closely as benefactor, there would be a convergence of political interest.[1]

* * *

The political machinery for processing urban problems has, as shown, changed since the 1930's. The question now is how federal urban programs have reflected the influence of the urban lobbies, and whether the programs have in fact been in the urban interest. How successful the lobbies have been in representing the interests of geographically-organized constituents to a functionally-organized Congress and Administration is difficult to assess. In fact, evaluation of urban lobbying in general is difficult because it varies so greatly in both nature and level of influence. Sometimes, as with Model Cities, the urban lobbies' functions have been to facilitate consent and dramatize support mainly after a program has been devised within government. Other times, as with urban renewal, they initiate an issue, propose a program, organize governmental allies, and pressure their project to fruition. As a third variation, their influence can take the form, as with control of poverty agencies, of simple but firm management of conflict created by issues not subject to earlier attempts at "preventive guidance." As with forms of influence, levels of influence of urban lobbies have also varied greatly. "The most significant feature of group politics is that it is a dynamic process, a constantly changing pattern of relationships involving continual shifts in relative influence."[2] Moreover, the federal urban policy subsystem deliberately minimizes the importance of who initiates ideas, and therefore obscures their origin. Its looseness and fluidity facilitate consent for policy generated from anywhere within the system.

Of more importance, therefore, is the ordering of priorities for action. The most urgent urban problem is, and has long been, the poverty of municipal governments, perpetuated, and to some extent even caused, by a circularity of legal, political, and social restraints over which cities have had very little control. Reasons are familiar and trite. The Constitution gives the power to raise money by taxation to the federal government, which has used this power to tap the richest source of revenue—income. The states also may raise money by taxing income as well as other things, but as a fact of life they are limited in how much they can raise by federal choices of sources and methods. Constitutionally, cities are creatures of states and completely subject to their control. Even home rule provisions and city charters are ultimately revokable or alterable by state governments. Thus, in the first place, cities have no inalienable legal rights to raise any money at all. In reality, they have been granted contingent authority to do so, but this authority is carefully controlled as to source, amount, and method of funds raised.[3] Constraints imposed by state law may be even further tightened by highly complex and seemingly irremedial legal, political, and jurisdictional limitations within cities themselves. Federal and state taxation has preempted, precluded, milked dry the sources, or, for a number of reasons, made it politically impossible for cities themselves to raise money commensurate with their responsibility to provide and administer municipal services.

The guiding rationale for the priorities of the urban lobbies are perhaps best illustrated by a series of intentionally oversimplified observations. City governments must do certain things for their residents which cost money. They perform an increasing number of functions and services on which a city depends for its very operation. Movement of large numbers of people into cities meant these same functions and services had to be provided for many more people. But those who came had greatly varying backgrounds (cultural, national, sectional, racial, occupational, etc.), and, along with the rest of the urban population, came to have increasingly greater expectations. Augmented by other factors this situation brought demands for a greater number of services, for different kinds of functions, and for greater involvement by cities in formerly non-governmental spheres of concern. At the same time that the need for funds grew, the cities' ability to raise them declined. The most significant aspect of this inverse relationship is that the convergence of reasons which caused it also compounds and perpetuates it. The reasons themselves matter less than that the situation exists, and seems, even now, insurmountable.

The cities' reaction was, by hindsight, simple: they had, and by any projection would continue to have, insufficient funds to perform services; the federal government had funds, collected in large part from the urban population which needed these services. Ideally, the cities could ask the federal government for money. However, the federal government does not give money; it "gives programs," and these would channel money into cities. Although these monies would be earmarked, controlled, contingent, and unstable, the cities would accept the program package rather than live with financial disability. Moreover, they could try to compensate for "money with strings" by attempting to influence the kinds of programs authorized. They could simultaneously try to abolish limitations on raising their own revenues. But income taxes, for example, as are levied by some cities, might still not provide enough funds. The same incomes were already the source for federal and state taxes, so how much could the cities hope to collect?

In any critique of federal urban lobbying, and in determining whether supported programs ultimately were in the cities' best interests, one must therefore remember that the lobbies' primary *raison d'etre* was to enable cities to provide services by gaining them access to other sources of funds. The success of their efforts would be measured by any increased expenditures a city could make without having to pay. Federal-urban programs were to be the means, however poor a substitute for money itself. Lobbying efforts to increase and shape these programs were thus derivative from the overriding goal.

Whether the federal urban programs supported by the lobbies have been effective must, in other words, be discussed within the framework of money. Substance was important, to be sure, but the strongest endorsement was simply for programs promising increased revenue to the cities. By the lobbyists' criteria, therefore, the very proliferation of these programs would be proof that they have been in the urban interest. However, an evaluation must also take into account substantive effects, and whether these programs have been beneficial in terms of today's urban crisis.

Within large cities, a major urban problem is the ghettoization of the non-white poor. They are congregated within a core of the central city which cannot house or employ them. To some extent this has been the result of past national housing policy, and to the degree that the USCM and its "urban interest" allies shaped that policy, they must bear some responsibility for lack of foresight. Because the large cities have always been a settlement for immigrants—whether from Europe, from the Far East, or from the deep South—there has always been a need for low cost housing, even if only as "half-way houses" on the journey of upward mobility. To accommodate this need, the mayors, through the USCM, lobbied for public housing—and got it in the National Housing Act of 1937.

As HUD Secretary Romney pointed out, early FHA mortgages, which were part of the National Housing Act of 1937, required racial homogeneity of the neighborhoods where a mortgage was insured. When the inner city began to deteriorate, middle-class whites used these mortgages to move to the suburbs. This deprived the city of revenues from middle class sources. And since the racial homogeneity requirement excluded Negroes from these "FHA suburbs," this shifting of residence reconfirmed patterns of racial segregation. The public housing section of the Act also had controversial effects, eventually causing the program to become politically unpopular. In some places public housing itself excluded the Negro and the very poorest elements. The Public Housing Administration encouraged development of segregated public housing projects according to a "racial equity" formula, meaning that units were to be separately constructed for whites and non-whites according to need. The formula, however, did not change with the changes resulting from immigration of blacks to the cities. In other places, public housing had different results. Some of the ramifications of the program for the current plight of cities are suggested by Scott Greer:

> . . . Few public-housing units were ever built in the middle-class areas of the outer city because citizens protested vigor-

ously at the threat of public housing nearby . . . Objections combined distaste for Negroes with distaste for the poor as neighbors. As a result of citizen pressure on local politicians, public housing was more and more often sited in the center of the Negro districts and, to avoid a net decrease in available housing, the structures grew taller.

. . . This was the exact opposite of the housing preferred by Americans who had a choice—the single family unit . . .

. . . Thus, typical public housing became slab towers filled with poor Negroes in the middle of Negro working-class neighborhoods; it developed its own critics among the liberals who once fought for it. They spoke of it as "immuring the slums" . . .[4]

Early low-rent housing programs, particular favorites of the urban lobbies, further complicated the urban housing problem by leaving out the very poor. Public housing projects had to be operated out of rental revenues, and, ostensibly to reduce possibilities of bankruptcy, local Housing Administrators could determine and select "acceptable" tenants. They usually selected tenants who were white, employed (therefore financially dependable), and who could afford to pay 20 percent of their income for rent (thereby keeping out larger families). Eligibility based on capacity to pay meant that the slum dweller who was most in need could not participate, especially since the Housing Administrator could fix the lowest financial limit.

Similarly, the 1937 Act indirectly accelerated a shortage of urban housing by calling for compulsory "elimination" of "unsafe or unsanitary dwellings" equal in number to those to be constructed. "Although experience has shown that slums disappear more quickly where there is an over-supply of dwellings, rather than where there is an under-supply, Congress saw fit to enact this provision."[5] Further, there was a statutory limit on cost allowable for construction per unit of public housing which naturally limited the number and size of rooms in each. This, coupled with financial requirements for eligibility, usually meant that large families, for whom shortage of housing was and still is the most acute, could not be accommodated. And in those instances where they were admitted, the per unit limit ensured that they would be crowded into small apartments. In turn, the crowding of people above a certain density has been suggested by scholars of human "territoriality" as a frequent catalyst for violence and anti-social behavior. Finally, as building costs continued to rise, the allowable cost per unit of housing became so unrealistic that in many instances federal housing programs could not be used at all.

Urban renewal has been another major interest of urban lobby groups. It, like the housing programs, has also been a mixed blessing. Early urban renewal projects simply "bulldozed poor people out of homes to make way for commercial establishments or high-income housing," on which a city could then collect more taxes.[6] They showed little concern for the problems of relocating people, and those displaced usually ended up in housing of even poorer quality. The urban renewal program, by ". . . the policy of destroying occupied houses without providing any compensating new housing, has had the effect of decreasing the supply of low-cost housing."[7] The effectiveness of urban renewal as a vehicle for revitalizing the central city business district has also been called into doubt. One expert maintains that the urban renewal program, in its assumption that a renewed downtown area would attract new enterprises, was mistaken from the start: "The key question is, how many enterprises will locate in the central business district that would not have done so anyway, and at what cost? Unless there is a net increase in the district's use, the new building is wasted."[8] Even new construction did not, he points out, profit by the fact that land was purchased and readied for sale at a cost above market value.

Legislation requires that renewed property be sold at market value, which in high-density areas is quite high. There is thus no economic incentive for businesses to relocate in urban renewal areas, and in fact, there has been difficulty in selling project sites. Yet the organizations most concerned with urban renewal, the NLC, NAHRO, the NHC, an the USCM, present estimates of urban renewal needs to the government without giving any consideration to disposition as a limiting factor. Professor Morton Schussheim makes the point that when there is demand for new downtown space, urban renewal comes about without public funds; when there is no demand, public funds are wasted on such a project.[9]

In retrospect, urban renewal and public housing have been a "national urban policy," but one whose effects may have added to some of the problems of the cities. They do not seem to have been in the long-run interests of cities in the sense of enhancing the viability, workability, or livability of urban areas as cultural, social, economic, or political communities. However, consistent with the most basic urban interest, they have created a flow of funds into cities. And once the large-city mayors accumulated large ghetto populations and public-housing constituencies, these voters had to be courted.

The generally "upper-class bias" of American pressure politics of which the "elite" association of mayors in particular has been accused, is untenable in the light of the large-city mayors' constituencies. Necessarily they had to speak for their urban poor—the ghettoized, the alienated, the jobless. Entirely apart from humanitarian concerns, they could not be assured of electoral victory without the "poor vote," and were therefore early spokesmen for programs aimed at the urban ghetto. These programs, moreover, became a useful form of patronage.

On the other hand, once the "liberal" mayors had made these groups part of their electoral base, they were no longer politically free to support programs which would disperse the ghetto. They would forfeit this base of support. It has therefore become a political necessity for these mayors to try to "fix up" their ghettos and to make living in the central city more bearable. It may be that this policy postponed what the mayors and a large number of constituents now want—metropolitan area distribution of the lower class population—and thereby added "ghetto unrest" to the list of explosive situations which became political dangers for large-city mayors in the 1960's.

On the other hand, quite a different interpretation may be put on the effects of Conference-sponsored policies in housing and urban renewal. A by-product of ghettoization is that the blacks have become a concentrated rather than a dispersed minority. This gives them the kind of political power which enables them to participate in the political system with greater results.

In some cities they hold the balance of power in mayoral elections, while in others they elect their own state and national legislators who can make their grievances more visible. In Cleveland, Gary, and Newark, they have even been able to elect black mayors. Moreover, black poverty did not become a politically urgent issue (compared, for example, with rural poverty) until the blacks became concentrated in the urban areas.

The fact that a passionate minority has been able to act so as to have its demands reverberate throughout the entire political system may in some way be a result of the past policies which encouraged Negro accumulation in a politically relevant area. The attention being paid this group may be due to their continuously increasing consolidation in large cities and their ability to voice dissatisfaction with conditions there. The situation may have intensified the social protest movement and the urban violence of the 1960's—uncomfortable to all, to be sure. But most waves of significant social change—the agricultural movement, the labor movement—have been accompanied by considerable, not dissimilar, turmoil. And if the central cities are to be left to the blacks as a result, then it may be they who will end up revitalizing them in their drive for self-identity, self-determination, and achievement. Urban programs, by hindsight, may not have contributed to the *general* well-being of urban areas, but if they facilitate representation and self-improvement of a deprived minority, one must give credit to the inter-governmental lobby as a catalyst for social change.

The substantive side-effects of federal-urban programs pushed through by lobbying groups, as stated, do not indicate as much about urban lobbying as they might suggest. The interest groups have been forced to work within the constraints imposed by the traditional methods of federal government participation, namely, specific programs for which funds are earmarked and distributed. Urban needs (as determined by the cities) have had to be tailored to appear as a "program" acceptable for presentation. This means, first, that whatever the need, it must be given legislative appeal, saved for a politically appropriate moment, and made to include (or exclude) objectives capable of gaining support from other interests.

Given these rules of the game, the urban lobbies *have* managed to get things done which have been in the interest of cities. To the agenda of items eligible for federal largesse they have added programs to aid urban mass transit, control of urban air and water pollution, and manpower training for increasing the employability of the jobless. Some housing has been built, some slums have been eliminated, and some central business districts have been saved.

Moreover, federal-city aid programs do bear an imprint of the efforts of urban lobbies to change aspects of federal government participation and to include within the programs some underlying and unifying motives. There are three such basic themes that the major lobbies have continuously stressed: to secure jurisdiction and authority for urban chief executives commensurate with their administrative responsibilities and equal to the need for mayoral leadership; to increase local autonomy; and to head off the threat of municipal insolvency. These are, so to speak, the most "real" urban interests as represented by the urban interest groups, and pressure to embody these goals is a steady undercurrent in all of the federal-urban programs they support.

The quest for urban financial viability is reflected in group demands for outright grants versus loans, for raising the percentage of the federal share in those grant programs contingent on a matching contribution by localities, for authorization permitting construction of facilities rather than cash to meet the city outlay required by these grants, and for even further liberalization of local matching contributions already allowable as non-cash credits. This "heart-of-the-matter" financial concern is also seen in the urban interest groups' fight with the Treasury Department to maintain the tax-exempt status of municipal bonds and in their manipulations attendant to the Model Cities legislation.

In short, the urban lobbies' first approach to federal urban programs may be summed up by two words—more money— and it is the financial plight of the cities, above their need for "policy" or "program" that is chosen by the USCM, NLC, and inividual mayors as the major urban issue for presentation to the mass media.[10]

It is not that the urban lobbies are unconcerned with what kinds of programs they support. On the contrary, they give much thought to the allocation of priorities among possible subject areas for federal attention. But they do this from a perspective that recognizes several factors: First, that precise definition of program priorities is difficult given the diffuse and changeable nature of the urban interest; second, that one of their tasks is to *add* the missing "urban aspect" to proposed or existing federal programs which thereafter become of interest to cities; third, given that maintenance and expanded funding of their own programs is a "survival" objective of federal agencies, the lobbies can come away with more friends and more funds by acting as agency allies. They make enemies by proposing abolition of a program which may have become outdated or even counterproductive, and make few allies by proposing something wholly new. Finally, almost any federal program which brings money into urban areas allows a city government to take some kind of political credit, to avoid other kinds of political blame, and to use some form of political patronage.

The urban lobbies discussed are guided in their approach to proposed projects by another of the three concerns unquestionably basic to the urban interest—increasing local autonomy. For this they must fight two battles on the same front. The first, the struggle to have federal programs bypass states and deal directly with cities, attempts to avoid having state regulations imposed which could interfere with local usage. Direct federal-city programs tend to prevent delays caused by going through state administrative staffs, and enable a mayor to win the inevitable competition with a governor for control over available federal funds. Finally, direct federal urban programs are viewed as a form of *de facto* municipal home rule because they permit more freedom from state participation. This can be cleverly exploited to achieve greater local autonomy, especially when a city has not been granted substantial home rule by its state.

It is a paradox that the second battle or local autonomy is made necessary in part by the consequences of winning the first; to bypass states is to trade state strings for federal guidelines. The urban effort continues as an attempt to eliminate federal guidelines hindering freedom of action.

The obstacles to local autonomy posed by federal programs are many. The steps required to remove them present a formidable task for urban lobbying. The grant system is a vehicle used by the federal government to promote *its* own priorities by subtly influencing the conduct of local government. Cities are encouraged to perform a function that might not be among its priorities, by the very fact that a grant for the specific function has been offered. The federal government also restricts local autonomy through conditions and regulations imposed by its programs. Participating cities must meet eligibility requirements, file plans which conform to federal standards, accept reviews of performance and guidelines for hiring personnel, and risk subsequent withdrawal of funds.

The urban interest is best served by those programs which offer some "ideal" mixture of financial gain, local autonomy, and desired activity. In pursuit of this ideal the urban lobbyist must try to simultaneously maximize the flow of federal dollars into cities, minimize the amount of federal control over local activities, and choose programs which meet the substantive area of most immediate need. Sometimes the differences between federal and local institutional arrangements, values, and ways of conducting public business are so great that involvement in a federal city program can bring about, in the words of one commentator, "a clash between two Americas." [11]

The complexities of choice in achieving this mix are staggering, and adding irony to intricacy, sometimes the most effective path is through the traditional "enemies"—the states. Many states have weak administrative capacities, partly as a result of having been successfully bypassed by cities, and therefore, less used. A city may subject itself to less federal influence by having its grant programs filtered through those states administratively too weak to monitor conformity with federal regulations. In addition, grants distributed through state governments tend to involve a continuous flow of funds and no fixed time duration, while grants going directly to local governments involve greater risks of discontinuity and are of more limited duration.[12]

Even after grappling with a proposed federal program to filter out foreseeable constraints on the activities, procedures, and plans of a participating city, urban lobbies must still contend with the unforeseeable effects it might have on local political relationships after its passage. The poverty program, as noted, turned out to have unintended implications for local government in creating intense competition for control between large-city mayors and militant leaders of the poor. In this case, as one analyst observed, "The stakes could hardly be higher. . .(since) a mayor's. . .power. . .has depended in no small measure on control of the welfare industry and the millions of federal dollars that flow through city hall en route to the poor." [13]

The demand for greater executive authority equal to executive responsibility, the third of the continuing principles that the urban lobbies have sought to uphold in federal urban programs, is well reflected in their efforts to alter the poverty program.

As the USCM convincingly stated at the Congressional hearings for poverty program amendments, the urban interest was that of control by mayors over the public functions within their cities. Responsibility for administration, policy, and distribution of public funds by private groups who could not be held accountable to any electorate or official was regarded as tantamount to heresy. Raising the sense of political efficacy of deprived minority groups by encouraging greater control over their own environment was not considered unimportant; but the main issue was that a chief elected official should control public administration on principles of democratic accountability. This control would sustain government "by the people." It would enable a mayor to carry out policy promises made to his electorate, and would help the voters identify who was responsible for what. With this knowledge they could make more meaningful choices in replacing their leaders.

Executive leadership and control (and therefore, the idea of accountability) is so weak on the local level (especially in large cities), that one might refer to the situation as a "crisis of executive leadership." The typical governmental structure of a large city encourages proliferation of special independent authorities, plural elective offices, and deadlocks between mayors and local legislatures controlled by different political parties. Large-city bureaucracies have become cumbersome, independent, inefficient and unresponsive to executive leadership as well as to the demands of the urban population. They seem, so to speak, to rule a city and with a thousand voices (that is, when not on strike). Interest groups, neighborhoods, factions, and unions seem less and less able to resolve their differences, and refuse to be led. The largest cities appear to be dissolving into warring factions, becoming unable to function as political communities. Moreover, public authority is so fragmented that sources of control are difficult to trace and most any action is difficult. The power vacuum inherent in this fragmentation thus becomes crippling and critical. Nothing has yet replaced the political machine to act as connective tissue, and mayors seem unable to lead.

Given these conditions, or, for that matter, any other elements which might underline the impression that "large-city governments just don't work," the term "urban crisis" takes on the additional meaning of a crisis in urban leadership. Impotence of leadership, unresponsive unaccountable bureaucracies, and government inability to act, all interfere with legitimacy—the acceptance of a regime by the governed.

Popular reactions take a variety of forms—community control, decentralization, illegal strikes, multiple separate charismatic leaders—all of which seem to involve a further rejection of existing official authority. In fact, they are often a quest for *more* authority, or at least, for "legitimate authority." To be held "legitimate," authority ideally must consist of acceptability, the jurisdiction to act, a mandate for action, responsibility for that over which it presides, and accountability for performance. Splintering executive authority confuses the issue of where ultimate responsibility rests. This, in turn, prevents possibilities for strong and vigorous political leadership, the lack of which may have led to the crisis of authority and legitimacy in the first place.

Another aspect of the urban crisis is the sense of alienation and powerlessness felt by the urban masses. Do people feel powerless when their leader is powerless? Administrative control commensurate with responsibility may be especially important in areas of social upheaval. Discontented citizens seize on "lack of government responsiveness," "breakdown of services," or "allocation of resources" as reasons to march on city hall. If "city hall" has insufficient control over public programs and their administration to change anything, the discontent multiplies further. Those who perceive the situation as such feel even more frustrated and powerless. Those who are told, but do not believe, may become more enraged and convinced of the necessity to "act from outside the political system." And further, if the effective power of an elected official is negligible, it is the alienated and deprived who may suffer most. If their vote is their only means of political expression, electing new leaders would provide no alternative if the leaders themselves are powerless.

The large-city mayors, perceiving this crisis of urban government, reacted by increasing their lobbying of the federal government. In effect, they have asked that this superseding source of authority and revenue share more of both with the mayors who, as representatives of local government, wish to increase the quality and accountability of urban leadership. The federal government, by the proliferation of its federal-urban programs in the 1960's, in effect "consented." It has increased a mayor's authority, possibilities for leadership, and sources of funds through those programs which assign local allocation of benefits, control of their execution, and staffing, to the city chief executives.

This aspect of "government lobbying government" has been aimed at compensating for those weaknesses and incapacities of city government which hinder its ability to lead and respond to its residents. To this extent, it is lobbying properly defined as "urban interest representation." It is also suitably defined both as inter-governmental lobbying, and as "government acting on government for interests of its own."

Now that this phenomenon has been viewed in so many of its aspects by analyzing the USCM in action, it becomes possible to make some tentative evaluation of how it fits into democratic theory and practice. "Government acting on government for interests of its own" can, in fact, be reconciled with the idea that democratic governments exist to carry out the expressed wishes of the governed.

Inter-governmental lobbying by groups of elected officials may be viewed as a demand for greater executive control for purposes of democratic accountability to the electorate and to counter "democracy by bureaucracy." It is an effort by the poorest level of government to re-channel revenues from the richest level into programs through which it can provide services for local populations (from whom the coffers of the richest level were originally filled).

Direct democracy becomes confused and inefficient when millions of people are involved, so participation has come to mean saying "yes" or "no." The focal point of popular participation has become the election, which presents these manageable alternatives in terms of a choice between competing sets of leaders. It is the chosen leaders who then make complicated public policy decisions in the context of their electoral mandate. This is meaningful only if the leader chosen can lead and can be held responsible by being accountable at the next election. A mayor who is prohibited from managing what theoretically is in his domain, cannot be held responsible for undesired or improper actions. This makes control of his administration by an elected public official an important value of democracy because it is a vehicle for accountability.

One level of government lobbying another for this control within its own jurisdiction, and the collective efforts of local officials to protect the integrity, autonomy, and financial viability of local government, can be seen as an effort to make electoral choice more meaningful to voters. The interests represented are governmental interests, but equally important to the governed and to the man who governs. It is not inconsistent with democratic theory, then, for government to have interests of its own.

Whatever its democratic legitimacy, there are important questions to ask about urban lobbying for the 1970's. Are there perhaps ways to achieve the same goals of greater revenue, autonomy and accountability that might involve fewer costs? Are the urban interests that lobbies define as paramount best represented by a continued pressure for special function federal-urban programs? Finally, going back to Moynihan's question with which this discussion began, can we find a way to meet the demands of the urban crisis in terms of policy as well as program—with "something like a national urban policy?"

Many and complex though these questions are, they could conceivably be answered within the context of a single idea—revenue-sharing. Despite the uncertainties involved in such an assertion, it is the responsibility of the policy analyst to attempt at least a preliminary judgment. The reasoning and speculation which follow are based on an "ideal type" revenue-sharing plan.[14]

Revenue-sharing is a plan by which the federal government would redistribute a portion of federal income tax revenues to state and local governments, with minimum restrictions on the

use of the funds. It is intended to permit states and cities to
exercise maximum discretion in providing public services and to
give relief to financially-pressed state and local governments.
Through this plan, therefore, cities would receive their much-
needed revenues, but with fewer of the strings that reduce local
autonomy. The major features of revenue-sharing are that it
provides for distribution of funds which would be predictable
as to amounts; unfettered as to specific programs, processes, or
requirements; shared on the basis of population, but adjusted
for relative tax effort; and guaranteed as to the percentage which
cities, counties and states would receive. The flow of unearmarked funds would reduce federal controls, thereby encouraging maximum accountability and control at the local level. If the
cities themselves were to be responsible for the allocation of
funds among services, local officials would be answerable to
residents on the issues of function and priority. The predictability
of amounts would remove some of the uncertainties and in-
stabilities which enter into local politics as a result of the vagaries
of special function federal-urban programs.

Ultimate control of those urban services and activities now
provided through the categorical grant-in-aid could be removed
from the professionalized federal bureaucracy whose accountability to anyone at all, much less to local electorates, is open to
question. If revenue sharing were to work ideally, responsiveness
of local urban bureaucracy to citizen access and participation, as
well as to mayoral management, might increase. The more subject
to federal guidelines and review, the more local agencies responsible for the same programs establish relationships of "mutual rein-
forcement," which insulate bureaucracy from effective control.

If a fixed portion of redistributed and unearmarked federal
revenues was to go to states and cities, revenue sharing would
also be consistent with the continuous struggle by urban lobbies
for direct federal-city relations. At the same time, the competition
between governors and mayors might lessen somewhat; each
would have a pre-determined share of funds to allocate according
to his own priorities, and control of specific programs would
cease to be a "zero-sum game." By eliminating programs with
matching fund requirements that significantly pre-determine
budgetary allotments, both cities and states could conceivably

end up with even more revenue that is not automatically obligated; their action options would thereby increase by an even greater extent than the incoming "shared taxes."

The most important aspect of revenue-sharing is that it would reverse the trend currently pushing the urban decision-making process more and more into the federal arena. Urban politics, the making of decisions pertaining to urban areas, would become more a matter of local politics. In fact, a much more intense and competitive part of political decision-making would devolve to the local level than it now exercises because the stakes would be higher. New groups might form to claim access to funds, and could expect a more responsive attitude from local government because of the proximity of constituency and decision-makers. Disadvantaged urban groups whose organizational capacities are too weak for mobilization at a national level might have more chance for success if revenue-sharing were to cause a shift in the location of a major portion of value and resource allocation.

Despite the inter-group, inter-agency, executive-legislative conflicts that would attend an inflow of unearmarked funds, the point is that tax sharing would put the mayor in the position of leading and mediating this process, the local bureaucracies fully in charge of executing its results, and urban electorates able to represent their interests with respect to more decisions. In short, urban politics might become urban policy-making and enable community control of programs.

To some extent, the states would still be operating programs of importance to large cities—perhaps even a greater proportion under revenue-sharing than at present. Those functions which have traditionally fallen under state jurisdiction would, of course, remain. But more important, programs aimed at "urban problems" such as air and water pollution or mass transit would have to be handled at the level which had regional jurisdiction. Revenue-sharing, especially since the proportion of funds to go to each city within a state might be subject to negotiation, would mean that cities would engage in intensive lobbying of state legislatures to represent the "urban" interest.

This probability suggests some of the greatest political changes vis-a-vis urban lobbying that might come about. Relations between the urban interest groups and federal officials would change significantly. Senators and Congressmen would no longer be as strategic for sponsorship on support of specific urban problems. The urban input would not have to be pressured through Congressional committees and administrative agencies (except for those programs which would remain under federal auspices). The urban lobbying process would shift its location of emphasis to the state and local level in proportion to the amount of federal revenue redistributed and the number of federal programs dropped or restricted.

Urban interest representation at the federal level would revolve around different sets of participants. For example, if responsibility for public welfare programs were to be removed from states and cities and assumed by the federal government, the urban interest spokesmen might revolve around the Congressional Committees on Labor and Public Welfare, Ways and Means, and Appropriations, and the Executive institutions of HEW, ACIR, and OIR.

The group network would re-align around whatever cluster of issues at the federal level was of greatest importance to cities. Most likely this would be the tax-sharing issue itself, and would involve pressure to increase the percentage of revenues to be redistributed, the proportion to be divided between states and cities, and the relationship between the income a state produces and the revenue it would receive. No doubt, the USCM and the Governors Conference would remain very much involved at the federal level. However, the roles of the functional urban interest groups and of the NLC would probably be to focus their efforts on states. The large-city mayors (like the New York "big six') might organize by states so as to operate at both levels.

Finally, revenue-sharing could conceivably constitue a national urban policy—an answer to the demands that have come from so many quarters. It would avoid the impediments to a national urban policy that have been discussed—"rationalization," or making coherent the multiplicity of existing federal-urban programs. It would fill the primary goals of the major groups representing the urban interest, it would be national in scope, it would permit specific urban policies to meet the differing priorities and needs of individual cities, and it would place the major policy-making responsibility in the places at which urban policy is directed—urban areas themselves.

It may even be that revenue-sharing should take a more radical form than has been proposed. Instead of a redistribution of federally collected revenues, perhaps a large part of these revenues could be collected locally in the first place. Under such an arrangement, the plan would have to include an agreement whereby the federal government would cease to pre-empt the income tax. It would include an obligation for the cities to tax incomes, in exchange for which the federal government would substantially lower its own use of that source. The idea would be that revenue which is raised and spent locally might allow city residents greater control of their governments. Moreover, citizens might be made more aware of the purposes for which their tax money is used, and of the relationship between taxation and the services government is able to provide. They themselves might, in effect, be forced to become more knowledgeable and responsible in their attitude toward taxes in general, and toward the accusations hurled at their governments. Cause and effect might at least become more visible, resulting in a political learning experience.*

Proposals for some form of tax sharing have been considered seriously for several years, and have been supported by both the mayors and the governors. In September 1969, President Nixon made a public commitment to preside over the legislation which could implement it. The proposition, therefore, becomes a possibility for the immediate future. However, there are many serious political impediments which must first be overcome. If revenue-sharing on an extensive scale were to replace federal programs as presently handled, the federal bureaucracy would

---

* The many disadvantages to this more radical approach, however, are likely to outweigh the advantages. To list just a few: people might relocate on the basis of "lowest tax rate"; the advantages of nationally uniform taxes forfeited; the amount of revenue for national (federal) expenditures (such as defense) in proportion to amount necessary for local needs impossible to calculate; and the redistributive aspects of the more orthodox revenue-sharing proposals impossible to apply, meaning the poorest cities with the greatest need would be able to raise the least.

no doubt shrink, agencies would "lose" programs to administer, and federal officials—the President as well as legislators—would cease to be identified as benefactors. They would lose patronage as well as "sponsorship" credit. The implications for the federal government are enormous. Moreover, the federal government would have to retain enough control to ensure that nationally uniform guidelines are followed in instances where national policy is at stake; in the application of anti-discrimination legislation, for example.

There may also be considerable opposition on the *local* level that is not generally vocalized. One might assume mayors would prefer to have their own tax base from which to exercise control, and that petitioning the federal government for programs is only a second choice. This may not be the case, however. Local governments may prefer the present situation in which they can avoid the political unpleasantness of levying taxes, and at the same time benefit from spending them. Although this may still hold under a revenue-sharing scheme, local public officials would have to take more "blame" for decisions on the allocation of funds. With the increased availability of funds, local officials may incur the responsibility, rightly or wrongly, for "solving" urban problems themselves. By endorsing "federal solutions" mayors are relieved of some responsibility: if the federal program does not work, or if the problem to which the federal solution is addressed is not susceptible to solution in the first place, then blame rests elsewhere than on the mayors' shoulders.

Assume, for the moment, that Edward Banfield is right in his assessment that the fundamental problems of the urban crisis cannot be "solved," especially by government. According to Banfield, government cannot "eliminate slums, educate the slum child, train the unskilled worker, end chronic poverty, stop crime and delinquency, or prevent riots." [15] Even if we knew how to do these things, Banfield points out, the knowhow would be unusable because those actions which government could take to ameliorate the less intractable situations are unavailable because of the jeopardy in which these actions would put elected public officials.

To illustrate his point Banfield lists recommendations for some of the visible urban problems; without even analyzing the merits of the recommendations, one could project that a group of elected public officials—especially mayors of large cities with heterogeneous constituencies—would have trouble supporting any of them. "Indeed," says Banfield, "with respect to most of the items on the list, the politically feasible thing is the exact opposite of what has been recommended."

It is possible, therefore, that to the extent revenue-sharing would place more responsibility for solving urban problems in the hands of public officials whose election is decided by a purely urban constituency, they might prefer to have solutions "imposed" by the federal government through special programs.

Nevertheless, given certain national guidelines, the proposal whereby the federal government would automatically redistribute part of its revenue back to the states and cities, to be used according to their own priorities, has great potential. It certainly seems to be an alternative worth trying. It would appear to achieve the goals advocated by urban lobbies of more funds, local autonomy, and authority equal to responsibility, with fewer disadvantages than exclusive reliance on the special category federal-urban program.

Finally, it may be a method of meeting the need for "something like a national urban policy."

Since the emergence of federal urban lobbying in the 1930's, federal urban policy has come to be made by a reasonably operating political subsystem that has just come of age. The urban lobbies have re-routed federal revenues directly back to their urban sources to a significant extent. The idea of an "urban issue" has been accepted. And, perhaps most important, we are at the brink of what could become a national urban policy which would emancipate the cities. Progress is being made, but it is necessarily slow. Urban lobbies must strive to formulate relevant policy options in a phenomenally complex area, and to shift their formations and strategies with each new political or social tide. One may venture a guess that the Nixon Administration will be a watershed for urban lobbying. It may pose to urban lobbies a challenge as great as did that posed by the Roosevelt Administration of the 1930's.

Other Examples
of Formal Consultations
Between Urban
Groups and Government

FOLLOWING are several examples of the formal consultation process:

1. Members of the 1958 ad hoc Legislative Committee on Urban Development coordinated by Hugh Mields included leaders of the USCM, the NHC, the IMCA, NAHRO, HUD, and future leaders of Urban America, and the Urban Coalition. All of them were also involved with the 1961 "Legislative Recommendations Group" and the USCM's Community Development Committee in 1963 and 1965.

The group affiliations indicated for these people have not been dated because the purpose is to show interaction flows and potential circulation of ideas among institutional participants during the time period of the whole subsystem. The people referred to are as follows (not *all* of each person's affiliations are listed):

John Barriere—staff director, House housing subcommittee; Director, Democratic Steering Committee; 1960 Kennedy Task Force;

Lawrence Cox—Redevelopment Director, NAHRO, ASPO, HUD;

William Rafsky—Redevelopment Director, NAHRO, NHC;

William Slayton—NAHRO, NHC, UA, HUD;

John Gunther—USCM, NAHRO, ICMA, ASPO, redevelopment official;

Nathaniel Keith—NHC, HUD;

Hugh Mields—NLC, USCM, NAHRO, HUD, Urban America, Urban Coalition;

Edward Logue—Redevelopment Director (New Haven, Boston, New York); 1959 Task Force, New York State Urban Development Corp.;

B. T. Fitzpatrick—NHC; 1959 Task Force, HUD;

Charles Farris—Redevelopment Director, NHC; private urban programming consultant;

John Lange—NAHRO;

James Lash—NHC;

William Wheaton—Director, Institute for Urban Studies, Univ. of Penn.; NHC;

Neal Hardy—HUD; assistant to Mayor Lindsay of New York, Urban Coalition (Non-Profit Housing Center);

John Robin—USCM (consultant on slum clearance since 1949 and testified for Conference in 1954); Redevelopment Director; NAHRO;

Richard Lee—Mayor, New Haven; USCM (Executive Committee); NLC (Executive Committee), Urban America (Advisory Board); Chairman, 1959 Task Force.

2. The 1969 Urban Coalition Task Force on Housing, Reconstruction and Investment includes leaders of the NHC, the Urban Coalition, Urban America, the NLC, the USCM, the 1968 President's Advisory Committee on Urban Housing (Kaiser Commission), individual city and state community development commissioners, and the National Corporation for Housing Partnerships (set up by the Housing Act of 1968; see Urban Coalition, Task Force on Housing, Reconstruction and Investment, list of participants, "Agenda" for meeting July 28, 1969);

3. A meeting on October 3, 1967, of the Urban Alliance, an ad hoc group that was created in 1966 to work on Model Cities legislation and which was dissolved in 1967 after the legislation was enacted and funded, is illustrative of the formal consultation among subsystem members that took place during the Alliance's existence. Present (among other more peripheral urban groups) were representatives from the USCM, NAHB, NAHRO, the NHC, the NLC, the Joint Council of Urban Development (a cooperative project set up by the USCM and the NLC), as well as mayors' assistants, and members of the Presidential urban staff, the Vice President's urban staff, the Banking and Currency Committees staffs, and of HUD.

4. The Special Committee to Study Welfare System, created by the USCM in 1969 to

> work with other groups including organized labor, the Urban Coalition and the National League of Cities, to study our entire welfare system and produce recommendations for Congress. . .distinguished officers and members of this association were appointed to this special committee (USCM, *Proceedings*, 1969).

5. Members from different areas of the subsystem appear in a formal capacity at meetings and conventions held by other actors. This practice engenders a "filtering through" of ideas and attitudes, and is illustrated by those "urban actors" addressing the USCM conventions. To illustrate:

In 1962: From the White House:
        Address   John F. Kennedy
        Address   Brook Hays

    From City Halls:
        Administrative
            Organization of the
            Mayor's Office   Arthur L. Selland
                            Robert F. Wagner
                            Henry W. Maier

Governmental
Development in
Metropolitan Areas Richard J. Daley
Samuel W. Yorty

From Federal Departments:
Cuban Refugees and
the Cities Abraham A. Ribicoff
Unemployed Out—of
School Youth Arthur J. Goldberg
National Civil
Defense Policy Stuart L. Pittman
National Defense and
the Nation's
Economy Robert F. Steadman

From Federal Agencies:
Urban Renewal—A
Progress Report
Discussion William L. Slayton
Public Service
Responsibility of
Radio and
Television Newton N. Minow

In 1964: President Johnson, Secretary of Labor Wirtz, Senator Harrison Williams (Banking and Currency), Congressman Rains, Attorney General Robert F. Kennedy, HHFA Administrator Robert Weaver.

In 1966: Message President Lyndon B.
Johnson

Address Vice President Hubert
H. Humphrey

Slums and the
City Beautiful
Address HUD Secretary, Robert
C. Weaver

Address   Secretary of Interior,
                                   Stewart L. Udall

In 1969: On Poverty and Public Welfare
        Ben W. Heineman, Chairman, President's Com-
        mittee on Income Maintenance Programs, and
        Robert Harris, Executive Director of the Com-
        mittee.

        On the new Administration's Urban Programs
        George Romney—Secretary, HUD.
        Lawrence Cox—Ass. Sec., HUD.
        Charles Rogovin—Law Enforcement Assistance
        Administrator
        Dick Lam—Urban Mass Transit Administrator
        Floyd Hyde—Ass. Sec. for Model Cities, HUD.

        Report from Capitol Hill
        Thomas L. Ashley—Chairman, Subcommittee on
        Urban Growth, House Banking and Currency
        Committee.*

Also, the following federal officials were officially "available"
for consultation" at the 1969 USCM convention so that participants could "contact them to discuss their particular federal city
interests." (From USCM, "Federal Officials Available for Consultation," 1969, p. 1)

Community Relations: Ben F. Holman, Director,
                                   Community Relations,
                                   Dept. of Justice
                                 Lawrence Hoffheimer,
                                   Special Assistant to
                                   Director, CRS, Dept. of
                                   Justice

* The above information is documented in USCM, *Annual Proceedings*,
1962, 1964, 1966, and 1969 respectively.

Health, Education, and Welfare: Sidney L. Gardner, Center for Community Development, HEW

Housing and Urban Development: Lawrence M. Cox, Assistant Secretary, Housing and Urban Renewal Assistance, HUD

ArDee Ames, Executive Assistant, Renewal and Housing Assistance, HUD

Andrew S. Bullis, Director, Division of State and Local Relations, HUD

W. Gerard Lyons, Sr. Assistant for Congressional Relations, HUD

Intergovernmental Relations: Nils A. Boe, Director, Office of Intergovernmental Relations

Wendell E. Hulcher, Deputy Director, Office of Intergovernmental Relations

William Colman, Executive Director, Advisory Commission on Intergovernmental Relations

William K. Brussat, Bureau of the Budget

Law Enforcement: Charles H. Rogovin, Administrator, Law Enforcement Assistance, Dept. of Justice

Manpower: Arnold R. Weber, Assistant Secretary of Manpower, Dept. of Labor

Model Cities:

Floyd Hyde, Assistant Secretary, Model Cities and Governmental Relations, HUD

Robert Baida, Deputy Assistant Secretary, Model Cities and Governmental Relations, HUD

Lawrence O. Houston, Jr., Director, Program Development Staff, Model Cities Administration, HUD

Poverty:

William H. Bozman, Deputy Director, Community Action Program, OEO

Robert C. Crawford, Assistant Director for Governmental Relations, OEO

Louis H. Ritter, Assistant for Public Officials Relations, OEO

Transportation:

Michael Cafferty, Deputy Assistant Secretary for Urban Systems and Environment, Dept. of Transportation

Dick G. Lam, Program Manager, Center City Transportation Program, Urban Mass Transportation Administration, DOT

Carlos Villereal, Administrator, Urban Mass Transportation Administration, DOT

Carroll C. Carter, Assistant Administrator, Urban Mass Transportation Administration, DOT

Water Pollution Control:

Fred L. Jones, Chief, Division of Land and Water Conservation Fund, BOR, Dept. of Interior

Further Examples
of Rotation and Overlap
# of Leadership and Staff

PAUL Betters, Executive Director of the NLC from 1932 to 1935, became the Executive Director of the USCM in 1935. Mields, in 1969 a private consultant for other groups and individual actors, has been with the NLC, the HHFA, NAHRO, the USCM, and the Urban Coalition. John Feild of the USCM was Director of the President's Committee on Equal Employment Opportunities. John Gunther, Director of USCM, is also a member of the International City Managers Association, NAHRO, ASPO, and a Commissioner of the Washington, D.C.'s Redevelopment Land Agency. William Slayton, Executive Vice President of Urban America, is a former consultant to the USCM and a former Commissioner of the United States Urban Renewal Administration. In 1969, he is also a member of NAHRO and ASPO, and a Director of the NHC. David Lawrence, a member of the Executive Committee of Urban America, was formerly a President of the USCM, a member of the NLC, and Chairman of the President's Committee on Equal Opportunity in Housing. Trustees of Urban America include Andrew Heiskell, Chairman of the Urban Coalition, and John Gardner, President of the Urban Coalition. Urban America's staff includes people who have been with HUD, as well as several former members of local planning or redevelopment agencies.

The President of the NHC, Nathaniel Keith, is also a former Administrator of the United States Urban Renewal Administration and consultant to the USCM. The 1969 makeup of the Board of Directors of the NHC is especially illustrative of the amount of overlap in the subsystem and, for this reason, will be treated in detail. Lee Johnson, an assistant to Mayor Currigan of Denver (who is on the Advisory Board of both the NLC and the USCM) is first Vice President of the NHC. He was Director of the NHC from 1949 to 1960, a frequent consultant to the USCM, and a member of the Eisenhower task force. Walter Reuther, third Vice President of the NHC, is also on the Steering Committee of the Urban Coalition and a union president. He was a member of the 1959 Democratic Advisory Committee on Urban and Suburban Problems.

Some of the other directors, all formerly with HUD or the HHFA, are Robert Weaver, Richard Steiner, Sidney Spector, William Slayton, Milton Semer, Edward Lashman, Jr., B. T. Fitzpatrick, Nathaniel Keith, Phillip Brownstein, Ralph Taylor, and Leon Keyserling. Directors who are either former members of Congress or members of Congressional staffs are Paul Douglas, David Walker, Milton Semer, Albert Rains, and Joseph McMurray. Other leaders of urban interest groups and task forces are: Jack Conway, Urban America; Robert McGrath, NAHB; William Rafsky and William Slayton, NAHRO; David Walker, the ACIR; Paul Douglas, the Douglas Commission; William Kaiser, the Kaiser Commission; Ernest Bohn, the Eisenhower task force on Housing; and seven men who represent the USCM and the NLC through their efforts as frequent consultants to the Conference's Community Development Committee: Nathaniel Keith, Knox Banner, Richard Steiner, William Rafsky, William Wheaton, B. T. Fitzpatrick, and Laurence Henderson.

William Rafsky, President of NAHRO, in addition to being a director of the NHC, is also a consultant to the USCM's working policy subcommittee. He is a former Development Coordinator of Philadelphia. Indeed, the entire NAHRO membership shows a wide overlap with other groups. John Gunther, the Executive Director of the USCM, for example, is also a member of NAHRO.

John Gardner, President of the Urban Coalition, is a former Secretary of the Department of Health, Education and Welfare. Andrew Heiskell, co-chairman of the Urban Coalition, is also a Vice Chairman of Urban America. The Urban Coalition's National Steering Committee (1967 list) represents the USCM and the NLC by including John Feild of the USCM staff as National Coordinator and by including nine mayors from Executive Committees of the USCM and the NLC. It also shows an overlap with the leaderships of Urban America, the NHC, NAHRO, the AFL-CIO, and four civil rights groups.

David Walker, a consultant to the USCM and a former Director of the Redevelopment Authority of Philadelphia, became staff director of the Senate Subcommittee on Intergovernmental Relations and, since 1967, has been Assistant Director of the ACIR. He is also a director of the NHC. Howard Moskoff, Assistant Director of the Kaiser Commission and Director of the National Corporation of Housing Partnerships in 1968, was loaned in 1969 to both the USCM's Community Development Committee and the Urban Coalition Housing Task Force. John Feild of the USCM is also national coordinator of the Urban Coalition. Ron Linton is a partner of Mields in the urban consulting firm of Linton, Mields, Coston and Cogan, and a national coordinator for both the Urban Coalition and Urban America. Norman Beckman "rotated" from Assistant Director of the ACIR in 1964 to Assistant Secretary of HUD. Donald Lief moved from the NLC to Urban America. Herbert Franklin, also a director of the NHC in 1969, moved from Urban America to the Urban Coalition. Don Slater went from the NLC to HEW. Jonathan Lindley was administrative aide to Senator Douglas in 1964, a member of the Senate Banking and Currency Committee staff in 1965, and subsequently has joined the Economic Development Administration.*

* This data was compiled in June, 1969. Some people changed positions in 1970, but in most cases moved simply to still another "urban policy" type of job.

Individual Influentials
and Informal Communications

ALTHOUGH no attempt has been made to "count" informal transactions among urban groups, the files of several of the groups indicate a continuous and voluminous amount of informal contact, as letters to one actor with copies for others, items of interest received by one and sent on for the attention of others, telephone conversations, meetings, and social gatherings. Typical of this material are the following examples:

1. Speeches drafted by the staff of one group to be delivered by a member of a second urban group at the meeting of a third group;

2. Letter from Hugh Mields (December 29, 1950), when he was with the NLC, to Urban Renewal Commissioner Steiner, with copies indicated for Cox, Gunther, Logue, and Rafsky (already identified as key individual actors);

3. Letters from Wheaton (February 6 and 21, 1961), a consultant to the USCM, Director of the NHC, and Director of the Institute for Urban Studies, to Mields, at the NLC, commenting on the conclusions of the 1961 Ad Hoc Committee for Legislation Recommendations with copy to Semer, counsel to HHFA. Also on the "1961 Legislative Recommendations—

Housing and Urban Renewal," a memo (February 10, 1961) from Mields (when on NLC staff) to Lawrence Cox, Charles Farris, B. T. Fitzpatrick, John Gunther, Neal Hardy, Nathaniel Keith, John Lange, Edward Logue, D. E. Macklemann, William Rafsky, John Robin, William Slayton, and William Wheaton;

4. Most groups hold frequent luncheons to "develop relations with the representatives of our supporters." A good example is an Urban Coalition luncheon in November, 1969.

Further Examples of Informal Consultation

1) To illustrate graphically:

July 20, 1964

Mr. Carl A. S. Coan
Senate Subcommitte on Housing

Norman Beckman, Assistant Director
Advisory Commission on Intergovernmental Relations [now HUD Assistant Secretary]

Enclosed is a statement (an almost identical version of which will be distributed to Committee members by Senator Muskie) proposing two amendments to the Housing Act of 1964 as reported by the Subcommittee on Housing. Following up on our phone conversation of today and with Hugh Mields, please let me know if we can answer any questions or provide further information on these two amendments affecting the FHA and Community Facilities Loan Programs.

cc: Hugh Mields [then Assistant Director, USCM]

2) Letter dated October 26, 1960, from the Director of the USCM to staff director of the Housing subcommittee of the

Senate Banking and Currency, thanking him for the opportunity to discuss the question of a survey of local housing
needs and plans. "This letter is in response to your invitation
to submit thoughts in writing which might be taken into
consideration in further pursuing this matter." . . .

After commenting on general considerations he then referred
the Banking and Currency staff to another member of the system:

"experts in the National Association of Housing and Redevelopment officials would be the appropriate persons to make
suggestions with details . . ."

3) Proposed petition to the President of the United States asking
him not to veto the Housing Act of 1959 was circulated with
request for comments among NLC, the USCM, several mayors,
and James Sundquist (Assistant to Senator Clark, in 1960 Secretary and Democratic Platform Committee, then with
Brookings Institution.)

4) Informal meetings are frequent occurrences throughout the
subsystem. For example, in January, 1969, the "U.S. Municipal
News" (a USCM publication) reported that a top agenda item
for the USCM was to develop,

"working relations with the administration of Richard M.
Nixon, his Cabinet-level Council on Urban Affairs and the
men named to run it—staff officer Daniel Patrick Moynihan,
HUD Secretary George Romney, HEW Secretary Robert
Finch and Transportation Secretary John Volpe."

The bulletin also noted that members of the Conference held
a series of meetings with this group. Similarly, a delegation
from the Urban Coalition had met with President Nixon in
New York on December 13th. One week later "a group of
mayors active in both USCM and NLC also met with Nixon.
On March 1, 1969, a 10 man Urban Coalition delegation
headed by John Gardner, President of the Urban Coalition, and

former Secretary of HEW and Mayor James Tate of Philadelphia, Vice President of the USCM met with Moynihan and
the Council on Urban Affairs."

The following lists of "influentials" is intended only to suggest that there *is* at least a nucleus of *individuals* (as well as institutions), around whom the urban policy subsystem revolves:
(The numbers following each name identifies the type of participation involved, according to the legend.)

Legend—numbers indicate types of participation

1. Mayor
2. Urban America (affiliated with in any capacity)
3. USCM
4. Community Development Committee of USCM
5. NLC
6. Urban Coalition
7. HUD (past or present official or staff of any constituent
   agency.)
8. Included as "influential" by Professor Wolman in his
   research on the housing policy subsystem
9. Active in "urban-oriented" legislation
10. Douglas Commission (any connection)
11. Kaiser Commission (any connection)
12. Congressional staff (committee or aide)
13. Congress member, Banking and Currency or Govern-
    ment Operations Committee
14. Executive Office of the President (any unit)
15. President's urban staff
16. Kennedy task force connection
17. AFL-CIO
18. Urban Alliance
19. National Housing Conference
20. Eisenhower task force
21. 1959 Democratic task force on urban problems
22. Johnson task force
23. NAHRO

24. ASPO
25. Local or state "urban" staff (redevelopment officials and mayors' staff)
26. Urban affairs plank in Party Platform
27. HEW
28. ICMA
29. Bankers interest groups that participate in urban policy
30. ACIR
31. New York State Urban Development Corporation
32. National Housing Partnership
33. Civil rights groups especially active in urban affairs

Allen, Ivan	1, 2, 3, 5, 6, 10
Ames, ArDee	4, 7, 9, 12, 23
Ashley, Thomas	8, 13
Barr, Joseph	1, 2, 3, 4, 5, 6, 10, 11, 14
Barriere, John	4, 8, 12, 16
Biemiller, Andrew	6, 8, 17, 18
Brownstein, Phillip	7, 8, 11, 19
Burrows, Kenneth	12
Califano, Joseph	8, 15, 16
Cavanagh, Jerome	1, 2, 3, 4, 5, 6, 8, 10
Clark, Joseph	6, 9
Coan, Carl	8, 12
Cole, Albert	7, 13, 20
Collins, John	1, 2, 3, 4, 5, 6, 14
Conway, Jack	2, 6, 8, 11, 17, 18, 19
Cox, Lawrence	7, 10, 11, 23, 24, 25
Daley, Richard	1, 3, 4, 5, 6, 8, 26
Douglas, Paul	10, 13, 18, 19
Feild, John	3, 6, 14
Fitzpatrick, B. T.	4, 7, 19, 21
Gardner, John	2, 6, 27
Gunther, John	2, 3, 6, 8, 23, 24, 25, 28
Hardy, Neal	2, 4, 7
Heiskell, Andrew	2, 6
Healy, Pat	5, 6, 8, 18
Henderson, Laurence	3, 4, 5, 9, 19

Hyde, Floyd	1, 3, 7
Johnson, Lee	19, 20, 25
Kaiser, Edgar F.	6, 8, 11, 19
Keith, Nathaniel	2, 3, 4, 7, 10, 19, 23
Klaman, Saul	8, 9, 22, 29
Krooth, David	2, 8, 10, 11, 19
Lash, James	3, 19, 25
Lashmon Edward	2, 8, 17, 19
Lawrence, David	1, 2, 3, 14
Lee, Richard	1, 2, 3, 4, 5, 10, 21 30
Lindley, John	4, 7, 12
Logue, Ed	4, 10, 11, 21, 25, 31
Maier, Henry	1, 3, 5
McGabe, Robert	7, 8, 11
McMurray, Joseph	12, 19, 25
Mields, Hugh	2, 3, 5, 6, 7, 11, 23
Muskie, Edmund	13, 30
Moskof, Howard	6, 8, 11, 32
Naftalin, Arthur	1, 3, 5, 6, 30
Patman, Wright	8, 13
Percy, Charles	8, 13
Pritchard, Allan	2, 5, 6
Rafsky, William	3, 4, 8, 11, 19, 23, 25
Rains, Albert	13
Reuther, Walter	2, 6, 10, 19, 21
Ribicoff, Abraham	8, 13
Robin, John P.	3, 4, 23, 25
Rouse, James	2, 3, 6, 10, 29
Semer, Milton	7, 4, 10, 13
Schussheim, Morton J.	7
Slayton, William	2, 6, 7, 8, 10, 19, 23, 24
Sparkman, John	8, 9, 13
Stahl, David	4, 6, 19, 23, 25
Steiner, Richard	3, 4, 7, 10, 19, 25
Tate, James	1, 3, 5, 6, 10
Taylor, Ralph	7, 8, 10, 11, 19
Tufo, Peter	4, 6, 25
Weaver, Robert	3, 7, 19

* Positions were compiled in June, 1969. Some reshuffling occurred in 1970. This list leaves out a great many urban policy activists because it is intended only to briefly illustrate the point that a number of *individuals* as well as institutions continuously reappear in the federal-urban decision-making process.

Overlap Between Task Forces, Established Government Officials and Interest Groups;
Further Examples of Linkage in the Urban Policy Subsystem

1. The Kaiser Commission task force on Urban Housing (President's Committee on Urban Housing, 1969) named the following as "consultants."

   National Association of Housing and Redevelopment Officials

   National Association of Home Builders

   National Association of Real Estate Boards

   National Housing Conference

   James Nelson
   Peter Kiewit Sons Co.

   Mary Nenno
   National Association of Housing & Redevelopment Officials

William Rafsky
President, National Association of Housing and
    Redevelopment

Robert C. Wood, Under Secretary
Department of Housing and Urban Development

Robert E. McCabe
Deputy Assistant Secretary for Renewal Assistance
Department of Housing and Urban Development

Edward J. Logue, President
New York State Urban Development Corporation

James A. Lyons, Jr.
National Association of Home Builders

Lawrence M. Cox, Executive Director
Norfolk Redevelopment and Land Agency

William C. Wheaton
Dean, College of Environment Design
University of California, Berkeley

John Williamson
National Association of Real Estate Boards

Hugh Mields, Consultant
Washington, D. C.

Philip N. Brownstein
Assistant Secretary-Commissioner for Mortgage Credit and
    Federal Housing, Department of Housing and Urban
    Development

Ralph Johnson
Staff Vice President
NAHB Research Foundation

Thomas Appleby
Executive Director, D. C. Redevelopment & Land Agency

Jack Conway
United Automobile, Aircraft and Agricultural Workers of
America, CIO

David L. Krooth
Attorney at Law, Washington, D.C.

Ralph Taylor
Assistant Secretary for Demonstrations and Intergovernmental
Relations, Department of Housing and Urban Development

U.S. Conference of Mayors

Nathaniel Rogg
Director, National Association of Home Builders

Most of the above individuals and groups are well established
members of the urban policy subsystem (see Appendix III). The
President of the USCM (Barr) and of the NAHB (Weiner) were
full members of the Kaiser Commission.

2. *The Douglas Commission* (President's Commission on Urban
   Problems, 1968) was headed by former Senator Paul Douglas,
   floor manager of the 1949 Housing Act and Chairman of the
   subcommittee on housing. Some of the other members include:

Richard Ravitch
Director, NHC
Member, N.Y. State Urban Development Corporation

Lewis Davis
Mayor's Advisory Commission on Housing, NYC

Chloethiel Woodward Smith
Former chief of research and planning, FHA
Director, NHC

Tom Vandergriff
Mayor, Arlington, Texas
NLC

Coleman Woodbury
Formerly Executive Director, NAHRO;
Assistant Administrator, NHA

Secretary Robert Weavery and Under Secretary Robert Wood, of HUD, both played a considerable role in this task force. Nathaniel Keith and Milton Semer, both important individual participants in the urban policy system (see Appendix III) served as consultants.

The following mayors from the USCM Executive Committee (and members of NLC) served as witnesses: McKeldin (Baltimore), d'Allessandro, Barr (Pittsburgh), Currigan (Denver), Cavanagh (Detroit), Allen (Atlanta), Tate (Philadelphia), Welch (Houston), Lindsay (New York), Lee (New Haven).

Witnesses and consultants also included James Rouse, Richard Steiner, David Krooth, Lawrence Cox, William Slayton, Edward Logue, Walter Reuther, and ArDee Ames, all shown in Chapter 3 to be important individual actors (see Appendix III for other affiliations).

Finally, the following organizations were officially thanked by the Commission for their cooperation and participation:

ASPO
AIP
RPA
NAHB
NAHRO
USCM
NLC
ICMA
ACIR

Programs Administered by the Department of Housing and Urban Development*

Federal Housing Administration

    FHA home mortgage insurance
        Regular homeownership housing
        Servicemen's housing
        Low- and moderate-income housing
        Homeownership housing for low-income families
        Rent Supplement program
        Regular rental housing
        Low- and moderate-income rental housing
        Cooperative housing
        Nursing homes
        Housing for the elderly or handicapped
        Condominiums
        Experimental housing
        Home improvement loans
        Land development and new communities
        Group medical practices facilities

* U.S. Senate, Committee on Banking and Currency, 90th Congress, 1st Session, "Progress Report on Federal Housing Programs, May 9, 1967.

282

Metropolitan Development Programs

    Land and facilities development administration
        Urban planning grant program
        Incentive to planned metropolitan development
        Open space land and urban beautification
        Basic water and sewer facilities grants
        Advance acquisition of land for community facilities
        Public facility loans
        Public works planning advances

Demonstrations and Intergovernmental Relations Programs

        Model cities program
        Urban information and technical assistance
        Metropolitan expeditor program
        Community development training program
        Fellowships for city planning
        Urban research and technology
        Low-income housing demonstration programs

Veterans' Administration

        Home loan guarantee program
        Direct loan program

Federal Home Loan Bank Board

        Savings and mortgage lending activities
        Federal Savings and Loan Advisory Council

Example of Joint
USCM-NLC
Urban Renewal Survey

Urban Renewal Survey	*Summary of Results*	
1. Questionnaires sent		896
2. Questionnaires returned		548
3. Questionnaires returned blank		−98
4. Useful questionnaires		450
a) Cities with urban renewal projects under contract	387	
b) Cities with only completed projects, none now in planning or execution	16	
c) Cities not now in program, planning to start	47	
	450	

(dollars in thousands)

5. Total Renewal Grant Dollars under contract (387 cities)
This represents 77.7 percent of the total $5,400.0 authorized by

the Congress through June 30,
1966 $ 4,162.1

6. Total renewal grant dollars in
   applications pending for survey
   and planning, loan and grant,
   increases; codes, demolition, rehabilitation and relocation (219
   cities) $ 1,517.8

7. Total requests to be made 1967-
   1969
   Approximately $212.1 million of
   this is for relocation (337 cities) $ 3,888.7

8. Total requests to be made 1970-
   1976 Approximately $494.8 mil-
   lion of this is for relocation (229
   cities) $ 4,969.5

9. GRAND TOTAL OF RE-
   QUESTS FROM 450 CITIES
   FOR PERIOD 1966-1976 $10,376.0

Membership Chart

Population	1966 *Number of Cities in the U.S.*	*Non-Members*
750,000 and over	10	None
500,000-750,000	16	San Francisco* San Antonio Seattle*
400,000-500,000	9	None
300,000-400,000	12	Oakland* St. Paul
200,000-300,000	19	Albuquerque* Des Moines Tucson*
100,000-200,000	69	19 Non-Members Salt Lake City Spokane, Springfield, Mass., Savannah, Tacoma*, Patterson, Erie, Chattanooga,* Kansas City (Kansas), Topeka, Beaumont Canton, Berkeley, New Bedford
50,000-100,000	183	75 Non-Members
30,000-50,000	267	144 Non-Members

Total eligible 569 Total Non-
members 246

* Cities that have since rejoined.

Notes

CHAPTER I

1. T. S. Eliot, "The Hollow Men," in *Collected Works* (New York: Harcourt, Brace, and World, 1934), p. 79.

2. These two phrases were borrowed from an unpublished lecture by Professor Irving Kristol, given March 15, 1970, at New York University.

3. Quoted from an unpublished lecture by Professor Robert Wood, Radner Lecture Series, March 1970, at Columbia University.

4. Kristol, *op. cit.*

5. Daniel P. Moynihan, "Towards a National Urban Policy," unpublished speech delivered at Syracuse, New York, May 8, 1969.

6. Bruce L. R. Smith, "The Study of Science Affairs," *Journal of International Affairs* (1969).

7. Frederick Cleveland, *Congress & Urban Problems* (Washington, D. C.: Brookings Institute, 1969), pp. 2-3.

8. For a thorough discussion of the growth of federal programs operating in urban areas, see Robert Connery and Richard Leach, *The Federal Government in Metropolitan Areas* (Cambridge: Harvard University Press, 1960).

9. That the cities now have this status has been documented by Roscoe Martin in *The Cities and the Federal System* (New York: Atherton Press, 1965).

10. Moynihan, *op. cit.* p. 20.

11. See U.S. Bureau of the Budget, Circulars A-85 and A-90.

12. Some of these models of community power structure are: Floyd Hunter's "hierarchical" model in *Community Influentials*, Edward Banfield's "issues bubbling to the surface and ratified by the mayor" in *City Politics*, Robert Dahl's "executive centered coalition" in *Who Governs*, and Wallace Sayre's "separate issue sovereignties" in *Governing N.Y.C.*

289

13. Definition in *The Public Interest,* quarterly (New York: Basic Books) cover page, motto.

14. An excellent discussion of the role of the USCM in poverty program changes is found in Steven David, "Leadership by the Poor in the Poverty Program," Academy of Political Science, *Proceedings,* Summer, 1969.

15. David Truman, *The Governmental Process* (New York: Alfred Knopf, 1954).

16. See L. Dexter, R. Bauer and I. de Sola Pool, *American Business and Public Policy* (Cambridge: MIT Press, 1964).

17. E. E. Schattschneider, *The Semi-Sovereign People* (New York: Holt, Rinehart, and Winston, 1960).

18. Theodore Lowi, "Interest Groups Liberalism," *American Political Science Review,* June 1966.

19. This is a very diverse group, some of whom are PPBS practitioners, some admirers, some analysts, some critics, and some idealists who would simply *like* to think in terms of "overall policy," "rational choice," "comprehensive planning" and "cost benefit analysis." Different aspects of the PPBS dialogue may be found in the recent writings of Robert Wood, Briton Harris, Mancur Olsen, William Gorham, Daniel Bell, Bruce L. R. Smith, David Novick and Charles Hitch.

20. Robert Wood, "Incremental Policy Making: On Tides and Trends," unpublished lecture delivered at the University of Alabama, no date indicated. The ideas about intervening elites are his as well.

21. David Easton and Robert Dahl.

22. Harold Wolman, *The Housing Policy System,* unpublished doctoral dissertation, University of Michigan, 1968.

23. See Cleveland, *op. cit.* pp. 375 ff.

24. *Ibid.,* p. 7.

25. This observation is also made in an introduction to Cleveland's book by Kermit Gordon, President of the Brookings Institute.

CHAPTER II

1. For early history of these groups and their inter-relations, see Louis Brownlow, *A Passion for Anonymity* (Chicago: University of Chicago, 1958), *passim.*

2. *Ibid.,* p. 235.

3. The activities of the USCM in bringing about these results are documented in *Materials Sent to Mayors,* unpublished, but compiled by USCM. These contain records and accounts of meetings, hearings, correspondence, drafts of legislation and other material quoted or referred to throughout the section of the USCM in the early 1930's. The material for the sections on the Relief and Public Works activities of the Conference

was also pieced together from other unnamed and unpublished files of the USCM.

4. Scott Greer, *Urban Renewal and American Cities* (New York: Bobbs-Merrill Co., 1965), p. 19.

5. A good discussion of the difficulties in interpreting these definitions may be found in Greer, *op. cit.*, pp. 20-27.

6. A few more examples of these relations are the following: the House version of the Taft-Ellender-Wagner Bill was introduced in 1947 by Congressman Jacob Javits (Republican, New York). He later moved to the Senate and became a member of the Banking and Currency Committee, the Government Operations Committee, and of the Appropriations Committee, all strategic places for urban legislation. Senator John Sparkman, a freshman in 1946, became increasingly active in the processing of the Act of 1949, became chairman of the subcommittee on housing of the Senate Banking and Currency Committee and then of the full committee (as of 1970).

The Urban Alliance's lobbying strategist for Model Cities in the House was Albert Rains, who had, in 1966, retired as chairman of the House Banking and Currency Committee as well as of the subcommittee on housing. Rains was another key legislator whose close relationship with the USCM and continuous involvement in urban legislation developed during the period immediately after passage of the 1949 act. Sparkman and Rains occupied central positions in the process of accommodation required to pass legislation considered critical by urban groups, especially during the Eisenhower years. Other individuals who have been important in the field of urban policy and established close relationships with the USCM and its allies, and who began their "urbanist" careers during this period were Hubert Humphrey and John Barriere. Humphrey, then Democratic Senator from Minnesota, was active in the 1949 bill. He eventually became a member of the inter-governmental relations subcommittee of the Committee on Government Operations, another strategic spot for urban affairs. Later, as Vice President of the United States, he served as President Johnson's liaison man for the cities.

John Barriere was chief of staff of the housing subcommittee of the House from 1949 to 1965, during which time he developed stable working relations with the staffs of the urban interest groups, the housing and urban bureaucracy, and the Congressmen interested in establishing "urban" records. He has been a member of the 1960 Presidential urban task force, a frequent guest at the working subcommittee meetings of the USCM, and since 1965, assistant to speaker of the House John McCormack as staff director of the Democratic Steering Committee.

7. Cleveland, *op. cit.*, p. 11.

8. James Sundquist, *Politics and Policy*, (Washington, D. C.: Brookings Institute, 1968), pp. 325-326.

9. *Ibid.*

10. The inter-relations among groups discussed here and in succeeding chapters were discovered by the author by going through early publications and internal documents of all of these organizations, correlating names with those found in United States Government organizations manuals and Congressional Directories. They are not documented as such in any other single place.

The general reference material has come from the author's direct interviews and correspondence, from letters, telegrams, bulletins, and reports found in interest group files, and *Proceedings* for the years referred to of the meetings of the various groups. In addition, the following items and publications not previously footnoted were of particular use in this chapter:

Truman, *op. cit.,* passim.

Resolution on the permanent organization of the USCM, February 17, 1933.

USCM, *The USCM: History, Activities and Organization,* 1953.

American Municipal Association, *Proceedings,* 1931-1935 (Chicago).

Connery and Leach, *op. cit.*

NHC, "This is NHC," undated pamphlet.

Correspondence to the author from Mr. Nathaniel Keith, President, NHC, July 8, 1969.

NAHRO, *Public Housing Surveys* (Chicago: 1934).

NAHRO, "State Laws for Public Housing," prefatory note (Chicago: Lakeside Press, 1934).

Letter to the Chairman and Executive Officers of local housing authorities from Charles Asher of NAHRO, dated June 12, 1934.

Helen Ingram, "Congress and Housing Policy" (unpublished Ph.D. dissertation, Columbia University, 1967).

William E. Leuchtenberg, *Franklin D. Roosevelt and the New Deal* (New York: Harper Torchbooks, 1963).

Ashley Foard and Hilbert Fefferman, "Federal Urban Renewal Legislation," *Law and Contemporary Politics,* XXV, No. 4 (Autumn, 1960).

U.S. Congress, House, Committee on Banking and Currency, *The Housing Act of 1949: A Handbook,* July 27, 1949.

U.S. President's Commission on Government Housing Policies and Programs (Eisenhower Task Force), *Report to the President* (Washington, D. C.: Government Printing Office, 1954).

CHAPTER III

1. Selecting one year as typical, in 1960, the Senate Banking and Currency Committee included members from New York (Jacob Javits), New Jersey (Harrison Williams), Illinois (Paul Douglas), Pennsylvania (Joseph Clark), and Connecticut William Bush). All represented highly urbanized states containing some of the largest cities in the United States. Senator John Sparkman (Alabama), whose expertise has already been noted, and

Edmund Muskie (Maine), whose special interest in urban matters is now familiar to the public, were also members.

2. These qualifications are especially true of Senators Clark (retired), Douglas (retired), Muskie, Williams, Javits, Sparkman, and Congressmen Albert Rains (retired), Thomas Ashley, and William Widnall.

3. The six who have been on the Banking and Currency Committee for at least ten years are William Barrett, Leonor Sullivan, Thomas Ashley, Henry Reuss, William Widnall, and Florence Dwyer. Considering the full committee, Chairman Wright Patman has been on the Banking and Currency Committee since 1937, Albert Gore since 1937, Albert Rains from 1948 to 1966, and Abraham Multer since 1948.

4. To give a few other examples: Senator Javits of New York has been a member of the Banking and Currency Committee and the Government Operations Committee, as was Senator Robert Kennedy of New York. Javits also has been on the Appropriations Committee. Senator Hubert Humphrey served on the Banking and Currency and Government Operations Committees; Senator William Proxmire was on the Banking and Currency and Appropriations Committees; Representative Dwyer of New York is also on Banking and Currency and Government Operations Committees and ACIR. These are only examples and do not represent the full extent of overlap or rotation.

5. Professor Harold Wolman, in his research on the politics of housing, found that "influentials" in federal housing policy were identifiable and that these individuals vary according to the stage of the policy process.

6. This was found to be the case in the three years analyzed (1967 to 1969) among the USCM, the NLC, the Urban Coalition, Urban America, the NHC, NAHRO, and several individual spokesmen from HUD and the Congressional Banking and Currency Committees.

7. ACIR, *Report* (1968), Chapter 2, pp. 11-12, and Chapter 1, p. 1.

8. Urban America, *City* (1969), p. 2.

9. Urban America, *The Non-Profit Housing Center* (Washington, D. C., 1968), p. 1.

10. USCM and NLC, *America's Urban Challenge*, (July, 1968), p. 1 and p. 7.

11. USCM, *Proceedings*, 1969, p. 164.

12. Urban Coalition, "Resolutions," 1967.

13. *Ibid.*, January 23, 1969.

14. NAHRO, "Program and Resolutions," October 15, 1958, p. 3.

15. NHC, "Resolutions," 1968, Chapter A.

16. Congressional Record, 90th Cong., 2nd sess., (307-187-12742).

17. President Richard Nixon, as quoted by Assistant Secretary of HUD, Lawrence Cox, in an address to USCM, June 17, 1969. Reprinted in USCM, *Proceedings*, 1969, p. 55.

18. President Nixon, Message, "Transmitting the First Annual Report on National Housing Goals," *House Doc. No. 91-63*, 91st Cong., 1st sess., January 23, 1969.

19. Remarks by George Romney to USCM, *Proceedings*, 1969.

20. Remarks by Lawrence Cox to USCM, *Proceedings*, 1969, p. 61.

21. Remarks to USCM by Representative Thomas Ashley, *Proceedings*, 1969, p. 82-85.

22. For HUD position, see Assistant Secretary Cox's remarks in USCM *Proceedings*, 1969, pp. 66-67; also interview data; for ACIR position, see ACIR, *Report*, 1968, p. 12; for USCM's position, see *Proceedings*, 1969, Resolution No. 4 or discussion at Community Development Committee meeting on June 16, 1969 (attended by author); for NLC's position, see NLC, National Municipal Policy, 1967, paragraph 1:29; also interview with Director; for the Urban Coalition's position, see Urban Coalition, "Working Papers for Task Force on Housing," July 28, 1969; for Kaiser Commission's position, see President's Committee on Urban Housing, 1968, "Summary of Recommendations"; for Douglas Commission's position, see President's *Commission on Urban Problems*, 1968; for Sparkman's position, see Address by Senator Sparkman before the 37th Convention of the NHC, inserted in *Congressional Record, op. cit.*, p. 1; for Urban America's position, see Urban America, *Housing Center;* for NHC's "Resolutions," 1968, Chapter G, No. 8.

23. ACIR, *Report*, 1967 and 1968.

24. USCM, *U.S. Municipal News*, XXXVI, No. 4.

25. Sparkman speech, *Congressional Record, op. cit.*

26. USCM, *Proceedings*, 1967-1969, *passim.*

27. NLC, *Policy*, 1967.

28. Correspondence to author from William Slayton, Director, Urban America, dated July 8, 1969.

29. For example, the ACIR refers to the list of reports issued by the Urban Coalition. Likewise, the NLC comments that "several Congressmen are considering the possibility of introducing legislation this year which will follow the recommendations of the Advisory Commission on Intergovernmental Relations to the end that the larger cities will receive a fairer share of the grant funds being made available. Found in ACIR, *Report*, 1968, p. 2, and NLC, "Federal City Reporter," January 22, 1963, p. 3.

30. Urban Coalition, *Action Report*, October 31, 1967, list of National Steering Committee Members.

31. ACIR, *Annual Report*, 1967.

32. NLC, *National Municipal Policy*, (Washington, D. C., 1967) and USCM, Annual Proceedings (Washington, D. C., 1967).

33. USCM, Bulletin from the Director, March 23, 1960.

34. See references to these in speeches by HUD officials in USCM, *Annual Proceedings*, 1969.

35. Letter to the author from Nathaniel Keith, President of the NHC, dated July 8, 1969.

36. See, for example, letter to Senator Sparkman from Ira Robbins, President of NAHRO, 1964, commenting on NAHRO's subcommittee on

legislation and thanking Senator Sparkman and staff member Coan of the Banking and Currency Committee for their attendance. Also, see Urban Coalition, task force on Housing, Reconstruction, and Investment members.

37. Since 1967, (and as of Fall, 1970), the six Congressional ACIR members include two who are on *both* the Government Operations Committee and Banking and Currency Committee, and one on the Banking and Currency Committee and Appropriations Committee.

38. The annual convention of the USCM provides just such an opportunity. For example, Proceedings of the 1960 Annual Convention indicate that the meeting was addressed by Representatives David M. Walker and Albert Rains of the House Banking and Currency Committee; Representative John A. Blatnik of the House Public Work Committee; Senator Paul H. Douglas of the Senate Banking and Currency Committee, and Mayor Robert F. Wagner of New York. Similar examples are in the Appendix.

39. USCM, *U.S. Municipal News* (Washington, D. C., January 1, 1969).

40. Remarks by Vice President Agnew recorded in USCM, *Proceedings*, 1969, p. 156.

41. For expansion on the theme of the importance of bureacracy and the political process, see the works of Karl Deutsch.

42. Report of the working subcommittee to the Committee on Community Development, USCM, January, 1965. These people were Ralph Widner, William Slayton, Andrew Hickey, Laurence Henderson, Charles Horsky, Nathaniel Keith, and Jonathan Lindley.

43. Some of the members of the committee were: Don Slater, formerly NLC, of HEW; Ralph Taylor, NHC; Norman Beckman, formerly ACIR, of HUD in 1969; Kurt Aller of the Department of Labor; Bill Bozman of the Office of Economic Opportunity; Ross Davis of HUD; Jonathan Lindley, formerly Senate Banking and Currency staff, and legislative assistant to Senator Clark, of the Economic Development Administration; John Sweeney of the Department of Transportation; Walter Pozen of the Department of Interior; Patrick Murphy of the Office of Local Law Enforcement Assistance.

44. August 23, 1963.

45. Letter to author from Nathaniel Keith, President of the NHC, dated July 8, 1969.

46. Letter to author from William Slayton of Urban America, dated July 8, 1969.

47. All unattributed quotations throughout this book are from confidential interviews with USCM staff, mayors, HUD officials, Congressmen, committee staff, or others who have asked to remain anonymous.

CHAPTER IV

1. This author received substantially unanimous opinions from all respondents on most of the topics discussed. These opinions were substanti-
ated by the evidence found in analysis of documents. They were also
confirmed by the author's observations of the USCM during its five-day
Annual Conventions in both 1969 and 1970, and by other observations
made over a two-year period (1967-1969) during which time twelve trips
were made to Washington and a substantial amount of time was spent at
the Conference (with free access to the offices and files and staff).

Interviews with mayors were ½ hour; interviews with others were
usually one hour interviews. Since all were promised anonymity, material
quoted from the interviews will be identified only by the general position
of the speaker, i.e. "mayor" or HUD personnel. Quotations will be used to
illustrate a point only when the quote used represents a consensus.

The author is extremely grateful to the members of the USCM staff
for giving freely of their time, making available all files and correspondence, and for permitting almost constant use of the Conference offices
during these visits.

The analyses in this and the next chapter are based on interviews and
correspondence with 26 mayors, 17 city government staff people, eight
people working on the staff of the Banking and Currency Committees or
of Senators or Congressmen who are members of the committees, eight
officials of the Department of Housing and Urban Development, four city
lobbyists, seven other Executive branch officials (Office of Intergovernmental Relations, the Bureau of the Budget, Office of Economic Opportunity, Department of Transportation, Justice Department and Vice
President's office), and 12 members of urban interest group staff.

2. This is the purpose put forth by HUD Secretary Romney. There
will be one field office in each state and ten regional offices.

3. Jerome Cavanagh (Detroit), Samuel Yorty (Los Angeles), Kevin
White (Boston), Arthur Naftalin (Minneapolis), and Joseph Alioto (San
Francisco). Except for White, who had just been elected, the mayors were
very active in the organization—Naftalin and Cavanagh on the Executive
Committee, Yorty on the Advisory Board, and Alioto on the Resolution
Committee.

4. The staff members of several mayors indicated that this was the purpose of Agnew's early appearance and private meetings with their mayors.
However, the author has no way of verifying this point.

5. It must be pointed out that the constitutional membership of the
Conference consists of cities (as represented by their mayors), and the
actual membership consists of mayors. Therefore, there are two possible
kinds of turnover—withdrawal of cities themselves and change of repre-

sentation of the cities due to changes in their mayors. The ten to fifteen percent figure refers to mayoral turnover.

6. Naftalin (Minneapolis), Barr (Pittsburgh), Cavanagh (Detroit), Lee (New Haven), and Van Tassel (Tuscaloosa).

7. This observation is based on interviews and analyses of the issues and votes by the full membership at the annual conferences, and by the leadership in Resolutions Committee meetings. Minutes from several Executive Committee meetings were also analyzed. The data covers the period from 1960 to 1969. Since fairly homogeneous results were obtained it is not necessary to discuss all issues debated and voted on which produced one of the three types of cleavage. Any year's annual proceedings of the USCM reveal typical voter patterns, of which only select representative examples will be discussed. The North-South cleavage will be illustrated by the controversy surrounding passage of a "civil rights" resolution; the liberal-conservative division by the "school prayer" resolution; and the big city-small city cleavages by the controversy over a Cabinet-level Department of Urban Affairs. These three issues were chosen from among the many available because they were being concurrently debated in Congress. Analyses of Congressional debate, of the Congressional personalities involved, of the hearings held, and of the final votes on the measures were thus available to establish how they involved North-South, liberal-conservative, and big city-small city controversies, as these are generally recognized.

Data on the existence and type of cleavages in the organization was obtained mainly from six, one-to-two hour intensive interviews with each of the major staff members of the Conference. In addition, the discussions at the annual meetings and minutes of the Executive Committee and Advisory Board were analyzed. All unattributed quotations throughout this book are from interviews with Conference staff members. All quotations attributed to mayors are from the Annual Proceedings in the year indicated. However, since no discussion from the Annual Meetings was included in the records until 1961, and since the minutes do not include discussions, Conference documents were less valuable as a source of information than the interviews. The interviews are the main source for the material in this chapter.

8. Address by President Kennedy, USCM, *Annual Proceedings*, 1963.

9. Address by David Lawrence, USCM, *Proceedings*, 1963, p. 7.

10. USCM, "Resolutions," in *Proceedings*, 1963, Res. No. 28.

11. Discussion of Resolutions, *Ibid*.

12. Savannah, Memphis and Seattle. Interview with USCM staff.

13. This resolution and the discussion which follows was taken from the 1966 Proceedings of the USCM.

14. Truman, *op. cit.*

15. The account which follows is based on an article by Stephen David, "Leadership of the Poor in the Poverty Program," in *Proceedings of the American Academy of Political Science*, XXIX, No. 1, 1968.

16. USCM, *Proceedings*, 1964.

17. Wagner (New York), Daley (Chicago), Cavanagh (Detroit), Tucker (St. Louis), and Walsh (Syracuse) thus testified in Congress that control should be vested in the local government unit.

18. Donovan, *The Politics of Poverty* (New York: Pegasus, 1968).

19. See David, *op. cit.*, pp. 94 ff.

CHAPTER V

1. Quoted from interview with Conference staff.

2. It is not entirely clear whether it was really Betters or Mayor LaGuardia who was "running" the Conference during these first few years. However, it seems most likely that LaGuardia was quite busy getting New York "in order," at least during his first year in office (1934), and that since Betters was already entrenched with the Conference as of 1933, Betters had a great deal of influence. It is also not entirely clear that Betters himself had as much access to Roosevelt as the present Conference staff now attributes to him; thus "access" might have been "thanks to" LaGuardia. Complete clarification of this matter is not available. It seems sufficient to say that for whatever reason, Betters and Roosevelt did deal directly with each other, and that whatever LaGuardia's initial role, Betters did provide strong leadership for the organization.

3. November 11, 1942. Correspondence between Mayor LaGuardia and the USCM is filed with LaGuardia's papers in the N.Y.C. municipal archives.

4. Meeting of the Executive Committee, January, 1966.

5. In 1966, as one example, $80,000.00 out of a budget of $127,000.00 went for salaries.

6. USCM, *The Mayor and Federal Aid*, Washington, D. C., 1968.

7. *Ibid.*

8. USCM-NLC, "This is NLC-USCM," undated pamphlet.

9. *Ibid.*

10. For example, during 1963, the following people were connected with the Community Development Committee's working subcommittee: Robert Goe, Executive Assistant to the Mayor of Los Angeles and in 1969 Director of the Office of Intergovernmental Relations in the White House; Justin Herman, Director of the San Francisco Redevelopment Agency and NAHRO member; Thomas Appleby, Administrator of the New Haven Redevelopment Authority and NAHRO Vice President for urban renewal; John Duba, Director of Urban Renewal in Chicago; Robert Knox, Charles Farris, and Robert Pease, Directors of Urban Development in Detroit, St. Louis, and Pittsburgh, respectively, and all NAHRO members; Richard Steiner, Director of Housing and Urban Renewal in Baltimore, on the Board of Directors of the NHC, and previously a Federal Urban Renewal commissioner; Edward Logue, Administrator of the Boston Redevelopment

Authority, formerly a member of the subcommittee on Urban and Suburban Problems (1959), part of the Democrat's Advisory Committee (a policy Task Force) headed by Adlai Stevenson, the Development Administrator in New York City, and in 1969 head of the new New York State Development Corporation; William Rafsky, Development Coordinator of Philadelphia and in 1969 President of NAHRO and director of the NHC; Lawrence Cox, Director of Housing and Redevelopment in Norfolk, past President of NAHRO, and presently, President of the American Society of Planning Officials and in 1969 Assistant Secretary for Urban Renewal for HUD; B. T. Fitzpatrick, formerly general counsel of HHFA, a member of the 1959 Advisory Commission on Urban and Suburban Problems, and in 1969 a director of the NHC; Nathaniel Keith, President of the NHC, a member of the first USCM Committee on Slum Clearance in the 1940's and Urban Renewal Administrator of the HHFA from 1949 to 1953; John Barriere, staff director of the housing subcommittee of the House Banking and Currency Committee, assistant to the speaker of the House on the Democratic Steering Committee; Carl Coan, staff director of the Senate Banking and Currency Committee; Ralph Widner, legislative aide to Senator Joseph Clark of Pennsylvania, who was one of the most active senators in urban matters; Ardee Ames, legislative aide to Senator Harrison Williams of New Jersey and in 1969 assistant to Cox at HUD; Ira Robbins, President of NAHRO; Milton Semer, HHFA general counsel and formerly counsel to the Senate Banking and Currency housing subcommittee, and to the FHA and a director of the NHC; Phillip Brownstein, Commissioner of the FHA and also a director of the NHC; and William Wheaton, a director of NHC and the Director of the Institute for Urban Studies, University of Pennsylvania.

This list of people connected with the Community Development Committee in 1963 is not complete, but serves to show how different participants in the subsystem interact and overlap. The identity of the people involved was culled from the documents pertaining to the Committee for 1963; however, their various other urban-connected activities were gathered from lists of officials of all the other institutions mentioned.

11. The story which follows was told to this author by a HUD assistant secretary.

12. ACIR, *Report*, May, 1967.

13. Bureau of the Budget Circular A-85, June 28, 1967.

14. Easton, "The Child's Acquisition of Regime Norms," *American Political Science Review* (March, 1967), p. 25.

15. Members of the ACIR serve for two-year terms, but are eligible for re-election on an unlimited basis. As a result, the composition of hte ACIR has been quite stable, and this is important as far as its program-generating capacity is concerned. For example, Mayors Blaisdell, Naftalin, and Maltester have served as the mayor members since 1960. Mayor Walsh makes the fourth mayor member. Blaisdell is a past President of the Conference and on the Executive Committee of the NLC; Naftalin is Chairman of the

Advisory Board of the Conference, on the Advisory Board of the NLC, and the steering committee of the Urban Coalition; Maltester in 1969 is President of the USCM, and Walsh is on its Advisory Board. All these mayors have been continuously active in these various urban groups.

One of the Executive branch members of the ACIR is Price Daniel, Director of the Office of Emergency Planning. This body also has mayor members who, in 1967 to 1968 were Barr, Currigan, and Collins. Barr is a past President of the USCM, member of the NLC, and active in Urban America; Currigan is on the Advisory Board of the USCM and of the NLC and active in Urban America; Collins was a leading member of the Conference and active in Urban America. Thus, through Daniels who, as Director of OEP worked closely with these mayors (who in turn represented the attitudes of their group membership), ACIR incorporates an even wider spectrum of representation of members of the urban subsystem. Moreover, the assistant staff director of ACIR is David Walker, formerly Director of the Redevelopment Authority of Philadelphia, staff member of the House Government Operations Committee, and also on the Board of Directors of NHC. Consultants to the ACIR include such other participants in the urban policy process as the Assistant Director of the National Municipal League, Frank Cassella, and James Sundquist, former assistant to Senator Clark (a major "urban" Senator) and secretary to the Democratic Platform Committee in 1960. Finally, among the Congressional members of the ACIR are two members of the housing subcommittees, one from the House (Florence Dwyer) and one from the Senate (Edmund Muskie) through which most of the urban-oriented legislation has passed. In 1968, Governor Spiro Agnew of Maryland was added to the ACIR, and, as Vice President, he is now the President's chief man in charge of urban affairs and inter-governmental relations. Such overlapping membership, rotation of leadership, continuous contact, and other linkages among actors have been shown to be common to the urban policy subsystem in general and are, in fact, what constitute it as a subsystem.

This information has been accumulated from the 1968 records of the organizations mentioned.

CHAPTER VI

1. Although most of these people were those who wanted the Conference to take a more active role and may, therefore, be considered biased, it also is true that Conference policy vis-a-vis external targets must be viewed in terms of how much support it gives to those who request it for issues they consider "controversial."

2. NLC, *Policy*, 1967, p. 70.

3. USCM, "The USCM," undated pamphlet.

4. Patrick Healy, "The USCM and the NLC: A History of their

Activities and Relationship," unpublished working paper, January 25, 1967.

5. *Ibid.*

6. USCM, Draft Statement on National Priorities, Executive Committee, January, 1966.

7. USCM, *Proceedings,* 1966.

8. Pittsburgh Press, June 16, 1969, p. 1-2.

9. *New York Times,* June 16, 1969.

10. USCM, Resolution 1A, 1969.

11. USCM, *Proceedings,* 1966.

12. *Ibid.*

13. Urban America, Report, 1968.

14. Urban America, *City,* April, 1969, p. 3.

15. USCM, "Community Relations Service Report Special," June, 1968, decried these activities.

16. Letter to the author from William Slayton, Executive Vice President, Urban America, July 8, 1969.

17. Truman, *op. cit.,* 264-265.

18. USCM, "The USCM."

19. *Ibid.*

20. USCM, *Proceedings,* 1948.

21. *Ibid.,* 1955.

22. Lester Milbraith, *The Washington Lobbyists* (Chicago: Rand McNally, 1963), p. 83.

23. See Section 501 C3.

24. See Section 501 D3.

25. See, for example, U.S., Congress, Senate, Committee on Government Operations, *Federal Role in Urban Affairs,* Hearings before a subcommittee on Executive Reorganization, of the Committee on Government Operations, Senate, Parts 106, 89th Cong., 1st sess., 1966. This same situation may be seen in the hearings on the establishment of HUD on Demonstration Cities.

26. USCM, *Proceedings,* 1937.

27. Milbraith, *op. cit.,* pp. 227-228.

28. USCM, "Urban Renewal Survey," unpublished, 1966.

29. U.S. Congress, House, Committee on Banking and Currency, *Hearings* before a subcommittee on housing of the Committee on Banking and Currency, House of Representatives, on H.R. 12341, H.R. 12946, H.R. 13064, and H.R. 9256, 89th Cong., 2nd sess., 1966.

30. H.R. 642 and H.R. 644.

31. Memorandum to the mayors from John Gunther, January 31, 1967.

32. Copies of these letters were in the USCM file on this legislation.

CHAPTER VII

1. Analyses of resolutions of the NLC and USCM, 1960–1969, discussions with their staff, and interviews with Congressional and agency staff indicate these areas to be those in which NLC and USCM activity has been greatest.

The role of some of the urban groups in air and water pollution control is discussed in Sundquist, pp. 349-353 and pp. 367-371. Its contribution to mass transit legislation is mentioned by Royce Hanson in Cleveland, ed., *op. cit.*, pp. 331 ff., and some aspects of the USCM's involvement with the poverty program are discussed by David, "Programs," pp. 86-100.

2. This suspicion is shared by Royce Hanson in "Congress Copes with Mass Transit, 1960-1964," in Frederick Cleveland, ed., *op. cit.*

3. The "Green Amendment" to the poverty program had the effect of returning to local public officials (mayors) some of the control which had been given to citizens under the "maximum feasible participation" clause of the Economic Opportunity Act; it also moved the Head Start Program from OEO to HEW.

4. James Sundquist, *Politics and Policy*, p. 351.

5. Professor Robert Wood uses the term "Innovative Policy" for what I have called macro-policy. Both terms are used in contradiction to "incrementalism."

6. See Wheaton and Ingram, *op. cit.*, *passim*, and Greer, *American Cities*, p. 158.

7. Letter to mayors from Betters, July 28, 1949.

8. NAHRO and the NHC, for instance, felt that for the first time in our history, we now have a declaration of national policy defining the responsibility of the federal government on the right of every American to adequate shelter.

"There, at long last, is a national policy and purpose. The Housing Act of 1949 affords machinery every community may use . . ." This is by Lee F. Johnson, Executive Vice President of NHC, in "Victory at Last for Housing," *The Survey* (1949), p. 538. Johnson also identifies the major opponents as the well organized opposition of the real estate lobby, composed of spokesmen for the National Association of Real Estate Boards, the United States Savings and Loan League, the National Association of Home Builders, the United States Chamber of Commerce, the Producers Council (supported by materials manufacturers), and numerous satellite organizations. The supporters were identified as Administration, labor, all major veterans groups, citizens organizations, religious bodies, women's organizations, the United States Conference of Mayors, other municipal and state organizations, most of the American press, and others who consolidated the efforts of those who believed that the consumer's interest comes before that of the speculator.

This is of interest because the support-opposition dialogue on slum clearance, public housing, and low-income housing is still basically between these two coalitions.

9. Letter from Betters to mayors, July 28, 1949.

10. Memo to mayors from Executive Director, October 13, 1949.

11. The Mields document is unpublished and is dated February 8, 1961. The digest referred to is, "Brief Digest of the Principal Provision in Housing Act of 1961" (S. 1922) "as agreed to by the conferees," June 27, 1961.

12. The particular "preferences" of the Conference have been ascertained from analysis of Conference documents, Congressional hearings, and interviews, at which the interviewee was asked, "What would you say are the particular characteristics of the Conference's role in these programs? What specific kinds of things has it stressed that in some way distinguish it from other groups?"

13. Letter to the President of the United States from Mayor Lee of New Haven (on the Advisory Board, Executive Committee and President of the Conference), dated June 29, 1959. Copies to Hugh Mields of NLC-USCM and James Sundquist.

14. Greer, *American Cities*, p. 19.

15. Foard and Fefferman, *op. cit.*, p. 675, as quoted in Greer, *op. cit.*, p. 28. Both of these works document the role of the USCM's in raising the percentage of funds allowable for commercial renewal and in raising the percentage of federal contribution.

16. The locality's contribution may take the form of cash or non cash credits, such as donations of land, demolition and removal work.

17. Statement by USCM staff chairman to the 1969 Community Development Committee, June 15, 1969.

18. U.S. President's Commission on Housing Policies and Programs, *Report to the President*, December, 1953.

19. U.S. Congress, Senate, Committee on Banking and Currency, *Progress Report on Federal Housing Program*, Senate, 90th Cong., 1st sess., May 9, 1967, p. 87.

20. Greer, p. 10.

21. "Demonstration Cities," and "Model Cities" will be used interchangeably as is done in most federal documents. The name of the program has been officially changed to "Model Cities."

22. USCM, "The Urban Development Act of 1966," (S. 2977), April 21, 1966, unpublished analysis.

24. William Alonso, "The Mirage of New Towns," *The Public Interest*, Spring, 1970, p. 17.

25. *New York Times*, November 4, 1966.

26. *Ibid.*

27. USCM, *Proceedings*, 1966.

28. Mayor Collins of Boston in particular wanted this change; Minutes of Executive Committee meeting, January, 1966.

29. The "bargain" between these groups and the resulting addition of

new materials to the Model Cities Act is seen in the discussion of the act's passage by Dick Cherry, "History of Congressional Action Relative to Model Cities, 1966-1967," compiled for use by HUD, October 3, 1967, unpublished document.

30. This term was coined by Professor Robert Wood.

31. Theodore Lowi, "Interest Group Liberalism," *American Political Science Review* (March, 1967), p. 10.

32. U.S. Congress, Senate, Committee on Banking and Currency, *Progress Report on Federal Housing Programs, Hearings* before a subcommittee on Housing of the Committee on Banking and Currency, Senate, 90th Cong., 1st sess., May 9, 1967, p. 87.

33. Letter requesting this draft to Milton Semer, counsel to HHFA, from Hugh Mields. Reply from Semer to Mields July 25, 1963.

34. Morton Schussheim, "Housing Policy in the Sixties: An Assessment," CED, 1970 (Washington).

35. Interview data, as corroborated by Hugh Mields and unpublished files.

36. *Ibid*

37. Compare housing program recommendations, *Report of the National Commission on Urban Problems to the Congress and to the President of the United States;* House Doc. No. 91-34, pp. 180ff., with "Resolutions of the USCM" *Proceedings*, 1963-1968, especially Nos. 16, 1968; 3, 1964; 6, 1965; 29, 1963; 13, 1965; and 9, 1965.

38. *Report of the President's Commission on Urban Housing*, Appendix G, p. 235.

39. Robert Gladstone Assoc., *Housing Supply and Demand*, study done for Kaiser Commission. Mields himself did not participate in this study.

40. Staff memo to mayors Don Hummel and Richardson Delworth, January, 1961.

41. Nathan Glazer, "On Task Forcing," *The Public Interest*, Spring, 1969, p. 41.

42. *Ibid.*, p. 42.

43. Karl Deutsch, *The Nerves of Government* (New York: The Free Press, 1966), *passim.*

44. Micro-policy is intended to mean the results of the type of decision-making process widely described as "incrementalism," especially throughout the works of Aaron Wildavsky and Charles Lindblom.

45. Harold Wolman, "Politics and Public Policy: A Study of the Housing Political System" unpublished Ph.D. dissertation, University of Michigan, 1968.

46. Wolman, p. 322, 323.

CHAPTER VIII

1. A good discussion of this appears in Martha Derthick, *The Influence of Federal Grants*, (Cambridge: Harvard University Press, 1970), p. 15 ff.
2. Truman, *op. cit.*, p. 65.
3. This statement is incomplete and subject to qualification. However, it is simplistically put in order to make a point about municipal finances, and a discussion of federal rebates, deductions for state taxes, political constraints on state taxation, etc. would be extraneous here. For similar reasons, the various ways in which city authority to raise revenues are circumscribed (varying, of course, from state to state) are also not discussed here. However, the author is not unaware of oversimplification employed at this point simply to direct attention to why the cities lobby primarily for money.
4. Greer, *op. cit.*, p. 166.
5. Charles Abrams, "The Practical Administration of the U.S. Housing Act of 1937," published as a manuscript to be circulated by American Federation of Housing Authorities, Washington, D. C., September 2, 1937.
6. Remarks by Secretary Romney to the USCM, June 17, 1969.
7. Greer, p. 158, quoting from Brownfield, "The Disposition Problems in Urban Renewal," *Law and Contemporary Problems*, XXV, No. 4 (Autumn, 1960), p. 735.
8. Greer, *op. cit.*, p. 166.
9. Morton Schussheim, "Urban Renewal and Local Economic Development."
10. Some examples: *The Pittsburgh Gazette*, on June 16, 1969, when the USCM was meeting in that city, records on its front page:

> Mayor Kevin H. White of Boston, asked to comment on a recent statement by Pittsburgh Mayor Joseph M. Barr that American cities are going bankrupt, said, "That's our (the USCM's) highest priority, getting adequate finances.

Or similarly, in the *Pittsburgh Press*, June 18, 1969:

> The leaders of 500 American cities will be leaving Pittsburgh today, but not without issuing a stiff warning to Congress that they need money—and plenty of it.

> The warning is contained in 25 proposals expected to be passed in the final meeting of the U.S. Conference of Mayors at the Hilton Hotel today. Squeezed into the proposals are requests for Federal aid for poverty, housing, transportation, control of pollution, inner city decay and crime, to name a few.

> And the mayors want the money directly—without interference or delay from additional administrative staffs at the state level.

Similar articles appeared in the *New York Times,* the *Chicago Tribune,* the *Washington Post,* and most of the major newspapers in large cities. These articles suggest that the media has picked up not only the urban lobbyists' priorities for money—"and plenty of it"—but also reflect the implication that their demands must be made in terms of proposals for specific projects. This is relevant to appraising the responsibilities of the urban interest groups for the consequences of the programs they supported. If considerations of the program itself were secondary to consideration of the financial aid it would bring cities, and if the reason program considerations were secondary were that the federal government could not have granted aid except by vehicle of the specific project and formula grant, then the balance of merits and demerits awarded the urban interest group shifts. They should get more credit for implementing one of the cities' primary interests —channeling more funds directly to cities—and less blame for the perhaps unforeseeable ill effects of their secondary goals, or means—the specific programs themselves.

11. Derthick, *op. cit.,* p. 10.

12. *Ibid.,* p. 16.

13. John Donovan, *The Politics of Poverty* (New York: Pegasus, 1967), p. 45.

14. The many different versions of revenue-sharing plans will not be discussed. Even under the most extensive revenue-sharing proposals, however, there would be some federal guidelines, some programs still to be under federal administration, and some areas in which cities still had to deal with states.

15. Edward Banfield, "Why Government Cannot Solve the Urban Problem," *Daedalus,* Summer 1969.

Selected Bibliography

PRIMARY SOURCES

1. Interest Group Material

Advisory Commission on Intergovernmental Relations. *Annual Reports.* 1961-1969.

———. *Factors Affecting Voter Reactions to Government Reorganization in Metropolitan Areas.* Washington, D. C., 1965.

———. *Intergovernmental Relations in the Poverty Program.* Washington, D. C., 1966.

———. Membership lists, selected publications.

American Municipal Association. *Proceedings: 1931-1935.* Chicago, 1936.

Division of the Budget, New York State. "Congressional Action in Federal Grant in Aid Programs." 1968-1969. Unpublished document.

LaGuardia, Fiorello. Correspondence with the USCM, 1935-1945. Unpublished.

National Association of Housing and Redevelopment Officials. *Resolutions.*

———. *Public Housing Surveys.* Chicago, 1934.

———. *State Laws for Public Housing.* Chicago: Lakeside Press, 1934.

———. *A Housing Program for the United States.* Chicago, 1934.

———. Assorted documents, pamphlets, correspondence, annual reports, and membership lists.

National Housing Conference. *This is NHC.* Washington, D. C. Undated pamphlet.

————. *Resolutions.* 1960-1969, Washington, D. C.

————. Selected pamphlets, membership lists, resolutions, internal committee reports and annual reports.

National League of Cities. *National Municipal Policy.* Washington, D. C., 1960-1969. Separate volumes.

————. *Nation's Cities.* Selected issues.

National League of Cities. *Proceedings.* Washington, D. C., Selected years.

Office of the Mayor and City Administrator. "Study of Federal Aid Available to New York City." December, 1964. Unpublished document.

United States Conference of Mayors, *City Problems: The Annual Proceedings of the USCM.* Washington, D. C., 1933-1969. Separate volumes.

————. Minutes of the Advisory Board. 1963-1966. Unpublished.

————. *Federal-City Relations.* Washington, D. C. Selected issues.

————. *U.S. Municipal News.* Washington, D. C. Selected issues.

————. Reports to the Executive Committee by the USCM's Committee on Community Development and the Community Relations Service. Selected reports. Unpublished.

————. "Constitution." Unpublished.

————. *The USCM: History, Activities, and Organization.* Washington, D. C., 1953.

————. Memoranda from the Executive Director. Unpublished.

————. *Municipal and Intergovernmental Finance.* Washington, D. C., 1953.

————. *America Cannot Afford Slums.* Washington, D. C., 1947.

————. *The Federal Municipal Debt Adjustment Act.* Washington, D. C.

————. *Wartime Financial Problems of Cities.* Washington, D. C., 1942.

————. *The Municipal Airport in the National Airport Program.* Washington, D. C., 1945.

————. "Desk Files." Compiled for mayors. Unpublished.

————. *Economic Opportunity in Cities.* Washington, D. C., 1966.

————. *The Mayor and Federal Aid.* Washington, D. C., 1968.

————. "Permanent Organization of the USCM." 1933. Unpublished memo.

————. *Materials Sent to Mayors.* 1933-1969. Bound volumes for each year.

————. *Mayors' Bulletin.* Selected issues.

————. Files, **correspondence**, collected documents, communications with Congressional and Executive officials, with cities, other groups, drafts of bills, accumulated comments, and files on each subject matter of USCM activity.

United States Conference of Mayors. Minutes of the Meetings of the Executive Committee. 1963-1966. Unpublisher.

―――. *Reports of the Community Relations Service.* 1965-1969. Washington, D. C.

―――, and National League of Cities. "Urban Renewal Surveys." Selected years. Unpublished.

―――, and National League of Cities. "USCM and NCL: A Staff Paper Describing their History, Activities and Relationships." January 25, 1967. Unpublished.

Urban America. Selected pamphlets, membership lists, resolutions, internal committee reports and annual reports.

―――. Urban America. Washington, D. C., 1966.

―――. *City.* A bi-monthly publication of Urban America. Selected issues.

―――. *The Non-Profit Housing Center.* Washington, D. C. Undated pamphlet.

―――. *Annual Reports.* 1966-1969. Washington, D. C.

Urban Coalition. Resolutions, annual reports, committee agenda, and membership lists.

2. Legislative Material

U.S. Congress. House. Committee on Banking and Currency. *Amendments to the National Housing Act. Hearings* before the Committee on Banking and Currency, House of Representatives, on H.R. 8520, 75th Cong., 2nd sess., 1937.

U.S. Congress. House. Committee on Banking and Currency. *Amendments of 1939 to the United States Housing Act. Hearings* before the Committee of Banking and Currency, House of Representatives, on S. 591, 76th Cong., 1st sess., 1939.

U.S. Congress. House. Committee on Banking and Currency. *Amendments of 1939 to National Housing Act.* Hearings before the Committee on Banking and Currency, House of Representatives, on H.R. 3232, 76th Cong., 1st sess., 1939.

U.S. Congress. Senate. Committee on Banking and Currency. *To Amend the National Housing Act. Hearings* before a subcocmittee of the Committee on Banking and Currency, on S. 1097, 76th Cong., 1st sess., 1939.

U.S. Congress. Senate. Committee on Banking and Currency. *General*

Housing Act of 1945. Hearings before the Committee on Banking and Currency, Senate, on S. 1592, 79th Cong., 1st sess., 1945.

U.S. Congress. Senate. Committee on Banking and Currency. *Housing. Hearings* before the Committee on Banking and Currency, Senate, on S. 287, S. 866, S. 701, S. 801, S. 802, S. 803, and S. 804, 80th Cong., 1st sess., 1947.

U.S. Congress. House. Committee on Banking and Currency. *General Housing. Hearings* before the Committee on Banking and Currency House of Representatives, on S. 866, 80th Cong., 2nd sess., 1948.

U.S. Congress. House. Committee on Banking and Currency. *The Housing Act of 1949: A Handbook.* Washington, D. C., July 27, 1949.

U.S. Congress. Senate. Committee on Banking and Currency. *Housing Amendments of 1949. Hearings* before a subcommittee of the Committee on Banking and Currency, Senate, on S. 2246, 81st Cong., 1st sess., 1949.

U.S. Congress. Senate. Committee on Banking and Currency. *Middle-Income Housing. Hearings* before the Committee on Banking and Currency, Senate, on S. 2246, 81st Cong., 2nd sess., 1950.

U.S. Congress. Senate. Committee on Banking and Currency. *Housing Act of 1954. Hearings* before the Committee on Banking and Currency, Senate, on S. 2889, S. 2938, and S. 2949, 83rd Cong., 2nd sess., 1954.

U.S. Congress. Senate. Committee on Banking and Currency. *Housing Act of 1954: FHA Insurance Provisions. Hearings* before the Committee on Banking and Currency, Senate, on S. 2889, S. 2938, and S. 2949, 83rd Cong., 2nd sess., 1954.

U.S. Congress. House. Committee on Banking and Currency. *Housing Act of 1954. Hearings* before the Committee on Banking and Currency, House of Representatives, on H.R. 7839, 83rd Cong., 2nd sess., 1954.

U.S. Congress. Senate. Committee on Banking and Currency. *Housing Act of 1955. Hearings* before a subcommittee of the Committee on Banking and Currency, Senate, on S. 789, S. 1022, S. 1412, S. 1501, S. 1524, S. 1565, S. 1642, S. 1744, S. 1766 and S. 1800, 84th Cong., 1st sess., 1955.

U.S. Congress. Senate. Committee on Banking and Currency. *Housing Act of 1955. Hearings* before a subcommittee of the Committee on Banking and Currency, Senate, on S. 789, S. 1022, S. 1412, S. 1501, S. 1524, S. 1565, S. 1642, S. 1744, S. 1766 and S. 1800, 84th Cong., 1st sess., 1955.

U.S. Congress. House. Committee on Banking and Currency. *Housing Amendments of 1955. Hearings* before the Committee on Banking and Currency, House of Representatives, on H.R. 5827, 84th Congress, 1st sess., 1955.

U.S. Congress. Senate. Committee on Banking and Currency. *Housing Amendments of 1956. Hearings* before a subcommittee of the Committee on Banking and Currency, Senate, on various bills to amend the federal housing laws, 84th Cong., 2nd sess., 1956.

U.S. Congress. Senate. Committee on Banking and Currency. *Housing Act of 1958. Hearings* before a subcommittee of the Committee on Banking and Currency, Senate, on various bills to amend the federal housing laws, 85th Cong., 2nd sess., 1958.

U.S. Congress. Senate. Committee on Banking and Currency. *Housing Act of 1959. Hearings* before the Committee on Banking and Currency, Senate, on various bills to amend the federal housing laws, 86th Cong., 1st sess., 1959.

U.S. Congress. Senate. Committee on Banking and Currency. *Housing Legislation of 1960. Hearings* before a subcommittee of the Committee on Banking and Currency, Senate, on various bills to amend the federal housing laws, 86th Cong., 2nd sess., 1960.

U.S. Congress. Senate. Committee on Banking and Currency. *Housing Legislation of 1961. Hearings* before a subcommittee of the Committee on Banking and Currency, on various bills to amend the federal housing laws, 87th Cong., 1st sess., 1961.

U.S. Congress. House. Committee on Banking and Currency. *Housing Act of 1961. Hearings* before the subcommittee on housing of the Committee on Banking and Currency, House of Representatives, on H.R. 6028, H.R. 5300, and H.R. 6423, 87th Cong., 1st sess., 1961.

U.S. Congress. Senate. Committee on Governmental Operations. *To Establish a Department of Housing and Urban Development. Hearings* before a subcommittee on Executive Reorganization of the Committee on Governmental Operations, Senate, on S. 497, S. 1045, and S. 1599, 89th Cong., 1st sess., 1965.

U.S. Congress. House. Committee on Banking and Currency. *Demonstration Cities, Housing and Urban Development and Urban Mass Transit. Hearings* before the subcommittee on housing of the Committee on Banking and Currency, House of Representatives, on H.R. 12341, H.R. 12946, H.R. 13064, and H.R. 9256, 89th Cong., 2nd sess., 1965.

U.S. Congress. Senate. Committee on Governmental Operations. *To Establish a Department of Housing and Urban Development. Hearings* before a subcommittee on Executive Reorganization of the

Committee on Governmental Operations, Senate, on S. 497,
S. 1045, and S. 1599, 89th Cong., 1st sess., 1965.

U.S. Congress. Senate. Committee on Governmental Operations. *Federal Role in Urban Affairs*. *Hearings* before a subcommittee on
Executive Reorganization of the Committee on Governmental
Operations, Senate, on parts 1-6, 89th Cong., 1st sess., 1966.

American Enterprise Institute. *Legislation Analysis: Housing and
Urban Development Bills*. Washington, D. C., 1966.

U.S. Congress. House. Committee on Banking and Currency. *Demonstration Cities, Housing, and Urban Development and Mass Transit. Hearings* before a subcommittee on housing of the Committee
of Banking and Currency, House of Representatives, on H.R.
12341, H.R. 12946, H.R. 13164, and H.R. 9256, 89th Cong., 2nd
sess., 1966.

U.S. Congress. Senate. Committee on Banking and Currency. *Progress
Report on Federal Housing Programs*. 90th Cong., 1st sess., May
9, 1967.

U.S. Congress. *Congressional Record*. 90th Cong., 2nd sess., 1968.

3. Materials from Executive Branch

Bureau of the Budget. "Circular No. A-85." June 28, 1967.

Federal Emergency Public Works Administration. "Release No. 171."
September 29, 1933.

Housing and Home Finance Agency. *Housing Definitions*. Washington, D. C.: Government Printing Office, 1959.

Moynihan, Daniel P. "Towards a National Urban Policy." Syracuse,
May, 1969. Unpublished speech.

Office of Economic Opportunity. *Catalogue of Federal Assistance
Programs*. Washington, D. C.: Government Printing Office, 1967.

U.S. Department of Health, Education, and Welfare. *Strategy for a
Livable Environment*. Washington, D. C.: Government Printing
Office, 1966.

U.S. Department of Housing and Urban Development. "The Demonstration Cities Program." Unpublished collection. Undated.

U.S. President. "Message from the President Transmitting the First
Annual Report on National Housing Goals." (91st Cong., 1st sess.,
House Doc. No. 91-63). Washington, D. C.: Government Printing
Office, 1969.

U.S. President's Commission on Government Housing Policies and
Programs (Eisenhower Task Force). *Report to the President*.
Washington, D. C.: Government Printing Office, 1954.

U.S. President's Commission on Government Housing Policies and Programs. "Administrator's Shirtsleeve Conferences." Unpublished collection of hearings, discussions, and preliminary recommendations. Available at HUD library.

U.S. President's Commission on Urban Problems (Douglas Commission). *Report to the President.* Washington, D. C.: Government Printing Office, 1968.

U.S. President's Committee on Urban Housing (Kaiser Commission). *Report to the President.* Washington, D. C.: Government Printing Office, 1968.

U.S. Vice President. "Address to the USCM." Reprinted in *Annual Proceedings of the USCM,* Washington, D. C., 1969.

SECONDARY SOURCES

Abrams, Charles. *The Practical Administration of the U.S. Housing Act of 1937.* Washington, D. C.: American Federation of Housing Authorities, 1937.

Berger, Curtis, and Dodyk, Paul. "Law for the Poor in an Affluent Society." 1968. To be published.

Brownlow, Louis A. *A Passion for Anonymity.* Chicago: University of Chicago Press, 1958.

Cherry, Dick. "History of Congressional Action Relative to Model Cities, 1966-1967." Unpublished analysis for internal use by the Department of Housing and Urban Development.

Cleveland, Frederick, ed. *Congress and Urban Problems.* Washington, D. C.: Brookings Institution, 1969.

Connery, R., and Leach, R. *The Federal Government in Metropolitan Areas.* Cambridge: Harvard University Press, 1960.

Dahl, Robert. *Modern Political Analysis.* New York: Prentice Hall, 1963.

———. *Who Governs.* New Haven: Yale University Press, 1961.

David, Stephen. "Leadership of the Poor in the Poverty Program." *Proceedings of the Academy of Political Science,* XXIX, No. 1, 1968.

Dexter, L., and Bauer, R. and de Sola Pool, I. *American Business and Public Policy.* Boston; M.I.T., 1964.

Easton, David. *A Systems Analysis of Political Life.* New York: John Wiley and Sons, 1965.

———. "The Child's Acquisition of Regime Norms," *APSR* (March, 1967).

Fitch, Lyle. *Urban Transportation and Public Policy*. New York, 1963.

Foard, Ashley, and Fellerman, Hilbert. "Federal Urban Renewal Legislation." *Law and Contemporary Politics*, XXV (Autumn, 1960).

Freeman, J. Lieper. *The Political Process*. New York: Random House, 1955.

Glazer, Nathan. "On Task Forcing." *The Public Interest*, No. 15 (Spring, 1969).

Graduate School of Public Administration. *Financing Government in New York City*. New York: New York University Press, 1966.

Greer, Scott. *Urban Renewal and American Cities*. New York: Bobbs Merrill Co., 1965.

Ingram, Helen. "Congress and Housing Policy." Unpublished Ph.D. dissertation, Columbia University, 1967.

Leuchtenberg, William E. *Franklin D. Roosevelt and the New Deal*. New York: Harper Torchbooks, 1963.

Lowi, Theodore. "Interest Group Liberalism." *American Political Science Review* (March, 1967).

———. "American Business, Public Policy, Political Theory, and Case Studies." *World Politics* (July, 1964).

Martin, Roscoe. *The Cities and the Federal System*. New York: Atherton Press, 1965.

Milbraith, Lester. *The Washington Lobbyists*. Chicago: Rand McNally and Co., 1963.

New York Times. Selected articles.

Sayre, Wallace, and Kaufman, Herbert. *Governing New York City*. New York: Russell Sage Foundation, 1965.

Schattschneider, E. E. *The Semi-Sovereign People*. New York: Holt, Rinehart and Winston, 1960.

Schussheim, Morton. "Housing Policy in the Sixties: An Assessment." Unpublished manuscript, 1969.

Sundquist, James. *Politics and Policy*. Washington, D. C.: Brookings Institution, 1968.

Truman, David. *The Governmental Process*. New York: Alfred Knopf, 1951.

Wheaton, William. "The Evolution of Federal Housing Policy." Unpublished Ph.D. dissertation, University of Chicago, 1953.

Wheaton, W., Milgram, G., and Meyerson, M., ed. *Urban Housing*. New York: The Free Press, 1966.

Wilson, James Q., ed. *City Politics and Public Policy*. New York: John Wiley, Inc., 1968.

Wolman, Harold. "Politics and Public Policy: A Study of the Housing Political System." Unpublished Ph.D. dissertation, University of Michigan, 1968.

Wood, Robert. "Alabama Lectures." Six unpublished lectures on new trends in policy-making, 1965.

Interviews—Partial List

Richard Cherry, "Man-in-Washington Service," USCM-NLC
John Feilds, Community Relations Service, Director; also National
    Coordinator, UC
John Gunther, Executive Director
Clifford Henry, Community Relations Service
Janet Kohn, Associate Director (1968–1969)
Hugh Mields, Associate Director, left USCM 1968
David Wallerstein, Community Relations Service
Robert Josten, Legislative staff
Peter Harkens, Legislative staff
Charles Schneider, Federal Aid Coordination Service

OTHER GROUPS

Don Alexander, Assistant to Director, NLC
William Cassella, Director, National Municipal League
Patrick Healy, Director, NLC
Nathaniel Keith, Executive Director, National Housing Conference
Father Krahl, Director, New York Office, Urban America
Frank Kristoff, Assistant Director, New York State Development
    Corporation; author of part of Douglas Commission Report on
    Urban Problems
Allan Pritchard, Assistant to Director, NLC
William Slayton, President, Urban America

CONGRESSIONAL PERSONNEL

John Barriere, Professional Staff, Democratic Steering Committee
Steven Berger, Administrative Assistant to Congressman Jonathan Bingham
Kenneth Burrows, Professional Staff, House Banking and Currency Commission, Subcommittee on Housing
Carl Coan, Professional Staff, Senate Banking and Currency Committee
James Grossman, Legislative Assistant to Senator Jacob Javits
Norman Holmes, Professional Staff, House Banking and Currency Commission
Jerry McMurray, Professional Staff, housing subcommittee, House Banking and Currency Committee
Don Nicoll, Administrative Assistant to Senator Edward Muskie
Edward Rovner, Administrative Assistant to Congressman Jonathan Bingham, Washington Office

EXECUTIVE PERSONNEL

Ardee Ames, Assistant to Undersecretary Lawrence Cox, HUD
Nils Boe, Office of Intergovernmental Relations, Executive Office of the President
William Brussat, Bureau of the Budget
Fred Burke, formerly in charge of Congressional Relations, Department of Transportation
Ray Hay, Planning and Evaluation Service, HUD
Neal Peterson, Assistant to former Vice President Humphrey for Housing, the Arts and Urban Affairs
G. B. Ratcliff, Staff Assistant, Urban Renewal Administration, HUD
Louis Ritter, Office of Economic Opportunity
Arthur Rosfeld, Assistant Secretary for Renewal and Housing Assistance, HUD
William Royan, Assistant to Sidney Spector, Congressional Liaison Officer, Department of Housing and Urban Development
William Sorrentino, Director, Planning and Evaluation Service, HUD
Robert Wood, former Under-Secretary, HUD

FEDERAL-AID COORDINATORS, CITY LOBBYISTS AND OTHER LOCAL GOVERNMENT STAFF

Marvin Brown, Director, Human Resources, Detroit
David Cason, Director, Model Cities, Detroit
Raymond Duncan, Administrative Assistant to Mayor of Jacksonville
Conrad Mallett, Director, Detroit Housing Commission
Patrick McLaughlin, Federal Coordinator, Philadelphia
Hugh Mields, Federal Legislative Representative, Chicago
Jason Nathan, New York City Housing and Development Administrator
Robert P. Roselle, Director, Public Works, Detroit
David Stahl, Development Coordinator and Assistant to Mayor Richard Daley, Chicago
Kathleen Strauss (Mrs.), Assistant Director Community Renewal, Detroit
Joseph Sullivan, Commissioner of Purchasing, Detroit
James L. Trainor, Community Development Coordinator, Detroit
Peter Tufo, Assistant to Mayor Lindsay of New York; chief New York City lobbyist in Washington
David Wallerstein, Federal Legislative Representative, Los Angeles
Anthony Zecca, Deputy to Mayor, Philadelphia

OTHER

Frank Crane, Professional Staff, City Administrator's Office, New York City
Florence Haines, Assistant to Jay Kriegal, formerly Mayor Lindsay's Assistant for Federal Affairs
Charles Quinn, NBC News
Jack McInnes, Budget Office, New York City (telephone interview)
James Sundquist, Former Assistant to Senator Joseph Clark, Secretary to the Democratic Platform Committee (1960), currently with the Brookings Institution
Edwin Weisl, Jr., Assistant United States Attorney General

MAYORS

Hon. Joseph Alioto, San Francisco; USCM, Executive Committee

Hon. Joseph Barr, Pittsburgh; USCM, Executive Committee; Urban Coalition, National Steering Committee

Hon. Beverly Briley, Nashville; USCM, Advisory Board; NLC, President

Hon. Jerome Cavanagh, Detroit; USCM, Executive Committee; NLC, Advisory Board; Urban Coalition, National Steering Committee

Hon. Frank Curran, San Diego; USCM, Advisory Board; NLC, Vice President

Hon. Thomas D'Alesandro, Baltimore

Hon. Clyde Fant, Shreveport; USCM, Executive Committee

Hon. Palmer Gaillard, Jr., Charleston; USCM, Advisory Board

Hon. Oran Gragson, Los Vegas; USCM, Advisory Board; NLC, Advisory Board

Hon. Alan Jepson, Milford

Hon. Herschel Lashkowitz, Fargo; USCM, Advisory Board; NLC, Advisory Board

Hon. Henry Maier, Milwaukee; USCM, Executive Committee; NLC, Advisory Board

Hon. Jack Maltester, San Leandro; USCM, President; ACIR, member

Hon. Roy Martin, Norfolk; USCM Advisory Board; NLC, Advisory Board

Hon. Frank McDonald, Evansville; USCM, Executive Committee

Hon. Arthur Naftalin, Minneapolis; USCM, Executive Committee; NLC, Advisory Board; ACIR, member

Hon. George Seibels, Birmingham

Hon. Terry Shrunk, Portland; USCM, Executive Committee

Hon. Hans Tanzler, Jacksonville

Hon. George Van Tassel, Tuscaloosa

Hon. James Tate, Philadelphia; USCM, Executive Committee; NLC, Executive Committee; Urban Coalition, National Steering Committee

Hon. Louis Welch, Houston; USCM, Executive Committee

Hon. Judson Williams, El Paso

Hon. Ted C. Wills, Fresno

Hon. Samuel Yorty, Los Angeles; USCM, Advisory Board

Hon. Frank Zullo, Norwalk; USCM, Executive Committee

Index